THE HEADLESS HORROR

STRANGE AND GHOSTLY OHIO TALES

THE GHOSTS OF THE PAST SERIES

CHOSEN AND EDITED BY
CHRIS WOODYARD

AUTHOR OF THE *HAUNTED OHIO* SERIES

Kestrel
Publications

Also by Chris Woodyard

Haunted Ohio: Ghostly Tales from the Buckeye State
Haunted Ohio II: More Ghostly Tales from the Buckeye State
Haunted Ohio III: Still More Ghostly Tales from the Buckeye State
Haunted Ohio IV: Restless Spirits
Haunted Ohio V: 200 Years of Ghosts
Spooky Ohio: 13 Traditional Tales
Ghost Hunter's Guide to Haunted Ohio
The Wright Stuff: A Guide to Life in the Dayton Area
A Spot of Bother: Four Macabre Tales (Fiction)
The Face in the Window: Haunting Ohio Tales
The Headless Horror: Strange and Ghostly Ohio Tales
The Ghost Wore Black: Ghastly Tales from the Past
See the last page of the book for how to order your own copy of this book or other
books by Chris Woodyard

First Printing
Printed in the United States of America
Design and Typesetting by Rose Island Bookworks
Cover Art by Jessica Wiesel

Woodyard, Chris
The Headless Haunt: Strange and Ghostly Ohio Tales / Chris Woodyard
SUMMARY: A compilation of 19th- and early 20th-century newspaper and journal
articles on ghosts, hauntings, Forteana, and supernatural mysteries with commentary and
annotations by Chris Woodyard.

ISBN 978-0-9881925-0-8

1. Ghosts
2. Ghost Stories
3. Ghosts—United States—Ohio
4. Ghosts—Ohio
5. Haunted Houses—United States—Ohio
6. Haunted Houses—Ohio
7. Ohio—History
8. Curiosities and Wonders—Ohio
398.25 W912H
070.593 Wo
Z1033.L73

For Marsha, an editor who is cruel.
Cruel, but fair...

Acknowledgments

Joseph A. Citro

Curt Dalton, Dayton History Books Online

Marsha Hamilton

Whittney Mahle, Librarian, Marion Public Library

Michelle Mellor and the Information Services Department of
the Public Library of Youngstown and Mahoning County

New York City Public Library Reference Department

Nicholas Reiter, The Avalon Foundation

Jessica Wiesel

Table of Contents

Introduction
The Stories That Would Not Die

> Sometimes I am a collector of data, and only a collector, and am
> likely to be gross and miserly, piling up notes, pleased with merely
> numerically adding to my stores. Other times I have joys, when
> unexpectedly coming upon an outrageous story that may not be
> altogether a lie, or upon a macabre little thing that may make some
> reviewer of my more or less good works mad. But always there is
> present a feeling of unexplained relations of events that I note,
> and it is this far-away, haunting, or often taunting, awareness, or
> suspicion, that keeps me piling on.
>
> -Charles Fort, *Wild Talents* (1932)-

In *The Face in the Window: Haunting Ohio Tales*, I collected a scrapbook of Victorian hauntings and horrors, unearthing long-lost tales that still have the power to terrify.

In fact I exhumed enough stories from the antique newspaper morgues to create this volume, the second in the *Ghosts of the Past* series. Here you'll find not only more chilling ghosts, haunted houses, and spooks, but also witches, visions in the sky, bizarre history and mystery, and a host of strange Fortean wonders, all from 19th- and early-20th-century sources, because everybody likes a good Ohio volcano story.

"Fortean" comes from Charles Fort, a researcher of all things strange. Fort, who lived from 1874 to 1932, spent many years researching scientific literature in the New York Public Library and the British Museum Library. He collected accounts of fish falls, phantom soldiers, and mystery airships, rains of blood and stones, poltergeist people and apparitions in *The Book of the Damned* (1919), *New Lands* (1923), *Lo!* (1931), and *Wild Talents* (1932). He was skeptical of conventional science, noting how often scientists ignored or suppressed inconvenient data. You'll find several chapters here in a Fortean vein.

As for ghosts, I offer haunted jails, Women in White, phantom coffins, shrieking spirits, and a hoodoo chair as well as the headless ghost of poor, pitiful Pearl Bryan, murdered by the man she loved.

Here you will find messages rapped by a spirit in the séance room or tapped on a telegrapher's key, tales whispered through a spirit trumpet, or clacked into place in the typesetter's tray. The Dead are eager to return.

Now let us sit at the table and join hands. The ghosts of the past will speak....

Note on spelling and formatting:

I have kept most of the spelling as found in the original newspaper article except for obvious spelling errors. Punctuation was a little shaky at times, depending on the newspaper. I have not tried to regularize this or make it conform to any standard. Period newspapers often inserted headlines into the text of an article for emphasis and I have kept these intact. I have divided newspaper articles, which were often one long undivided column, into what I think are logical paragraphs for ease of reading. This is dense language and sometimes difficult to read. I have not censored any politically incorrect or bigoted remarks. The language is as it came from the pencil of the reporter. It should be understood that the sentiments expressed in these articles, no matter how odious or bigoted, are not my own, but those of the original journalist or newspaper in which they appeared.

The Headless Horror:
Strange and Ghostly Ohio Tales

1.

A House in Which Nothing Will Thrive

Haunted and Hoodoo Houses

"The concept of certain houses as unclean or forbidden—perhaps sacred—is as old as the mind of man...it might not then be too fanciful to say that some houses are born bad. Hill House, whatever the cause, has been unfit for human habitation for upwards of twenty years. What it was like before then, whether its personality was molded by the people who lived here, or the things they did, or whether it was evil from its start are all questions I cannot answer."

– The Haunting of Hill House –
Shirley Jackson

Houses with a curse on them, houses haunted by a murder or a death were known as hoodoo houses or "troubled houses." They go back a long way. An ancient account describes how a house in Athens, Greece was haunted by the ghost of an emaciated old man in chains. The philosopher Athenodorus heard the stories and rented the property out of curiosity. When he saw the old man's chained ghost beckoning to him, he followed it, and marked the ground where the spirit disappeared. A chained skeleton was discovered, buried at that very spot. Once it was properly laid to rest, the house was no longer haunted. This tale created some of the standard motifs of ghost stories ever since: a ghost who cannot rest until his body is buried, rattling chains, a ghastly face, a bony, beckoning finger. If we follow that ghostly summons, where will it lead us?

CLEVELAND'S LIVELY GHOSTS
THEY OCCUPY AN OLD FARMHOUSE AND DO MANY STRANGE THINGS

Cleveland, Ohio, Nov. 15. The following story is given on the authority of respectable citizens of Woodland Hills Avenue concerning one of the oldest farmhouses in the suburbs of Cleveland. When its owner, Dawson, died in 1868, his family moved to Iowa, and the old house passed into other hands. It was a farmhouse until 1872, when the land about it was cut into city lots, and its acres shrunk to less than a quarter of one acre. Since then it has been idle or rented to such persons as could not find a habitation in more cheerful quarters.

Four years ago a spiritual [sic] medium named Hollister and his daughter occupied the place, and almost nightly séances were held there, crowds coming from this city. One night the daughter of the individual disappeared, for weal or for woe to herself, no one knows until this day, as the father uttered no word about her, and the idea that she had eloped with a Western man who had attended many of the séances was only a suspicion that could be founded on nothing substantial. Old man Hollister gave up his public exhibitions after that and shut himself from the world and grew silent and morose.

One day no motion was seen about the house. The next day and the day after it was the same, and when a policeman and the neighbors broke into the house they found the old man hanging to a rafter in the garret, without a scrap of writing or any other hints as to his past or his connections. His body was started to a cemetery, but the students of the Cleveland Medical College saw it before any sexton placed eyes or hand upon it.

The old house stood idle, going to decay, and noted only by the boys who patronized the apple trees about it. Its windows were broken, the doors hung loose on their hinges and loosened bricks from the chimney lay scattered on the roof. Two weeks ago, as David Black, a neighbor, was passing near the place at a late hour of the evening, he was surprised at seeing a small light at one of the upper windows. Fearing a fire, he went close to the gate and saw the body of a man leaning from one of the garret windows.

Going a little nearer Black sang out, "Hello, there! What are you doing up there?" The man in the window made no reply, but beckoned Black to come nearer. He did so. The figure above dropped a small piece of paper which slowly fluttered to the ground. Black picked it up and striking a match read these words, written in a coarse, angular hand: "She has gone. I am dying of sorrow and starvation. I want--" Here the match went out. Black looked up and the figure and the light had disappeared. Still holding the paper in his hand, the man hurried on a few rods to his home. On reaching there the paper was a blank.

Black is vouched for by his neighbors as a sober, honest man. He is prepared to make affidavit to the truth of his statement. Said one of the leading citizens of that neighborhood, Mr. Andrew Belden, in conversation with a reporter: "I have known Black for years, and have never known him to tell a lie. He is not an imaginative man. I cannot explain this circumstance, but believe every word of it." All the neighbors spoke in a similar strain.

Two nights later another neighbor, George T. Griffin, was near the old house when he heard a sweet strain of music come from the same upper room. He stopped and listened attentively. Two voices were singing, that of a man and a young girl, apparently. The tune was low and soft, and he could make out none of the words. In two or three minutes it ceased, a bright light flashed through the upper part of the house, a shrill voice as of a frightened woman cried out "Don't!" and then all was silent and dark as before. Griffin is a man who does not look likely to be scared by a shot.

In telling his story to a reporter Friday night he said: "I had heard Black's story and felt a little shaky. I went up to Black's house after it was over, and he and I and two young fellows who were at my house got a couple of lanterns and two or three clubs. I slipped a revolver into my pocket, and over to the old house we went. We shook the side door loose and, keeping well together, went into every room. Not a thing did we see and not a thing did we hear. We went to the garret last and had to break a locked door to get up there. It was empty, and no sound was heard except the wind as it came in through one broken window and went out at another. Yes, I'll swear to the truth of my story, but I won't try to explain it, for I can't."

All the neighbors for half a mile about have kept a close watch on the old house for several nights, but nothing came of it. On Thursday night last, no one was near it, when suddenly several wild screams rent the air. They came from the lower end of the street and sounded as though a woman was in mortal agony. The neighbors rushed to their doors while Griffin, Black, and the other men rushed to the old house without hunting for their hats or waiting to ask questions. Three of them declare that the whole front of the house was lighted up, and that lights streamed from the garret windows in a great flood, and that they heard the word "Don't!" repeated in quick succession, followed by a moan, and that instantly all was darkness and silence as before. They remained on watch for an hour, not having the courage to go in, but nothing followed. Great excitement prevails in that neighborhood. All was quiet during Friday night and up to 12 o'clock to-night.
The New York Times 16 November 1884: p. 2 CUYAHOGA COUNTY

Just as railroad men had their "hoodoo engines," there were also hoodoo houses.

IT'S A HOODOO
A HOUSE THAT BRINGS TROUBLE TO ALL
ITS INMATES

McConnelsville, Ohio, July 9. The old belief in evil spirits and devils is gaining credence in Eastern Morgan and Western Noble. Near Keith's is a house that seems to have a baneful influence on all who dare to enter its portals.

About a year ago it was occupied by the family of Dr. Gatewood. The doctor had an extensive practice, and seemingly a bright future. In the midst of his success his beautiful wife became a raving maniac and the heart-broken doctor wandered off to Cleveland, where he took his own life. Recently Dr. J.W. Lindsay, a young physician, moved into the property vacated by the Gatewood tragedy. He had only resided in the haunted house a few months until he became a confirmed drunkard, and, to complete the ghastly history of the place, word is just received that his wife, in a fit of despondency, took morphine, and died from the effects.

Cincinnati [OH] Enquirer 10 July 1895: p. 10 NOBLE COUNTY

NOTE: None of the information I can find about Dr. Gatewood, who was a highly respected physician, mentions these dire events. Perhaps it was a different Dr. Gatewood or those memorializing the dead were being discreet. I can find no trace of Dr. J.W. Lindsay either. Perhaps a hoodoo hoax? "Keith's" may be Keith, Ohio.

A HAUNTED CABIN
A LOG HOUSE IN WHICH NOTHING WILL THRIVE
UNACCOUNTABLE GOINGS ON

Van Wert, January 7. Your correspondent, while out gunning to-day, met a farmer named Goodloe residing near the Indiana line. During a conversation, Mr. Goodloe pointed to an old log house in the vicinity of a strip of woods, stating at the same time that there was something unaccountably strange about the premises. Said he: "About ten years ago I moved my family to Van Wert County from near Pottsville, Penn., and bought eighty acres of land, upon which I built that cabin. We had no luck as long as we lived in it. When we came here, we were all well and hearty. After living in the cabin about a year I began to lose flesh. So did my wife and children. Before three years rolled around we resembled a family of skeletons. My wife wanted to return to Pennsylvania, but I said that I would build another house on the other side of the farm. I did so, and we have prospered ever since. We gained health and strength and now I am as strong as anybody. Nothing ever thrived in the cabin. I rented it to an old negro, who after living there six months moved away. He said the place was haunted, and I, too, am inclined to think it is. Everything about the place dies or shrivels up to nothing. When we cooked meat on the stove it would curl up or boil down almost out of sight. I planted a lot of young fruit trees on the south side of the house and in less than two months they twisted and shriveled to mere sticks. After we removed to our new house I used the abandoned hut as a shelter for hogs during the winter. The more corn I fed them the thinner they became, until I had to turn them out into the woods and nail up the cabin doors to keep them out. The last winter I lived there, just after butchering hogs, I hung eight hams on a joist. They were tied in sacks, and when I took them down to use them they were found to have shrunk to chunks no larger than your fist.

"Then, again, I could notice a difference in my corn crop this fall. I had a pretty fair yield all around, excepting the part of the field which was near the cabin. Close to the cabin the ears were nothing more than nubbins, and mighty poor ones at that. I'll bet I shingled that old house more than half a dozen times in the three years that I lived in it. Every time the shingles would warp and draw out the nails and finally drop off. I don't believe in ghosts nor spooks, but I can't for the life of me account for the queer antics of that blessed old cabin."
Cincinnati [OH] Enquirer 8 January 1885: p. 1 VAN WERT COUNTY

HEARD
STRANGE NOISES AT NIGHT
AND WEIRD TAPPINGS AT THE WINDOWS OF THE HOUSE.
MCDANIEL'S SUICIDE REVEALS A REMARKABLE STORY.
FAMILY HAS BEEN FRIGHTENED FROM THE RESIDENCE
IN WHICH OTHER MEN BECAME MANIACS.

Columbus, Ohio. February 2. It develops that John McDaniel, of Linden, who committed suicide a few days ago, took his life because he believed the house in which he lived was haunted.

The surviving members of his family deny emphatically that they are superstitious, but they say that no money could induce them to live in the house. Immediately after the funeral of McDaniel the family hurriedly left the premises.

Strange tales are told by the neighbors about "doings" in the McDaniel house. For a long time McDaniel complained about hearing footsteps in the attic and the tapping on a certain downstairs window. He repeatedly investigated these uncanny sounds, but could not explain them.

HEARD THE SAME SOUNDS.

Members of the family heard them, but gave them no heed until the head of the household was driven to take his own life because of the alleged spookish demonstrations.

A sister of Mrs. McDaniel, Mrs. Thomas, of Middleport, Ind., went to Linden, which is a few miles from here, to attend the funeral. She had not been told of the phenomena, but one night in the house convinced her that the family should get out. She heard the footsteps in the attic, and to her they sounded like the martial tread of a detachment of soldiery. She also heard the tapping on the window. That experience drove the McDaniel family out of the house, and the widow and children are with friends and relatives until they can settle elsewhere.

HISTORY OF THE HOUSE.

The history of the house and former occupants is also the subject of discussion in this peculiar matter. It was built about 12 or 13 years ago and so far as the older residents in that neighborhood are concerned they can never remember any crime having been committed there.

But the remarkable fact exists that three former occupants of the property became violently insane, two of whom are dead. The first insane victim of the place was a Mrs. Davis. The second was a man named Segrist, who died in the State Hospital about a year ago, and the third was McDaniel, who met a tragic death but a week or so ago.
Cincinnati [OH] Enquirer 3 February 1903: p. 1 FRANKLIN COUNTY

NOTE: "John McDaniels, a wealthy retired farmer of Columbus, committed suicide by hanging at the home of Jacob Kropp, near Rushsylvania. No cause is known." *Hocking Sentinel* [Logan, OH] 5 February 1903: p. 2

This story of an unlucky farm in Lorain County almost sounds like a parody of hoodoo houses.

In Henrietta Township, Ohio, a mile or so from Birmingham, is a farm which may well be called an unlucky one. A hundred years ago it would have been shunned as bewitched. Five different families have lived upon it, and in two instances life was lost. The farm was owned by a Mr. Akers. He first rented it to a Mr. Cole, who was so unfortunate as to lose a leg. Next it was rented by Mr. James Rockwell. One day, while at work, he accidentally cut his foot with an ax, and in consequence had to have his leg amputated. A son of Mr. Akers then went to live upon it. By some mishap he injured his knee, and was obliged to suffer an amputation of the leg, from the effects of which he died. The farm was afterwards sold to a German named Krause. One day while engaged about a sorghum mill his hand was suddenly caught in the machinery, and injured so badly that amputation at the wrist was necessary. Last spring Mr. Krause rented the farm to a brother-in-law. This last victim, if we may so term him, caught his leg in a mowing machine, and was wounded so seriously that the leg was taken off. He survived the operation but a few moments.

Helena [MT] Weekly Herald 8 October 1868: p. 2 LORAIN COUNTY

NOTE: This story is also a grim reminder of how dangerous farming is as a profession and how many people at this time lost limbs in work accidents—with or without a "hoodoo."

Some houses were haunted as the result of a curse by a former owner, such as this Unionville home, where a woman died of unrequited love and did not want the house occupied after her death.

KATY'S CURSE
CURIOUS CAPERS BY THE ALLEGED GHOST OF A DEPARTED UNIONVILLE DAME

Unionville, Ohio, October 29. Several months ago there died in this place a widowed, middle-aged woman named Katy Conkling. At the time of her illness a story was current that she was dying of unrequited love for a widower of about her own age, and well known throughout the country as a high kicker among the more susceptible women of the neighborhood. It was said, too, that before Katy died she pronounced a curse on her home, and declared her intention to hold ghostly watch and ward over the place and protect it against all manner of occupancy save that of owls and rats and such spiritual company as she will find genial companionship with after climbing the golden stairs. She had built and beautified the place with fond expectations that had been blasted, and she would see that it went to ruin with her ruined hopes.

Some time since, however, a man with a small family moved into the vacant house, and early this morning the neighbors were set on end by discovering his entire stock of furniture and household goods stacked in the street. The head of the family stated to an *Enquirer* man that during all the time he had lived in the house he had not had a night of undisturbed rest because of the ghostly presence of Katie, rattling at the stove, turning over the chairs, going up and down stairs, appearing at his bedside, and sometimes tramping over him and his wife.

"Night before last," he continued, "she came as usual, and spoke for the first time. She told me in a voice that appeared to come from away off to get out; that if I remained another night she would come with somebody I wouldn't care to see. Then she disappeared—sort of slid along the floor like a shadow, growing taller and thinner, till she wasn't as thick as a whip-lash, and went out in a kind of bluish light.

"We stayed, all the same, but last night fixed us. We hadn't been in bed two hours till she came down stairs, without opening the door, and Bill Wilcox following her with the halter that hung him around his neck. I couldn't stand that any longer, and yelled murder. My wife says she didn't see Wilcox, but I did; and here are my things and family in the street, and damme if I'd move 'em back into that house for a gold mine."

The man is of ordinary intelligence, with every evidence of good digestive powers, and the earnestness of his story, which is mainly sustained by his wife, has awakened an interest in the matter that will lead to an early and thorough investigation of the mystery attached to the deserted house.

Cincinnati [OH] Enquirer 31 October 1881: p. 1 UNION COUNTY

NOTE: I am unsure about the location of Unionville. There are towns named Unionville in Ashtabula, Columbiana, Holmes, Lake, Morgan, Union and Washington County. However, Bill Wilcox, who hacked his wife to pieces with a corn knife and was then found hanging from a hickory tree October 11, 1881 in Union County, suggests that county as the site of the house.

It's a moot point whether someone selling or renting a house is obliged to tell purchases/renters about the haunting. Is a ghost a disclosable defect? A couple in Nyack, New York sued to get back their deposit when they found the house they had purchased was haunted and the owner had not disclosed the fact. They won their case. I've found a number of similar historic cases where the residents were haunted either by spirits or buyer's remorse, such as this one:

GHOSTS AND HOB-GOBLINS IN COURT

Human credulity touching ghosts and hob-goblins has just been illustrated according to law in Tuscarawas County. We learn by the *New Philadelphia Advocate*, that in January, 1856, Levi Hull bought a farm of 250 acres of William Dunlap, in Sandy Township, for which he paid $5,000 down, and his note for $3,000 secured by mortgage on the farm. The note was not paid, and Dunlap brought suit. Hull set up in defense that shortly after taking possession of said premises, he became convinced that the house was haunted and that ghosts, hob-goblins, spooks, evil spirits, &c., were in the habit of making nocturnal visits to the inhabitants of the mansion, and of making night hideous—that the neighbors were afraid to come near the house—that he was unable to get work hands to cultivate the land—that his own and his family's health of body and peace of mind were destroyed thereby, &c.—and that therefore he ought not to be compelled to pay said note of $3,000, but ought to have judgment for $4,000 as damages sustained in consequence of getting so terribly "skeerd."

The hob-goblin plea, however, did not avail the frightened Mr. Hull, and instead of getting damages he got put in for the $3,000, interest and costs. The haunted farm can probably be bought cheap. *Cleveland [OH] Morning Leader* 21 March 1859: p. 2 TUSCARAWAS COUNTY

Here is a similar case from Marion, where a house was declared legally haunted.

A JURY AND A GHOST
EXCEPTIONAL CASE WHICH A MARION COUNTY
JURY DECIDED

ACCORDING TO WHICH
GHOSTS AND HAUNTED HOUSES HAVE A
LEGAL EXISTENCE
LEGEND OF THE TOWN OF PROSPECT, WHICH
REMAINS A MYSTERY

It is likely that many more people believe in ghosts and apparitions than would like to acknowledge the fact...superstition is yet part of our natures. But it is not often that a jury of enlightened Americans can be found who, in broad daylight, are willing to acknowledge their nightly fears, and to sympathize to the extent of their legal power with the victim of a witch, for example, or the tenant of a haunted house. The history of a little town in Ohio furnishes the only case within the knowledge of the writer of this, unless search is made in the records of a previous generation.

The town of Prospect, in Marion County, was formerly called Middletown, because it lay midway between the cities of Delaware and Marion. It lies on the banks of the Upper Scioto, in the midst of a flat country such as if there is anything in geographical theories about superstitions, should make its inhabitants quite skeptical on all these mysteries. The town is a thriving one now, and some of its new citizens may be inclined to doubt whether a jury was ever impaneled in one of its Justice's Courts that actually and frankly expressed in legal form its belief in haunted houses, but there are others who will certainly call to mind what happened not a great many years ago. The case caused a great stir in the town at the time and was even mentioned briefly in the newspapers as remarkable.

The house which was the center of interest in the affair was anything but a castle or a manorial hall in its appearance. Generations of moldy ancestors had not called it theirs for several hundred years, and consequently had no occasion to be pottering around on the look-out for their degenerate heirs. Nor had it ever been the scene of a crime.

The ghost that infested it did so out of pure wantonness or because the grave that had been made for him did not fit...The reputation of the house for queer carryings on was gained during a period in which it had no tenant. It began to be whispered about that strange beings and flitting lights and rapping noises disturbed its solitude at frequently intervals.

A harmless lunatic who went by the name of Doc Weights, and whose mania was to load himself with all the old coats, old hats and old boots that he could find and carry them around the country, was allowed to take refuge in the house one evening. He was as simple as an infant, and utterly devoid of superstition because he had not sense enough to be terrified at a ghost had he seen one. He might have asked for its shroud, if he had observed that there was a hole in the garment anywhere but he was incapable of fear. His experience was looked upon beforehand as a real test of the reputation of the house. So many people were curious about the matter and watched the place so closely that it seemed hardly possible that any mischievously inclined person could have played the simple-minded old fellow a trick. Yet in the small hours of the night he was seen emerging from the house with his pack on his back. He moved with some haste, and seemed considerably disturbed. He was asked what the trouble was, and answered gruffly: "Don't want to stay there. Man of the house makes too much fuss."

The madman's verdict was thought by many people to be conclusive evidence that there was really some mystery which nobody could pretend to solve. But a young farmer who worked some land near the village on the shares moved into the house with his wife, taking the chance because the rent was cheap. He had one or two hired hands, who boarded with them. For a few nights they all got along well enough. Then the hired men began to show some signs of fright. They insisted that when they were awake and fully conscious something would come silently and pull the quilts off their bed. They would hold on the clothes and pull with all their strength, but slowly and surely the quilts would slip away. Then the farmer and his wife began to have the same experience. There were strange noises about the house at night, too, snappings and cracklings, as if the woodwork was on fire, creakings as if doors opened which were known to be not only shut, but locked and bolted. The climax was reached late one night. Every room in the house was lighted with a brilliant ball of fire. The sleepers were all awakened, and each saw in his own room the same apparition. That was enough. The next day the young farmer and his wife and hired men sought other quarters.

The building remained empty for some time, until, at length, it was taken by a stranger unacquainted with the town and, of course, ignorant of the reputation of the house. He moved in with his family, and the neighbors waited to see what would happen. For a few days all was quiet enough. Then the stranger began to show signs of annoyance and discontent. When asked about the matter he stoutly insisted that he was not afraid himself, but there were queer things happening about the house, and he could not keep his wife and children from being frightened. The older residents, glad of a chance to gossip, gave him a full account of the events that had already happened, with such added details as their excited fancy dictated. In fact, without meaning to do it, they converted themselves into regular legend manufacturers. The women performed the same office for his wife. As a result the stranger and his household gathered up what belonged to them and sought a house not frequented by ghosts.

Farmer Landon, the owner of the place, had rented it for a month, and when his tenant vacated thus unceremoniously he determined to find out what the law was in the case. After demanding the rent for a month and getting a refusal, he brought suit before the village Justice of the Peace. The foreman of the jury was Errick, the saddler, an eccentric but sharp-witted and sensible man, and the panel was throughout quite up to the average of juries. In the trial the endeavor was made on behalf of Landon to show that the plea of the defendant was frivolous, that no house could be haunted and that the belief in such things was absurd. The defendant produced plenty of witnesses whose senses had convinced them that a house could be haunted and that his house in particular was haunted to a peculiar and surprising degree. They had seen and heard things that neither science nor common sense could explain to their satisfaction. The jury, without pretending to any knowledge of their own with respect to ghosts, accepted the sworn statements of these eye and ear witnesses and returned a verdict for the defendant. They laughed it off afterward, but what was really the matter with the house is still a mystery. It was tenanted anew after a length of time and turned out one of the best behaved domiciles in the town.

Cincinnati [OH] Enquirer 5 August 1883: p. 13 MARION COUNTY

NOTE: The New York state court case was *Stambovsky v. Ackley*, 1991. I was puzzled about the connection between flat country and "geographical theories about superstitions." I found some discussion among social theorists and geographers that geography, shaping a people's way of life, also determined their level of superstition. For example, "Among pastoral tribes and nations..their habits of contemplation and solitude...dispose the mind for the reception of superstitious rites...In agricultural life, the regular and continuous strain on the physical powers produces corresponding exhaustion; leisure is used for rest...The physical development is in muscular strength, the mental is overpowered by it, the religious belief...becomes often vulgarly and coarsely superstitious." *A Manual of Geographical Science*, Charles Grenfell Nicolay, 1852.

Some of the more notable testimony in what was dubbed "The Great Spook Trial" follows:

> The Defendant testified that he had heard sounds at different times like dogs fighting and running across the floor in the night. Also, that on the night of 17th of December, 1856, clouds of fire and smoke appeared in the room with a flaming sword in the midst of it. The effect of the fire and smoke seemed almost to kill him...A bad smell also pervaded the house, like some person dead and putrid. At different times noises were heard as if potatoes were thrown violently across the floor... A crock of new milk put in the buttery, would spoil in one hour, and would have that putrid smell.
>
> First Witness for the defendant testified that the smell was very sickening one—that new milk would spoil. Also, that a young man stayed at the house when he lived in it—slept upstairs—heard something walking up and down the stairs like a man—which came to his bed and pulled the bed clothes from him....Also states he is not afraid of spooks, witches, spirits, men, or the d---l.
>
> Second Witness heard noises at different times—smelt the offensive smell—testified to the spoiling of new milk—searched the house at different times, but could find nothing; believed there was something troubling the house uncommon and unnatural.
>
> Third Witness was passing by one evening, with his son, when they heard a mournful groaning in the house, such as no human person could utter...saw large lights in and about the house, as large as a washing tub...was acquainted with the smell....the cause of the trouble he did not know.
>
> The defendant himself...made awful denunciations—so much so, that it would make the hair stand on end to hear him. Among other things he said he would go to jail and be carried out of the keyhole by worms before he would pay the rent, and so went on until he got perfectly enraged, when he took his seat, greatly excited.
>
> Thus ends the great spook trial. Now for the decision. Well, the spooks got off victorious—the plaintiff had to pay the cost of suit; lose all the rent, and pay $15 damage!...We are a people to be looked up to as a very intelligent and progressive people! We are the first in the world

to bring to light and establish the personality of spooks by judicial litigation!

NOTE: Quoted in *News from Marion, Marion County, Ohio: 1844-1861*, Sharon Moore (Bowie, MD: Heritage Books, 1995): pp. 110-111 MARION COUNTY

The author of this next article, who sounds like a sensible man, points out the very real losses suffered when a house got a bad name. He also engagingly describes how he has laid "ghosts" in his properties.

GHOST POPULATION COSTS THE UNITED STATES A LARGE SUM ANNUALLY

'The ghost population of the world is passed over by census-makers as a negligible quantity yet you would be surprised to see what a large sum those coy retiring inhabitants cost the country annually,' said the real estate man.

'How? Why in lost rentals. There is many a house you can't keep a tenant in. After a week perhaps only a night in one of those queered houses the tenant is sure to show up with some excuse for moving—the cellar is damp, or the chimney doesn't draw, or the oven won't bake. It's very seldom that the fellow will tell you frankly that he doesn't intend to run a boarding house for spooks.

Whenever I hear of a ghost getting into a house in my charge I immediately go on the hunt for it. Not that I have any interest in psychic phenomena. It is a simple matter of dollars and cents with me. I want to dispossess the spiritual squatter and get in a tenant that is willing to pay rent.

In all my years in the business I have not yet come across one ghost story that has not had some foundation. The usual ghost is a very unobtrusive fellow who only asks the privilege of pattering up and down the stairs stalking through the halls opening and shutting some door or groaning to himself up in the attic or down in the cellar. Except to the very young or the very nervous he usually keeps himself invisible.

I must confess that even to an experienced ghost hunter like myself the task often puts a strain on the nerves. There is a peculiar musty atmosphere about a vacant house that sends a chill to the marrow the same sort of chill that is supposed to emanate from the near presence of a spook. Then come the queer sounds usually heard only in the dead of night.

My plan of action is to drop on my hands and knees and with an ear close to the floor creep forward. The chances are that before the night is over I will have laid that particular ghost—I will have discovered the board or beam in the house that needs to be tightened up.

You see in every house there is always a lot of shrinkage and expanding going on. Some board or beam is usually more responsive to the changes than the rest of the building and so it gives out a peculiar creaking noise as of someone stealthily walking back and forth.

The string beams that carry the stairs are peculiarly sensitive to this shrinkage and expansion and that is why the stairway is the favorite promenade of ghosts. An odd twist in a chimney flue will furnish a spook with good respectable groans.

Why do we hear these sounds only around midnight? Simply because our vitality is then near its lowest ebb we haven't a good supply of that two o'clock in the morning courage and because every man is intuitively suspicious of the dark.

My hunt, though, is not always successful. I remember two cases that came very near being in this class.

The first was a bedroom door that invariably swung open the moment the occupant of the room got into bed. It was a door in an old-fashioned country house and was provided only with a latch. It didn't make any difference whether it was day or night the instant a person got into bed the door would swing open and stay open unless a chair or some other obstacle was put in front of it.

It took a lot of studying before I discovered that the head of the bed rested on one end of the floor board that was not nailed down and that the door jamb rested on the other end. The moment a person climbed into bed his weight made the board teeter, the door jamb on the other end of the board was raised and the latch was released.

The second case was also in a country house. There was a window opening on a stair landing that was glazed with small, diamond-shaped panes set in lead. Like all glass similarly set, these panes were just a trifle loose.

Regularly at 12:13 every night they would begin to rattle as though someone were tapping on them. In about a minute they would stop as suddenly and mysteriously as they had begun.

'It took me a long time to solve this puzzle. I did it accidentally while inquiring about the last outgoing night mail. I was told that the mail bag was picked up by an express that passed the station at 12:13—the very instant when the window panes began to rattle. That gave me my clew.

Investigation showed that the foundations of the haunted house rested upon a ledge of rock that extended over a mile westward and passed under the station and the railway track. When the train rumbled over it this ledge simply carried the vibrations to the house but they had meanwhile grown so gentle that only the little window panes responded. 'But apartment houses are driving the ghosts out of business. With pianos and babies and phonographs above, below, and on both sides, the ghost doesn't get half a chance with his modest little creaks and groans. I have yet to hear of a haunted flat.

But out in the villages and country districts a ghost is still the same old-fashioned terror.

Sandusky [OH] Star Journal 17 August 1905

Nevertheless, there would always be people ready to take advantage of a landlord's fear of notoriety.

HOUSE HAUNTED?
LOW RENT!

When alien immigrants arrive in this country they often bring with them a stock of misapplied ingenuity. The tenant with a ghost is a game that is being played by foreigners in various parts of the United States, and, what is more, it is being played successfully.

The newcomer takes a house, and, after one or two payments of rent, complains that the premises are haunted. Quaking with simulated fear, he tells a tale of horror—of a headless man seen stalking from the coal cellar, a lady in white or of something invisible but groaning. Now, a ghost is the average landlord's prime aversion. Spectral visitors afford splendid subjects for gossip in the neighborhood, and prospective tenants seldom fail to hear and be warned off by the story.

Anxious that the report shall not get about, landlord confers with tenant, and in several such instances the result has been this—the tenant agrees to stay on, to say nothing about the matters to others and to put up with the ghost, providing the rent is substantially reduced.

The Logan [UT] Republican 4 April 1911: p. 2

Unlike the ghost-busting landlord from the *Sandusky Star Journal*, a Warren County "character" had his own way to clear a haunted house of its ghost.

SETTLED THE GHOST.
THE HAUNTED HOUSE IN WARREN COUNTY
AND HOW IT WAS CLEARED OF ITS
NOCTURNAL VISITOR
OLD DAN GALLAGHER DRIVES AWAY THE
BAD SPIRIT
WITH RELIGIOUS SERVICES

Morrow, Ohio, October 15. Dan Gallagher, who is one of the noted characters of Warren County, was in town to-day. He is a "son of the ould sod." And although 70 years old, is as vigorous and active as a man of half that age. Dan has several small farms in the eastern part of the county, but is best known as the owner of the haunted house, eight miles from Morrow, on the Oregonia and Harveysburg pike. Dan was telling to-day how he settled the ghost.

THE HAUNTED HOUSE

Is a one-story frame, rather isolated from its neighbors. It has stood there many years, and is in fact one of the pioneer dwellings of this section. Several months ago Gallagher rented it to William Fries.

Shortly afterward Fries' son John, a young man, died. In a night or two mysterious rappings were heard at the windows. They were sharp, quick taps on the sill and glass, and were most manifest at one particular front window. The Fries family naturally became alarmed, and the story quickly spread among the neighbors, that John Fries had returned from spiritland, until the whole eastern part of the county began to talk excitedly about the ghost at Gallagher's farm house. Investigating parties were organized. And sat up to meet the ghost. The

RAPPINGS INVARIABLY OCCURRED

Shortly before midnight and continued several minutes. Some of the boldest of the investigators would rush out to the window, but could see nothing. The tapping, however, would at once cease on their approach. The ghost's visits continued until they were the talk of this section, and scores of people went to see the house and hear the spirit.

Finally Dan Gallagher, declared that he would fix the ghost. He is a devout member of the church. A few days ago he secured a vessel containing holy water from the church at Oregonia. It quickly spread about that Dan was going to drive the spirit away or

MAKE IT SHOW ITSELF.

The plan was put into execution the other evening in the presence of many curious spectators, several of whom had come from a distance.

The scene was a most solemn, dramatic one. Dan approached the window and removed his hat, which was the signal for the others to uncover.

Sprinkling the window profusely with the holy water, Dan in tragic tones thus addressed the invisible visitor:

"If you are a bad spirit, depart hence, and never return. If you are a good spirit, come forth and show yourself."

Several minutes of profound silence elapsed, but there was no response.

Dan again sprinkled the window and repeated his invocation. Still no ghost appeared. Dan addressed the crowd with much satisfaction, saying that the spirit which had annoyed the family was undoubtedly a bad one, but he had settled it forever.

It is a strange fact that, since that evening no more tappings have disturbed the rest of the Fries family, and the ghost, or whatever it was, has certainly departed.

Cincinnati [OH] Enquirer 16 October, 1890: p. 8 WARREN COUNTY

Despite the debunking spirit of rationality displayed by some journalists, there were still stories of haunted houses that mystified.

SPIRITS AND SPOOKS
QUEER DEMONSTRATIONS NEAR MILLERSBURG, OHIO
SUPPOSED TO BE THE GHOST OF A WOMAN WHO WAS KILLED

Millersburg, Ohio, January 24. The question of the return of departed spirits is now being discussed by the people of a portion of Killbuck Township, this county, and this discussion is accompanied by actual demonstrations nightly, which has caused much excitement in the neighborhood, and abject fear by many.

The place where these alleged spirit manifestations take place is in a dwelling on a piece of land near Sharp's Mill, in Killbuck Township, and in a somewhat secluded spot. The place is now owned by Ransom Shilts, a young man, who with his wife and family reside in the dwelling.

Mrs. Shilts's life has been made miserable by the nightly occurrences which she says take place in the house.

She says that there is distinctly heard the slow and soft tread as of someone moving through the house in stocking feet, or with gum shoes on, as if hunting for someone or something. Then will follow the slamming of doors in different parts of the house, and a general disturbance kept up to the terror of the inmates of the dwelling.

Generally these manifestations are traced back to their supposed origin, and this strange case is no exception to the rule.

About twelve years ago, on the site of where this house now stands there stood a small log house in which lived David Heilman with his wife and six children. Mr. Heilman owned the land, and in the fall of the year 1877, after thrashing his wheat and oats (having no granary) he put his crop upstairs in his house.

Shortly after this, as Mr. Heilman, his wife and little child were sleeping in a bed directly under the grain overhead and two little boys in another bed in the same room, the logs of the house spread by the weight of the grain, letting the joist down and the whole pile of grain came down on the sleepers, smothering and almost instantly killing Mrs. Heilman, the babe, and the two boys. The husband and father having in some way escaped with slight bruises.

It is believed by some that the disturbances are caused by the return of the spirit of Mrs. Heilman, as the tread seems that of a woman, and that she is hunting from room to room for someone as if desirous of telling something. It is stated that these strange noises are of nightly occurrence, and a close investigation fails to reveal the cause. A further investigation will probably be made, and if possible, solve the mystery that is making the life of Mrs. Shilts very unpleasant.

Cincinnati [OH] Enquirer 27 January 1889: p 16 HOLMES COUNTY

NOTE: In the chapter "A Family Bewitched," in *The Face in the Window*, I told of the David Hoffman family, formerly of Millersburg, tormented by a clothes-slashing poltergeist. Mr. Hoffman was a miller at Sharp's Mill, mentioned here. The Hoffmans lived in a house which was apparently haunted and caused the entire family, except Mr. Hoffman, who remained behind for his job, to move to Wooster, where the manifestations continued and intensified. That was in 1871. It is curious that there were two afflicted houses so close to Sharp's Mill.

Although I've cut some non-ghostly details out of these next two accounts, they are, in substance, almost identical to modern accounts of paranormal investigations, including no resolution to the ghostly sighting.

HAUNTED HOUSES.
WEIRD AND UNEARTHLY SIGHTS SEEN IN AND ABOUT NEVADA, OHIO
DO THE DISEMBODIED SPIRITS OF THE DEAD RETURN TO EARTH AGAIN?

Nevada, Ohio, March 10. In December, 1840, there emigrated from Franklin County, Penn. and settled in Todd Township, Crawford County, about five miles from this place, an enterprising frugal, hard-working farmer by the name of S.P. Shaw... By dint of hard work and most rigid economy Mr. Shaw succeeded in amassing quite a fortune. Mrs. Shaw died soon after reaching Ohio, and ere-long his son and daughter married and left the old man alone.

Deprived of his only pleasure in life, the care and support of his family, Mr. Shaw devoted himself to the increase and preservation of his shekels. This was quickly noted by his neighbors, who soon learned to regard him as a miser...[Shaw died in 1875.]

Some time ago, Jacob Kinsey, a prominent well-to-do farmer residing near this now interesting property, purchased that portion of the Shaw farm on which the old buildings are situated, and converted the original dwelling, a hewed log house, into a store-room or warehouse for farming utensils. Returning from Bucyrus about ten o'clock on Saturday night, February 25th, with some plows, harrows, &c., Mr. Kinsey stopped at the old house with the intention of leaving his purchases where they would be soonest needed. The building was built nearly in the center of a field containing probably thirty acres and Mr. Kinsey, without thinking for a moment of witnessing anything unusual, drove up to the door and dismounted.

Pushing back the creaking door, what was his horror and aston-ishment to see, seemingly in a sitting posture, a human form clothed in white, in the act of counting apparentless money. Not of a supersti-tious or cowardly disposition, Mr. Kinsey, in his usual manner, saluted the figure with a "Halloo," which seemed to attract the attention of the ghastly form. For a few moments each gazed fixedly upon the other when the apparition with a horrid scowl, and without uttering a word,

motioned the disturber of his midnight revel away. Thoroughly terrified, Mr. Kinsey was unable to move, and seemed rooted to the spot.
After a short time the fleshless hands seemed to gather up its wonted
plaything and the whole to vanish speedily from view.

As quickly as possible Mr. Kinsey repaired to the residence of Jacob
Shoupe, situated on an adjoining farm, and related to Mr. Shoupe pri-
vately what he had seen. Imagine the surprise of Mr. Kinsey on hearing
Mr. Shoupe relate an experience almost identical with his own. Mr. S.
gave as his reason for keeping the matter a secret that his neighbors,
who did not believe in such things, would attempt to ridicule him out
of the idea, and make it the subject of innumerable jokes and puns, and
expressed his satisfaction at the experience of Mr. Kinsey, confirming
his belief in the spirit visitor.

The next day being Sunday, a number of neighbors assembled at
the house of Jacob Kinsey, among whom were Messrs. William Powers,
Aaron Chance, J.M. McCracken (Constable of the township) and Jacob
Shoupe. After thoroughly discussing the matter, it was decided that the
five gentlemen named should constitute a Committee to investigate the
weird and restless spirit of the honored dead, the following Saturday
night—March 4th—at nine o'clock sharp, being the time appointed for
the Committee to meet at the haunted house.

Your correspondent has succeeded in securing the history of that
horrid night through the kindness of Mr. Chance. Arrived at their des-
tination the committee found that, owing to the chilliness of the night,
and to keep up good feeling, it was necessary to build up a fire on the
long-unused hearth. The door was closed, and in the absence of a latch a
heavy plow was set against it. Seated around the fire, which gave the surroundings the appearance best suited to the occasion, they had entered
into a spirited conversation concerning mutual business, and had well
nigh forgotten the object of their visit when, suddenly, immediately
over their heads, there were such rumblings, crashings, and creakings as
might result from a full volley from the artillery of Heaven. At the same
moment the door swung slowly back upon its rusty hinges, the heavy
weight seeming no more of an impediment than a feather, and standing in full view on the threshold of the cabin he had reared appeared
the form of one they could not fail to recognize, its former owner and
occupant.

Had they not known that S. P. Shaw was dead, not a man present
could have been convinced that it was not he. Life-like, natural, and

appareled as in life, they could scarcely refrain from grasping the hand seemingly extended to greet them. Only for a moment did that hand seem so extended, quickly pressing it to his breast and then to his head, with the other he motioned the intruders upon the privacy of his domain grandly and silently away. As before the specter vanished, and after waiting several hours for its reappearance, the Committee returned silently, solemnly and thoughtfully to their homes, each convinced that he had seen and almost talked to their old neighbor.

The Committee have decided to revisit the house next Saturday evening, March 11, and your correspondent will form one of the party. *Cincinnati [OH] Enquirer* 11 March 1882: p. 5 CRAWFORD COUNTY

GHOST-HUNTING
A SECOND VISIT TO A HAUNTED HOUSE
AND ANOTHER UNSUCCESSFUL ATTEMPT
TO UNRAVEL
A BLOOD-CURDLING MYSTERY
THE APPARITION MAKES ITS APPEARANCE
AS BEFORE,
BUT THE WATCHERS FAIL IN THEIR MISSION

Nevada, Ohio, March 15. Your correspondent, although harassed by a most inclement and disagreeable night, desiring that the facts in the S.P. Shaw mystery, given you in detail in our dispatch of the 10th inst., should be fully and candidly presented to the many readers of the *Enquirer*, proceeded, according to promise, together with the members of the Committee before enumerated, to investigate as far as possible the foundation for the seemingly incredible event already given you....

Promptly at nine o'clock we repaired to the dilapidated cabin that had once sheltered the head and heart of as true a Christian as it was ever our good fortune to know. As before, everything seemed orderly and as it should be. The puncheon door creaked ominously on its rusty hinges, as was its wont; the same musty air pervaded the apartment as usual, and silence, dread and death-like, reigned supreme. Slowly and with silent tread, as one who views with tearful eyes the last frail fragment of a departed friend, or one who unwillingly passes the sunken mounds and leaning stones, we filed almost breathless, entirely speechless, into the little primitive mansion...

Again a blaze was kindled in the wide, old-fashioned, long-neglected hearth, and, improvising seats of plow-beams and wagon-tongues, we discussed the disagreeable business of the hour, each relating his experience and imparting to the others his belief or disbelief in the revisitation to earth of the spirits of departed dead. In this manner the first hour of our visit was spent. Eleven o'clock came, twelve o'clock passed and still no evidence that our weary, relentless watch was to be rewarded.... [Dinner was eaten.] Almost before our...meal was finished a little gust of wind, seemingly natural in its course, which led through the openings in the sides and roof, totally extinguished the fire that had already burned low from neglect, and that furnished us our only light.

Immediately a sound resembling the reverberations of distant thunder burst upon our straining ears and seemed to issue from the ceiling, walls, and floor, accompanied by the rattling of chains and such groans and exclamations as might reasonably be expected from those condemned to eternal suffering in the sulphurous regions of the damned; then all was quiet, and a stillness the grave could scarcely equal reigned again. Only for a brief period did this suspense obtain, when a faint glimmer of light from an unascertainable source flew through the place, growing brighter and still more bright at each succeeding moment, until so intense as to be almost painful.

At last our unremitting vigil was to meet its due reward. Standing in bold relief against the door we had taken the precaution to securely fasten, his body, surrounded by a halo of light rivaling in brilliancy the sun at midday, was the object of our search...The face, recognizable to those who knew it in life, wore a troubled, care-creased expression, as though weighed down by something yet undone, a sorrow yet untold.

Without deigning to notice our...presence, after a few moments apparently spent in careful meditation, the apparition strode grandly and majestically by us and halted in an opposite corner. He again seemed lost in deep reflection for a little time, when, without discernible cause, he commenced an ascension, bolt upright, disappearing through the ceiling, and again darkness filled the room. Then recommenced clanking of chains, creaking of hinges, rattling of keys, groans and moans more unearthly than before.

A second later the ghastly form reappeared, to our great surprise, in a part of the room removed from the point whence it had ascended. A marked change was noticeable on his countenance, the expression on entering have given place to one of satisfaction and joy, as though the object of his quest had been attained. Now, for the first time he realized our presence, and seemed pained at the intrusion. The sorrowful wave again passed over his face, even deeper and more profound than before, as he commenced moving stealthily toward the door. Barely halting at the threshold, he vanished as quietly and as inexplicably as he had entered.

The dying embers flickered into a sickly flame, and for the first time since the specter's appearance we found power to speak. We then examined the door and found it as securely fastened as we had left it. As on a previous visit, the little company, although still unconvinced, moved slowly and thoughtfully out at the rude doorway, each repairing to his respective home firmly impressed with what he had seen.

Incredible as the above may seem to the sceptical reader, its truth can be vouched for, and any of the Committee will deem it a pleasure to answer any questions in regard to the important subject mentioned in this article. Messrs. M. Powers, J.P. Phillip Shupp and Jacob Kinsey may be addressed at Bucyrus, Ohio and Messrs Aaron Chance and J.M. McCracken (Constable), at Nevada.

Cincinnati [OH] Enquirer 16 March 1882: p. 6 CRAWFORD COUNTY

Another seemingly cursed property, from Port Union, complete with a ghostly, beckoning hand:

A GHOSTLY HAND
AT MIDNIGHT WARNS A CARD-PARTY TO BREAK UP.
THE HAUNTED HOUSE OF PORT UNION, BUTLER COUNTY
STRANGE EVENTS FOLLOWING A FARMER'S TERRIBLE DEATH
HIS FAMILY, STRICKEN WITH LEPROSY, DECLINE AND DIE
FEARFUL NOISES HEARD IN THE PLACE, AND A MIGHTY SPECTER SEEN.

The denizens of Union Township, Butler County, residing near Port Union, for some time past have been considerably exercised over the fact that there is a haunted house in the community, and that ghosts with all the latest improvements are nightly seen by its occupants....

The house is situated about one fourth of a mile west of Port Union in that region known as the Miami Valley, and is at present occupied by a family named Nash.

Many a neighbor who entertained the belief that ghosts did not exist has abandoned such a belief after having passed a night beneath the roof.

During the year of 1844 a man named Jerry Mead, from Pennsylvania, with his family purchased the land and erected the house, which is provided with a mill roof.

Mead, with his family, resided there for a number of years, and the place was known as

THE "MEAD HOMESTEAD."

The family consisted of the husband and wife and two children—a son and daughter.

The head of the family lost his life there. He was engaged in digging a well near the north-east corner of the house, and had reached the depth of thirty-five feet, when it caved in, burying Mead under several feet of the fallen earth. After several hours of laborious work he was taken out dead, and was buried on a small knoll of ground about 200 yards north of where he lost his life.

Some five years after this event the remaining members of the family were stricken with a strange malady, much resembling leprosy, and all succumbed to the fatal disease and were buried beside the father.

The farm then passed into the hands of Clark Mounts, who for a number of years was employed as Superintendent of the Southern Division of the Miami Canal. It was during the occupancy of the premises by this family that the strange scenes were first witnessed.

There is a large hallway in the house, from which ascends a flight of stairs leading to the upper story, and at the head of these stairs is where the first manifestations were witnessed.

UNEARTHLY YELLS,

As of someone in great distress can be heard, and during these strange periods a ghostly shadow in the shape of a human form would appear upon the scene, and at a given signal from this form all turmoil would cease, and for a short time all would be as still as the grave.

One dark cold night in the winter of 1871 a party of young folks, consisting of two ladies and an equal number of gentlemen, were at the house, in the basement story, seated around a table, engaged in a friendly game of cards. The house is so constructed that two large windows are in the east side of this room, the windows being so arranged that the sash may be lowered from the top.

Among the party on the evening alluded to was a young man named Clark, whose position at the table afforded him a full view of these two windows.

A fierce storm was raging without, and, as the old family clock chimed the hour of midnight, Clark raised his eyes upward and gazed out of the windows in time to witness a spectacle that almost made him frantic with fear. The upper sash of one of the windows slowly lowered and instantly what seemed to be a human hand was thrust through the aperture and motioned, as if beckoning, to the party to depart. Clark made known what he had seen to those around him, and they

TRIED TO CALM HIS FEARS,

Telling him it was all imagination. The table was then so arranged that should the strange operation be repeated they might all witness it.

It was not long until a repetition of the scene occurred, and this time it was witnessed by the entire party, being at the other window.

The young ladies were so badly frightened that they immediately sought another position in the house, trembling with fear, and soon took their departure. All efforts to induce them to go to the house after this night's experience proved of no avail.

The query is, what is this, and is it the ghost of old man Mead returning to torment the occupants?

A party of young men of the neighborhood have banded themselves together with the intent to fathom the mystery, if possible.

Cincinnati [OH] Enquirer 23 March 1890: p. 12 BUTLER COUNTY

Let us close this chapter with a gruesome mystery that echoes that ancient Greek tale of a ghost who wanted his bones discovered.

A HAUNTED HOUSE
COVERED THE BODIES OF A FAMILY LONG MISSING

Chillicothe, May 29. A strange story of a supposed crime revealed after lying hidden for half a century was related to *The Enquirer* to-day by Charles Boice, who resides in Pike County. He states that while workingmen were engaged in removing the kitchen floor in an old farmhouse near Cooperville on Saturday, they were horrified to come upon an excavation under the boards, in which reposed three heaps of bones, undoubtedly those of human beings, but with the heads missing. Remnants of rotten wood were also discovered, which are supposed to be the remains of three coffins. This find, with the reputation the house has borne for years, has stirred up quite a commotion. The old structure is quite dilapidated, and has been almost deserted for years, owing to its reputation for being haunted.

Fifty years ago it was inhabited by a family named Burns, consisting of father, mother, and two daughters. They did not live happily, however owing to the old man's morose and miserly disposition and his unreasonable jealously of his wife, who was quite a good-looking woman. One day the wife and daughters were missing and the old man gave out the report that they had gone to visit relatives in Illinois. This story was believed, as such a trip had been talked of for some time, but the neighbors were surprised at the sudden departure. Burns remained in the house alone for nearly a year, when he also announced his intention of leaving. His family were so well pleased with their new quarters that they had determined to reside there permanently. This story was believed also, as he had received a number of letters in a woman's handwriting, which he said were from his wife. After selling off his possessions he departed and nothing has been heard of the family. Soon after he left, the house got the name of being haunted and has changed owners frequently, owing to the strange sounds and sights at night.

The present owner, however, not believing all he had heard, determined to remodel the interior of the place, and it was while such work was going on that the bones were discovered. Strange to say, in all these years this is the first time suspicion of foul play has been entertained.

The bones have been buried, and an effort will be made to trace the Burns family.

Cincinnati [OH] Enquirer 30 May 1894: p. 1 PIKE COUNTY

2.

The Bloody Hand of Findlay:
And Other Mysteries in the Skies

[The mirage] may have been a revelation of heaven, and for all I know heaven may resemble Sandusky, and those of us who have no desire to go to Sandusky may ponder that point, but our own expression is that things have been pictured in the sky, and have not been traced to terrestrial origins, but have been interpreted always in local terms.

– *New Lands*, Charles Fort, 1923 –

For most of the 19th century, man could only look wistfully up at the sky. There were no airplanes or airships. Balloons were only for military observers or daredevils at county fairs.

But that did not mean that the skies were empty. The night skies, more visible with less ambient light, blazed with falling stars and comets. The heavens were full of aerial marvels and prodigies, either curious or prophetic.

SAW CITY IN A MIRAGE.
TOLEDO (OHIO) MEN VOUCH FOR APPEARANCE OF THE SPECTACLE
WHILE THEY WERE FISHING

Toledo, Ohio, Dec. 22. A remarkable mirage, which appeared over Lake Erie, visible just beyond the bay, startled a large number of ice yachtsmen, and the strange phenomenon is the talk of the city. The story is vouched for by well-known citizens.

The men had been fishing through the ice, after fastening their yachts. Suddenly one of them, Harry Ashley, uttered an exclamation and pointed eastward. Many pairs of eyes were turned in that direction, and there, strongly defined against the sky, was the mirage of a large city. It gradually became clearer until the streets and large buildings could be plainly distinguished. Hundreds of buildings could be seen very distinctly.

Suddenly flames broke out of one of the large buildings, the smoke and flames appearing very plainly. The mirage continued to appear

brighter, and people and fire apparatus and horses were seen pouring from other buildings in different portions of the city. For fully thirty minutes the strange spectacle held the men spellbound, then gradually faded away.
New York Times 23 December 1901: p. 1 LUCAS COUNTY

A GREAT MIRAGE
A CITY APPARENTLY SUSPENDED IN THE AIR
NEAR ASHLAND, O.

Ashland, O., March 15. A remarkable instance of a mirage was witnessed here yesterday about 4 o'clock in the afternoon. It presented a picture of a clear and well defined city, full size, though of course inverted, and appearing like a large city suspended in the air or falling through it, as the ground on which it stood was not reflected. Church steeples and walls of houses were slightly inclined.

The phenomenon seemed to be only a few hundred yards above the earth and was visible for nearly three-quarters of an hour. The day was clear and calm with a cloudless sky. Many spectators claimed that the city reflected was Mansfield, thirty miles distant; others say it was Sandusky, eighty-five miles away, and each party professed to recognize buildings in those places.
Oshkosh [WI] Daily Northwestern 15 March 1890: p. 1 ASHLAND COUNTY

NOTE: The *New York Sun* of March 16, 1890 added that "The more superstitious declared that it was a vision of the New Jerusalem."

The most interesting of the sky prodigies are the visions. Some simply sound like cloud shapes; others like the aurora borealis. Yet they all had a symbolic value, which differed wildly, according to their observers.

CITY NOTES [from Newark]

A phenomenon, which is not easily explained, appeared in the heavens about 9 o'clock last night, remaining for about twenty minutes. It was in the shape of a finger and thumb, which pointed toward the east. In color it was of a milky whiteness. It was observed by many of our people, some of whom consider it a sign of turbulent times in the Far East.
Newark [OH] Daily Advocate 30 June 1895: p. 4 LICKING COUNTY

A STRANGE PHENOMENON.

Findlay, Ohio, May 22. A strange spectacle was visible in the northern sky here last night shortly after 11 o'clock, which has caused the greatest consternation among the people. It was the representation of a human hand of immense proportions and awe-inspiring in its realistic vividness. Early in the evening the sky in the north had a peculiar appearance, which as the night wore on took the form of flashes of light constantly changing in color, pulsing up from the horizon and again subsiding, but with each appearance becoming more brilliant. This continued until about 11 o'clock, when those viewing the phenomenon were terrified to see these plumes of light concentrating into a distinct object which assumed the proportions of a giant hand, well-formed and as distinct as if painted on the black background of the sky. The hand appeared to be a shadowy substance, through which waves of light of a blood-red color regularly surged and then fell off at the ends of the fingers in drops of the same color. The first finger of the hand pointed downward toward the sleeping city, as if warning the people of some evil about to fall upon them. The spectacle lasted for about an hour and was witnessed by hundreds, who were breathless with suppressed excitement, until slowly it began to fade away, and finally disappeared altogether. It was one of the strangest and yet most impressive exhibitions of nature ever witnessed, and speculation regarding its cause and significance will not abate for many a day.
Coshocton [OH] Semi-Weekly Age 25 May 1888: p. 1 HANCOCK COUNTY

The *New York Herald* gave an even more lurid description:

...A hand of giant proportions, through which pulses of flame, red as blood, throbbed and bounded as in human arteries, and then fell in huge ruby drops from the tips of the fingers, and were swallowed up in the darkness below....Banners of light, constantly changing in hue from amber to amethyst, rose, and fell as regularly as the heart throbs of a healthful maiden, while over and beyond this wonderful sky picture soft, fleecy clouds drifted like incense arising from some burning altar of the heavens...finally, as midnight laid her fingers upon the lips of care, the sky resumed its normal appearance. At least a hundred of Findlay's wickedest people witnessed this remarkable and impressive spectacle... The superstitious are thoroughly alarmed and insist it was the hand of

God portending some direful calamity or disaster to the State....
New York Herald 23 May 1888: p. 7

NOTE: The bloody hand even found its way into the pages of *The New York Times*. However, the *Bradford [PA] Era* had some skeptical editorial comment. The paper writes:

> "Findlay is to the front again. The imaginative reporter who used to write such tall stories about the natural gas boom, is now devoting all his energies to concocting thrilling tales of natural phenomena. Close upon the heels of the cat-eating cow, comes the following realistic description of a blood-red hand of flame in the heavens."

The reporter then inserts the story above, adding,

> "This finger of doom pointing downward at the most thoroughly advertised city in the United States is without doubt an indication of the fate predicted by the editor of the McKeesport *News*, that is to overtake Findlay when the Trenton rock blows out all its gas. Or, more dreadful still it may mean that the flame from the great Karg gasser... is to be drawn backward into the well by some disarrangements in the draught, fire the immense deposits of gas that remain in the Trenton and blow Findlay and the surrounding territory higher than she has yet been blown by the bombastic real estate agent or the most enthusiastic newspaper correspondent. Beside the stupendous occurrences in the great town of Findlay, Lima pales into utter insignificance."
> *Bradford [PA] Era* 25 May, 1888: p. 2

NOTE: The great Karg gasser was the Great Karg Gas Well, discovered at Findlay in 1886. "The Trenton" is the Trenton Gas Field in Western Ohio and much of Indiana, discovered in 1876 and the largest natural gas discovery up to that time as well as a giant oil reserve. Findlay's gas and oil boom roused much enmity among neighboring communities and states.

The cat-eating cow belonged to Joseph Tucker, of Marion Township, near Findlay: "The animal eats every cat that comes within its reach and has disposed of five so far this spring." *Logansport [IN] Pharos Tribune* 25 May 1888: p. 2.

The unusual vision of a woman clinging to a cross in the sky witnessed by two Coshocton ladies in 1916, corresponds almost exactly to a popular print of the time period, which could be seen on the wall of many a Victorian parlor. *Folie a deux?*

I was unable to find the original letter by Mrs. Danford and Mrs. Vance, but several people wrote to the Coshocton papers to offer comment and corroboration.

THAT VISION

Editor, the *Tribune*:

I was much interested in reading about the remarkable vision, which was witnessed on last Sunday by Mrs. L Danford and Mrs. Joseph Vance, as they claim, they saw a cross outlined on the sky on which was clinging a woman in white and a man kneeling by it.

Shortly before the outbreak of the Spanish-American War a "fiery sword" was seen in the heavens by some market men at an early morning hour which I think was significant.

In conversing with some friends about this matter they suggested that perhaps the vision of the cross may mean that peace is near. Let us pray that such may be the case.

Joel 11, verse 28: "And it shall come to pass afterward that I will pour out my spirit upon all flesh and your sons and daughters, shall prophesy and your old men shall dream dreams, your young men shall see visions."

Verse 30: "And I will show wonders in the heavens and in the earth blood and fire and pillars of smoke."

Ensign Thomas McMahon,
Salvation Army,
Boston, Mass.
Coshocton [OH] Morning Tribune 7 June 1916: p. 6 COSHOCTON COUNTY

APPARITION
IN WESTERN HEAVENS ALSO SEEN BY DR. WAGNER
OF MILLER TOWNSHIP
COSHOCTON STORY MUST BE TRUE

The strange apparition, in the form of a bright cross with a clinging form and the image of a woman kneeling at the foot of the cross, which was witnessed in the western heavens Sunday evening, June 5, by Mrs. Lorena Danford and Mrs. Joseph Vance, of Coshocton, was also visible over in Knox County. Since Mrs. Danford and Mrs. Vance told of the strange sight, other Coshocton people have verified their statement and it is now clear that the apparition was not an optical delusion.

Dr. Jos. Wagner of Miller Township, Knox County, writes: "Having read in the *Times-Age* of the strange phenomenon witnessed by two of your townsladies and their desire for confirmation of their statement, I hereby corroborate their story as my wife and I both witnessed the same strange sight."

Now let some student of astronomy come forth and explain what the strange apparition was.

The Democratic Banner [Mt. Vernon, OH] 16 June 1916: p. 6

COSHOCTON/KNOX COUNTY

NOTE: The image described seems to be a variation of a popular religious print of a woman clinging to a stone in the middle of rough water titled either "Rock of Ages" or "Simply To Thy Cross I Cling," which is a line from the hymn "Rock of Ages."

This next story may be a report of the aurora borealis. It also has certain features in common with the 1919 "Miracle of the Sun" at Fatima, Portugal:

A Martin's Ferry correspondent of the Pittsburgh *Dispatch*, under date of August 15th, says: "Your correspondent awoke this morning at 5 o'clock with a heavy feeling in his head and a kind of numbness in his limbs. When he got his eyes open he saw the room flooded with a peculiar orange tinted light. At first it could not be understood, but a glance at an open, unblinded window showed that all out of doors was in the same condition. It seemed so unnatural that he called other members of the household and found that two of them had already awakened under similar circumstances. In a few minutes windows were thrown open in many houses in the neighborhood, and half-dressed people pushed their heads out to look at the curious phenomenon. The entire space from earth to the sky seemed to be floating full with light clouds of this strange, bright orange color, while a steady pouring rain was descending. All objects appeared as they would look through a piece of orange colored glass, except that outlines of forms were shaded in blue, which faded away to green, and a bright orange color in the heavier parts. The sun had not yet risen, but one could see a distance of 300 or 400 yards distinctly, and all space seemed filled with the peculiar yellow light.

"The phenomenon lasted about a half hour, and at 5:30 it was again rather dark and only the natural gray dawn forcing its way through the

heavy rain could be noticed. The scene presented throughout the time the phenomenon lasted was weird and beautiful. Buildings were outlined in green and blue, while the walls and heavy parts assumed the yellow's golden tint. During the forenoon it was learned that many people were awakened at about the same time, and all felt a peculiar, startled feeling as if suddenly called from the midst of an unpleasant dream, or awakened by a cry of fire. No solution of the mystery is offered by our local meteorologists, and the sun not being up yet makes it all the more strange. Some superstitious people were very much scared, and several very fervent prayers were offered while the strange sight lasted."
East Liverpool [OH] Saturday Review 20 August 1887: p. 2 BELMONT COUNTY

A Fortean feature of the 19th-century papers was stories of mysterious falls of stones, animals, blood, sand, and, of course, fish. Ohio seems to have fewer fish and frog falls than other states, but I did find the following:

MUD STORM WAS MERE PIKER COMPARED TO DISPLAY BACK IN 1869

Norwalk, May 20. Huron County recently had its mud storm, but this evening was nothing to the reported marvelous shower of fish, snakes, eels, frogs and fishes that a New London correspondent described in the issue of the old *Cleveland Evening News* of June 23, 1869, owned by Dr. William R. Johnston of Collins.

The following item bearing a New London dateline and appearing under the heading "Singular," indicates that modern news correspondents are mere pikers compared with the resourceful journalists of the sixties:

"Singular—A correspondent writes to us from New London, O., under the date of June 21:

"Last night and today we were visited by one of the most remarkable rains that ever passed over this section of the Western Reserve. It is estimated that at least 14 inches fell in the short space of 10 hours. The most remarkable feature occurred this morning between five and six o'clock, which was a shower of snakes, eels, frogs and fishes. Every gutter and ditch in the village was filled with this promiscuous mass, which created the utmost excitement among us. They evidently fell a great distance as none was picked up alive."
Sandusky [OH] Register 21 May 1935: p. 2 HURON COUNTY

The following fish story comes from Wyoming, Ohio:

"A shower of fish fell this evening during the rain. The school children gathered them up by the bucketful from the sidewalk. They were several inches long."
Decatur [IL] Daily Review 18 June 1886: p. 2 HAMILTON COUNTY

High up in the topmost branches of a large tree that was felled near Winchester, Ohio, recently a petrified fish was found. It is supposed to have been dropped by an eagle or some bird of prey. And petrified with fright probably when he discovered that the eagle had the "drop" on him.
New York Herald 27 October 1888: p. 6 ADAMS COUNTY

Other strange things also fell from the Ohio skies.

There was a refreshing shower of frogs at Middletown, Ohio; on Friday last. They were about an inch in length, lively as frogs fresh from the skies might be expected to be, and the grounds was completely covered with them.
Springfield [MA] Republican 5 June 1855: p. 2 BUTLER COUNTY

NOTE: Another shower of frogs with no details was also reported at Newark in 1873.

SHOWER OF FROGS

Findlay, Ohio Friday, July 19. Residents of North Findlay declare it rained frogs during the last heavy storm. They aver that thousands upon thousands of frogs, none of which were larger than a half dollar, fell to the earth during the rain, but that few of them lived.
Seattle [WA] Daily Times 19 July 1912: p. 15 HANCOCK COUNTY

RAINED SQUIRMERS

Alliance, O., April 13. During the heavy storm Friday night millions of angle worms fell, making pavements so slippery that it was nearly impossible to walk on them.
Newark [OH] Daily Advocate 14 April 1895: p. 1 STARK COUNTY

NOTE: A story printed just below this squib told of a violent local storm that caused landslides. It seems more likely that the worms emerged onto the sidewalks after the drenching rain. But that doesn't seem to cover the facts as reported in this next shower from Tiffin.

HEAVY SHOWER OF SNAILS.
THE STRANGE PHENOMENON AT TIFFIN, OHIO

Cleveland, April 22. A special from Tiffin, Ohio records a strange phenomenon that took place there last night. It was no more nor less than a heavy shower of snails, from a pin head in size to some as large as a half dollar. The ground on Highland addition, a suburb of the town, was covered with them, and the noise made in their descent was like the falling of hail. In the eastern part of the city snails literally covered the sidewalks last night although it only sprinkled slightly.
Newark [OH] Daily Advocate 22 April 1889: p. 1 SENECA COUNTY

Of course, the sceptics explained away fish/worm/snail falls with whirlwinds and, more amusingly, tales like this:

A PRETTY FISH STORY SPOILED

There was a pretty story circulating along Vine Street, below Fourth and elsewhere yesterday about a shower of fish from the clouds during the morning storm. A number of minnows about an inch long were picked up in the street near the Albany Building, and quite a little sensation was started thereby. Everybody in the neighborhood accepted the story that the fish came down from the clouds. Investigation proved the rain theory a fallacy. A small boy had brought up from the river a lot of minnows in his hat and had given them to another small boy, whose father has a cigar store under Wilde's clothing house. The latter small boy put them in a basin and threw out in the street some that he thought were dying. These were revived by the rain, and flopping about in the mud, attracted the attention of people in the neighborhood, who jumped at the conclusion that the minnows came from the clouds
The New York Times 30 June 1885 HAMILTON COUNTY

Fishfall skeptics would appreciate this impassioned defense of rationality. You can practically hear the after-dinner audience crying, "Hear! Hear!"

A SHOWER OF FISH

Although it is quite late in the season for fish tales, such a piscatorial phenomenon is reported by the passengers on a steamboat plying the Ohio River between the Ohio and West Virginia shores that it merits a passing glance. As narrated by a West Virginia eye-witness quoted by the *Pittsburg Chronicle Telegraph*, there came a sudden and strange downpour upon the deck. After it had subsided sufficiently to permit of investigation, the passengers and crew discovered that there had been a rain of fishes, and when the count had been complete there were 72 as fine salmon and catfish as an epicure would desire to gaze upon. It follows of course, that the fishes were cooked and served to passengers and crew, and if every fellow aboard didn't get all he wanted it was his own fault. The most reasonable explanation of this wonderful fishfall is that the paddle-wheel of the boat had connected with a floating fish-box of large dimensions, and as a result had hurled the contents upon the boat's deck. At any rate, this hypothesis does not do such violence to the human reason as to be instantly rejected by scientists.

In a broad sense it may be called a miraculous draught of fishes, but above all things let us avoid error and seek out the truth. The credulity of both ancients and moderns has so often been taxed by fish tales which in the last analysis were fairy tales, that we must apply the accepted tests of historical criticism to all narratives of the species. When anything of this kind turns up, let the spirit of investigation be right on deck, even as the 72 fish were. Once we accept the paddle-wheel theory, we can swallow the story as easily as the passengers and crew did the sudden shower of ichthyology.

Men of high intelligence, broad culture, deep research, scholarly attainments and scientific cast of mind will never believe that the 72 fish dropped from the clouds, or were fired from a gun, or of their own free will and accord rose in a body and went on board the steamboat in a spirit of frolic, a vein of caprice, a mood of insanity, or a passion for scientific investigation. Let the paddle-wheel theory stand. When it comes to fish, gentlemen, let us be realists and materialists, not romanticists, visionaries, and mystics.

Anaconda [MT] Standard 17 November 1915: p. 6 OHIO RIVER

NOTE: I hate to be a spoil-sport, but...salmon in the Ohio River?

And finally, this tasteful, tongue-in-cheek rain in Darke County:

WONDERFUL PHENOMENON IN DARKE COUNTY

To the Editor of the *Cincinnati Gazette*:

Arcanum, Ohio, March 14.

We have just been informed by a reliable citizen that, a few miles north of this place, the people witnessed a most striking phenomenon about 9 o'clock to-day. While the sun was shining in a clear sky, there came down from the heavens a copious shower of ham and eggs. This strange shower lasted for the space of half an hour, and at this writing the whole face of the country, for miles around, is covered with slices of sugar-cured ham to the depth of about four feet. We have information that specimens have been forwarded to Cincinnati for inspection, which we have no doubt will give some light on this subject.

Cincinnati [OH] Daily Gazette 15 March 1876: p. 4 DARKE COUNTY

NOTE: Cincinnati was the hog-packing center for the United States, sometimes called "Porkopolis," so naturally they knew about ham. On the subject of fish-falls and other mysterious rains, Charles Fort suggested that there was a "Super-Sargasso Sea" above the clouds—"I think that things raised from this earth's surface to that region have been held there until shaken down by storms." See *The Book of the Damned*, Charles Fort and http://www.anomalist.com/features/sargasso.html.

While technology was advancing the study of the heavens, to the man on the farm, marvels such as comets and meteors and falling stars might still portend the end of the world. These next articles are eye-witness accounts of heavenly prodigies in 1841: a meteor fall and a parade of angels in the sky.

STRANGE HEAVENLY PHENOMENA

Witnessed by Miss Olive E. Coffeen of Hillsboro, O. and Mrs. Martha A. Ellis of [illegible], O., August 19, 1841. Writing of the heavenly hosts, Mrs. Ellis says:

This phenomenon occurred about 2 a.m. Mother was up at the time and was startled by the bright light of a strange appearance in the yards and streets. She soon had all the family up to witness the wondrous scene. The cry went up that the world was coming to an end, but as my father (Dr. Clancy) was a well-read man he soon quieted their fears, while the citizens were all excitement. Mother ran across the street to awaken another old lady so that she might see the great wonder. We called to mother to run back or she would be burned up, as the meteors were falling all around her, but they soon learned that there was little or no heat in them. They fell thick and fast like a heavy fall of snow. They fell within about a foot of the ground and then became extinguished.

This strange scene frighted the people right well. Our old neighbor, Mother Cunningham, got partly dressed and then rushed into the street calling out to all that the end of the world was at hand and the Day of Judgment had come and they were not saved. Repent and be saved, was the cry. By daylight but few meteors were to be seen and nothing remained on the ground to show what a curious thing in nature had occurred.

This great meteoric shower, known as "the falling stars," created a great sensation over all the country. Much fear and consternation were excited among the superstitious, many supposing the end of the world was near at hand. We believe that the cause of this phenomenon never was explained except theoretically.

Bellbrook [OH] Moon 16 March 1904 GREENE COUNTY

I will mention one more strange phenomenon that I witnessed in Bellbrook, August 19, 1841. We were sitting outdoors viewing what to us was a strange sight in the shape of an unusual band or circle of light in the northern heavens...when we noticed excited families of the neighborhood in the streets viewing the south-eastern sky. A glance in that direction showed her a phenomenon which in her own words consisted of angel forms in solemn procession, marching with stately tread through the realms of space in full view. In the heavens, marching by twos, was a parade of what appeared to be human forms clad in flowing robes. As fast as one company consisting of from ten to fifteen couples would disappear from view another would take its place, and the vision lasted ten minutes. The forms were so life-like that seemingly the movements of the limbs could be distinguished. The people at the time were greatly excited at the angelic visitation and in several instances families carried invalids out of doors that they might view the scene. The occurrence took place between nine and ten o'clock in the evening. The forms of the spirit visitors were to all appearances, covered by a gauzy substance, and their existence in companies was visible to the eye through a space of probably thirty degrees in a northwesterly direction....

Bellbrook [OH] Moon 16 March 1904 GREENE COUNTY

The 19th-century papers reveled in stories about falling stars and meteors. There was a whole genre of newspaper stories of houses set on fire by meteors or people killed by them. The shockingly high toll of aerolite victims (the unfortunate "David Misenthaler" and a Mexican sheepherder were two of the most popular) is explained by the fact that identical stories were recycled in newspapers all over the country, with a little editing to make the setting local. Like this plausible-sounding piece:

ONLY MAN EVER KILLED BY A METEOR

To the writer's certain knowledge there is but one case on record where a human being has been killed by an aerolite or fall of meteoric stone. The fatality mentioned occurred in Whetstone Township, Crawford County, O., in 1815, and is recorded in the *Bucyrus Journal* as follows:

As David Misenthaler, the famous stockman of Whetstone Township was driving his cows to the barn about daylight this morning he was struck by an aerolite and instantly killed. It appears as if the stone had come down from a direction a little west of south, striking the man just under or on the right shoulder, passing obliquely through him from the right shoulder to just above the left hip, burying the greater portion of his body under itself in the soft earth. The stone is about the size of a wooden water bucket, and appears to be composed of pyrites of iron.
Sandusky [OH] Daily Register 22 July 1892: p. 2 CRAWFORD COUNTY

Although killer meteors were legendary, the papers were still full of reports of aerolite falls.

FOUND A METEORITE

Last week while Thomas Richards, a resident of Alliance, Ohio, was standing on his porch during a heavy rainstorm he was startled by a bright flash and a hissing sound. The next instant he felt a concussion, which shook the ground and rattled the windows of his dwelling. Richards came to the conclusion that his home had been visited by a meteor, and has been hunting for it ever since.

He has found a hole in the ground within four feet of his house, around which the tall grass had been burned. Richards dug down into the earth and within a foot of the surface struck his meteor. The aerolite is in the shape of a spheroid, and weighs about 9 pounds. It is very hard, blows from a sledge hammer failing to crack it. Local scientists say it is mostly meteoric iron.
New Philadelphia [OH] Ohio Democrat 2 July 1896: p. 8 STARK COUNTY

A VESPER SMOKE DISTURBED.
MR. M'MULLEN CAPTURES A REAL AEROLITE

Cleveland, Ohio, May 29. As Mr. I.N. McMullen was enjoying his vesper smoke last evening in his house yard on Seelye Avenue his attention was arrested by a blazing object in the sky shooting his way. He called to his wife to step out and see it, and as she responded to the call, an aerolite imbedded itself in the ground within 10 feet of where he stood. When it struck, the mass of fire resolved itself into a ball large as a football and burned for a few seconds. The atmosphere was filled with a strong sulphurous odor. For a moment Mr. McMullen was struck dumb with amazement and terror, but on recovering he hastened to the spot where the mass had fallen. He found a hole in the ground from which a considerable amount of heat issued. Resolved at all hazards to find out what had entered the ground, he procured a light, and seizing a small hatchet, dug down for a distance of two feet, when he found a substance about as large as a small apple too hot to handle. He threw it out on the ground to cool, which took about half an hour.

After being sufficiently cooled to handle he took it into the house and proceeded to examine it. It is a half sphere in shape, weighs about 12 ounces and has the appearance of copper coated with a thin black substance. It is so hard that a sharp knife will not cut it. The bottom, which is flat, is punctured with small holes, making it somewhat resemble a sponge. One side is corrugated and has the appearance of beaten brass, only the color is a duller, coarser one. The mass is covered in spots with a thin, melted substance, which causes it to resemble a new casting. Mr. McMullen will place it in the hands of Prof. Morley of Adelbert College for analysis.

The New York Times 30 May 1888 CUYAHOGA COUNTY

NOTE: Perhaps Prof. Morley was included to add verisimilitude to a spoof, but he was the very real chemistry professor Edward Morley of the Michelson-Morley experiments on the speed of light. Adelbert College eventually became Case Western Reserve University.

I've run across a few early accounts of UFOs, but, like the meteor story above, they may be tall tales. This one has a delightful steampunk flair to it.

FROM THE LAKE
THE STRANGE BOAT ASCENDED AND SAILED AWAY

Cleveland, Ohio, April 15. S.H. Davis, of Detroit, was in Cleveland this week. He was out on his fish tug, the *Sea Wing*, Wednesday headed for Cleveland Harbor about 15 miles from the piers. The fisherman noticed a queer-looking boat about two miles away.

When the tug drew near it was discovered that the strange boat was a curio. Captain Joseph Singler, master of the tug, and Mr. Davis agreed in the statement that it appeared to be about 40 feet in length and was formed somewhat like a barge. It had a cabin covering about one fourth of the deck surface.

A man in a checked hunting suit and wearing a long, peaked cap, was fishing from the boat. He was apparently about 25 years of age. A handsome woman sat at his side. A boy of about 10 years sat at her feet. As the *Sea Wing* neared the curious craft, to the amazement of those on the tug, a gaily decorated object, which had been lying on a frame work over the boat, was slowly inflated and rose to the length of the ropes by which it was attached to the boat. It was a balloon, cylinder-shaped, about 50 feet long.

Slowly the boat rose into the air until it stood directly over the tug, about 50 feet from the water. It circled like a hawk for several minutes. Suddenly there was a splash in the water. A large sword fish had been dropped from the airship. The fish was stunned by its fall, and was picked up by Captain Singler, and is now on exhibition in a tank at the fire tug Cleveland, Ohio. After moving aimlessly about for a short time, a sail was dropped from the airship, and the mysterious people were carried away by the high wind.
Cincinnati [OH] Enquirer 16 April 1897: p. 6 LAKE ERIE/CUYAHOGA COUNTY

NOTE: The *Sea Wing* was a real tug built in 1881 and owned by E.A. Davis of Detroit, according to the 1899 *Blue Book of American Shipping*. This was during the 1896-1897 "Mystery Airship Flap." There are a number of theories about these mystery airships: inventors' prototypes on test flights, journalistic hoaxes, alien spaceships, and mis-identified flocks of birds. For more information see *The Great Airship of 1897* by J. Allan Danelek (Adventures Unlimited Press, 2009); *Solving the 1897 Airship Mystery*, Michael Busby, (Pelican, 2004) and, for a slightly later airship flap, the comprehensive, *The Scareship Mystery: A Survey of Phantom Airship Scares, 1909-1918*, Nigel Watson (Domra Publications, 2000).

VERY LIKE A WHALE

Zanesville, Ohio April 5, 1873
To the Editor of the *Herald*:

A most extraordinary phenomenon was observed near the village of Taylorsville, a few miles from this city, about a week ago. Mr. Thomas Inman, whom your reporter can vouch for as a respectable farmer of unquestionable truth and veracity, related the circumstances to the writer, and, with his son, who was also an eye witness, is willing to make oath to the truth of this statement.

One evening about two weeks ago, while Mr. Inman and his son, a young man, were returning to their home from Taylorsville, they saw a light, which they describe as looking like a "burning brush pile," near the zenith, descending rapidly towards the earth, with a loud, roaring noise. It struck the ground in the road a short distance from them. The blazing object flickered and flared for a few moments and then faded into darkness, as a man dressed in a complete suit of black and carrying a lantern emerged from it. The man walked a few paces and stepped into a buggy, which had not been observed before by either Mr. Inman or his son. There was no horse attached to this supernatural vehicle, but no sooner had the man taken his seat than it started to run, noiselessly, but with great velocity along the highway and this it continued to do until it reached a steep gully, into which it plunged, when buggy, man, and lantern suddenly disappeared as mysteriously as they came.

This phenomenon is certainly an extraordinary and unexplainable one, and sounds more like the vagary of a crazed brain than anything else. But both Mr. Inman and his son, who are sober men and not given to superstitious notions, agree precisely in their statements and maintain that they are strictly true. If it was an optical delusion, superinduced by a meteor or "Jack o' lantern," is it not strange that the same fancied appearances could be conjured up in the minds of two men at the same time? Here is a chance for scientists to explain the fantastical optical and other illusions and delusions which follow in the train of, and are suggested by, some strange and unexpected sight or occurrence.

W. A. Taylor.

New York Herald 8 April 1873: p. 7 HIGHLAND COUNTY

NOTE: The title is drawn from a dialog between Hamlet and Polonius in William Shakespeare's *Hamlet*, Act iii Sc. 2, where the two men are looking at clouds:

> *Ham.* Do you see yonder cloud that's almost in the shape of a camel?
>
> *Pol.* By the mass, and 't is like a camel, indeed.
>
> *Ham.* Methinks it is like a weasel.
>
> *Pol.* It is backed like a weasel.
>
> *Ham.* Or like a whale?
>
> *Pol.* Very like a whale.

The man carrying the lantern could be the prototype of the Men in Black. The horseless buggy and the falling, blazing brush pile sound like something from "the father of Science Fiction," Jules Verne, who wrote about space travel, submarines, and manned flight before such things were invented. He wrote extremely popular novels such as *Journey to the Center of the Earth* (1864) and *Twenty Thousand Leagues Under the Sea* (1870).

And finally, what was this thing, anyway?

AN EARLY UNIDENTIFIED FLYING OBJECT

Monday afternoon, May 1st, Henry Altman, who lives a mile north of Lockport, had an experience that created consternation in his soul for the space of a few minutes.

He was fishing on John Wyse's farm, back where a small stream empties into Bean Creek. All was quiet and no sound broke the afternoon stillness, till he heard a distant whirling sound that grew louder and louder. At first he thought it was a sound of a flock of birds coming through the air. He looked around and guided by the sound finally saw an object coming through the air.

When he first saw it he thought of a large chicken hawk, but as it came nearer he thought of a meteoric rock. A nearer view showed it to be a funnel-shaped affair with the small end forward and at an angle of forty-five degrees. Along the top was what appeared to be a large fan-shaped appliance.

The direction taken by this queer craft was south with a slight variation to the west.

It appeared to be about three or four times as high as the treetops and from 80 to 100 rods away and while it kept the same distance from the ground it moved with incredible velocity. When closest to him it looked to be about four feet long.

In describing his sensations he said he was frightened and wished he was not alone. The same object was seen by people near Burlington and Mr. Altman is not one of the kind that carries "bait" that is apt to make a person "see things." What was the thing, anyway?

Bryan [OH] Democrat, May 1899, quoted in *Stories of The Fountain City 1840-1900*, Paul Van Gundy (Bryan: OH: The Bryan Area Foundation, 1975) p. 111. WILLIAMS COUNTY

3.

Spooks in the Slammer:
Haunted Jails; Haunted Prisoners

I am forbid
To tell the secrets of my prison-house

– Hamlet, Act 1: Scene 5 –

As I wrote in the preface to the tale of the Woman in White haunting the Hamilton County Jail in *The Face in the Window*, there was a genre of haunted jail stories in the 19th-century papers. The usual explanation for such stories is remorseful convicts, but I find it hard to believe that all of the criminals of this era had such tender consciences that they hallucinated ghosts. Another recurring theme is superstition and its ruinous effects on character. There is an underlying assumption that only the ignorant and the criminal believe in ghosts; *ergo* belief in ghosts leads to a life of crime. You have been warned...

A HAUNTED JAIL.
A COLUMBIANA COUNTY MURDERER SAID TO BE PLAYING GHOST

The other night an event occurred in the jail at Leetonia that will be remembered by the prisoners to the full length of their existence, and which would have appalled the stoutest heart, being in its nature inexplicable and frightful. At about nine o'clock Tooley McKee, who is confined in jail for selling liquor in violation of the law, divested himself of his clothing and got into bed. Shortly afterward unearthly yells were heard to emanate from his cell, and all at once he brought up with a crash against the door, while still more frightened he drew a bed quilt over his head, exclaiming in pitiful tones, "My God, I see Mead!" He had hardly given utterance to the ejaculation ere a chair mysteriously dashed against the barred door and fell in broken fragments, a bucket leaped forward from the corner of the cell, and the foul contents fell upon his person, the shackles hanging in the hall commenced to clank with terrible violence, and the iron bed was wrenched from its fastenings and the bedclothes flew in the utmost disorder about the cell. As if to add to

the dire confusion, the prisoners in the other part of the building added demoniac yells of alarm. Tooley, his hair standing on end and his eyeballs starting from their sockets, leaped about his cell like a caged hyena, and with every leap a yell of agony; while upon the walls all around him there shone out a richly sulphurous light, dancing as in mockery of his terror. Human fortitude could endure this no longer and, with a cry to Deputy Gailey for help, he sank fainting to the floor. As in broken accents Tooley unfolds the terrors of that night, it is enough to make the hair of a tobacconist's Indian stand around on his head like a brush fence afflicted with the jim-jams. The prisoners are all firm in the belief that Mead has returned to earth to haunt the jail.
Cincinnati [OH] Enquirer 8 December 1877: p. 2 COLUMBIANA COUNTY

NOTE: Mead was Samuel Err Mead, who murdered Elijah Davidson, an 89-year-old veteran of the War of 1812 for his money. He was captured, tried, convicted, and sentenced to death, then given a new trial. However, he escaped and was at large for several years before he returned to see his wife. Authorities cornered him and he shot himself. The full story can be found at http://www.eastliverpoolhistoricalsociety.org/murwiout2.htm. The "tobacconist's Indian" is a carved wooden Indian used as a shop display.

A cruel and unusual punishment from the Ohio State Penitentiary:

GHOST SCARE WORKED WELL.
GUARDS AT OHIO "PEN" TRY NOVEL FORM OF DISCIPLINE

Columbus, Aug. 11. The guards of the Ohio Penitentiary have decided on the "ghost scare" as a sure cure for misbehaved colored prisoners and attempted their first experiment with ghosts Saturday night. The experiment worked to such good purpose that the prisoner experimented upon nearly went into hysterics.

Many of the colored prisoners are habitual criminals and spend most of their time in solitary confinement much to the annoyance of the guards in charge. One of the guards conceived the idea of giving a "ghost scare." Throwing a sheet over his head he went into the cellar about 11 o'clock and proceeded towards the cell of the one of the men confined.

With a yell that could be heard all over the big prison, the colored prisoner fell to the floor begging for his life and moaning as if he was about to die. The guard thinking that his man had enough went away, but the prisoner could not be quieted. He threw himself about and appeared to be in such agony that medical attention had to be called to quiet him.

In a short time the news that ghosts were about the prison was known to all of the prisoners, who had heard the scream of the scared man, and sleep was impossible the rest of the night.

The plan worked so well that the colored population have vowed that they will be good for all time to come and have promised the guards that if they will keep the ghosts away they will have no more trouble on their account.

It is the plan of the guards to try the "scare" as often as the occasion calls for. If it works again as it did Saturday night the "solitary" will be a deserted place for a long time to come. Many tricks have been used, but none of them has had the effect of the one lone ghost.

The subject of the experiment is in good condition again, but does not know the ghost he saw was not real. Much comment on the mysterious ghost is passed, and when the occasion requires the men to go near the cellar they waste no time in getting by the supposed headquarters of the whiteclad spirits.

Evening Independent [Massillon, OH] 11 August 1909: p. 2 FRANKLIN COUNTY

NOTE: A common theme in 19th-century papers was that African Americans were unusually superstitious and afraid of ghosts—hence this heartless "ghost scare," which does not seem to have been tried on the white prisoners. However, the following story suggests that the authorities at the Penitentiary, which housed some of the most hardened criminals in the country, did not mind encouraging ghostly tales to keep order among the inmates.

CRAVEN
BECOMES THE DESPERADO
CONFINED IN THE FATAL CELL THIRTEEN
STRANGE SERIES OF STARTLING AND UNCANNY OCCURRENCES

CREDIT A CELL IN THE PENITENTIARY WITH WEIRD TERRORS
THREE PRISONERS HAVE KILLED THEMSELVES IN IT AND SEVERAL MORE HAVE SEEN GHOSTS.

Columbus, Ohio, December 14. Down in the cellar of the penitentiary is a dark cell, credited by the imaginations of the more superstitious convicts with all the terrors properly belonging to an abode of departed spirits, who still feel the weight of sins committed upon earth preying upon them. A large portion of the felon population of the big prison will put up a very lively fight before consenting to a stay in that cell, and those morally more brave, or physically less courageous, who take their turn of punishment in the cell without a murmur, come out limp with the horror of the sojourn. Every colored convict in the institution will tell you, if he consents to talk of the matter at all, that Cell 13, Solitary, is "ha'nted," and most of the white men will swear to the statement.

The cell itself is a very innocent looking affair. It is the corner cell in the solitary block, better known as the cellar. Here

REFRACTORY CONVICTS

Are taken for a practical illustration of the great moral truth, that sins bear with them their own punishment. The fact that the punishment usually comes in the form of a six-foot paddle, wielded by a lusty convict, is ordinarily convincing to the victim. Occasionally the water treatment is administered, and once in a long while other punishment is resorted to. But only with the more determined case of sulkiness is the haunted cell brought into action. Then the recalcitrant is ordered to Cell 13, and the ceremonies begin which usually result in a change on the part of the object of this attention.

Cell 13's bad reputation is not entirely undeserved. Several men have committed suicide within its portals, and many others have made desperate attempts to get away from this life of care, and incidentally from the haunted cell, only to be cut down in time by the guards. Therefore, two superstitions have been fastened to the cell by the convicts who have occasion to resort to the cellar. The first is that the cell in question is the permanent abiding place of all manner of spooks and hobgoblins who delight in appearing to the unfortunate temporary occupant of their home amid gusts of red fire and to the accompaniment of rattled bones and jingling chains.

The second is that the cell itself exerts a malign influence over those unfortunate enough to be incarcerated in it. According to the tale which finds most favor among its occasional visitors, the cell is inhabited by a spirit, ghost, call it what you will, that impels poor convicts irresistibly toward self-destruction. Men who have been placed in the cell overnight come out worn with the strain in the morning and assert that throughout the hours of darkness they had to fight against the impulse to tear their bedding into strips and suspend themselves by the neck to the convenient bar above the door. A voice seemed to whisper in their ears of the beauties of an eternal release from suffering and prison and promise wonderful happiness in the indefinite future.

The cell's history is such as to lend an air of probability to these tales to those superstitiously inclined. Its first occupant was Harry Johnson, from the northern part of the state, serving a short term for manslaughter. He was, ordinarily speaking, a good convict, though he had the name of being "set in his ways" and a man of great determination. The

NEW SOLITARY BLOCK

Had just been completed then, and the hospital had been removed from the old hall into its present commodious and elegant quarters. Johnson appeared at the morning clinic with a complaint of sickness. He was pronounced a malingerer, and ordered back to work. He went to the shop where he was employed, and worked a short time. Then he went to the hospital and demanded medicine, saying he was too sick to work.

He was refused medicine and sent back to the shops. He utterly declined to do any work and was sent to the cellar for punishment. He was "hung up" by the hands until his agony became so apparent that the guards cut him down. A physician examined him, and for some unknown reason ordered him hung up again, but the guards refused. Whatever the man might have been, he was certainly sick enough after his punishment. That night he was locked in Cell 13, and in the morning, when the guard was making his first round, he came face to face with Johnson, grinning through the bars. He had torn his shirt into strips and hung himself in earnest. His feet hardly cleared the floor, but his hands hung clenched at his side, showing the determination of the man.

The story of Johnson's death got abroad and aroused much sympathy for the man. It was generally believed that he had been cruelly treated, and soon the story started that his spirit walked o' nights. It was whispered about that in the quiet of the cellar night, where darkness reigns at all times, Johnson's voice could be heard in impassioned protest against the manner in which he had been treated. Then his pain-wrenched body could be heard brushing about in the empty cell. A fierce whisper of defiance to the guards, to the world which had mistreated him and to the God who had deserted him, preceded the gurgle which announced that strangulation was slowly ending his life. That performance began early in the evening, according to the story, and kept up all night.

Sam Tyler was the next man to venture upon the uncertainties of the next world after an unfortunate experience with the realities of this life. Sam had been a bad Indian for some time, and in his own cell had tried to shuffle off by the gas route. He was foiled in this, and removed to solitary for punishment. Sam was penitent by this time, and was willing to quit and be good, but in spite of his protests he was given the cell where Johnson had committed suicide. That night Johnson appeared to Tyler, and Tyler tried the rope. The cellar guards were on the lookout for such an attempt, and cut him down. Tyler shouted and raved all day and most of the night. Toward morning

HE BECAME QUIET,

And when the guard investigated the reason for the sudden stillness he slipped on a pool of blood. Tyler had cut the arteries of both wrists and stayed quiet while his life blood poured out. It is still a mystery where he got his knife.

Then Frank Campbello happened along. He had been sent from Cuyahoga County for cutting to wound, and was due to stay a year. Campbello undertook to revolt and was subdued. Ennui overcame him and he tried to vary the monotony of his existence. He went to the cellar because his attempts were ill-advised. He took Cell 13, and the next morning was found facing the bars of his door, grinning into the future. A rope of bedding was twisted about his neck, and he was free again.

The last man to succeed in shuffling off in this cell was Johnny Jones, of Hamilton County. Johnny was a thoroughly bad man, and was serving a ten-year sentence for criminal assault. He had been cantankerous for some time and was sent to the cellar for treatment. Cell 13 was prescribed and though Johnny protested with all the force of his lungs and fists, he was locked safely in. On the morning of December 2, 1898, Guard Prittner discovered that Johnny had escaped from the cell. He had twisted the sleeves of his shirt into a rope and suspended himself from the same old bar. He had to hold his feet up to make suffocation possible, but he stuck to it until he was dead as Caesar.

Many others have tried to commit suicide while locked in this cell, though, owing to the watchfulness of the guards, they have failed. The last was George Penrose on Wednesday night of this week. George was locked in the cell overnight because there was no other place to put him. He knew nothing of the eerie reputation it has, and did not object to going in. But toward morning a gurgle aroused Guard Prittner, and he cut George down. His face was then black from suffocation, and a minute more would have done the work.

Dan Watkins, a colored man from South Carolina, was absolutely impervious to the ordinary methods of punishment. He took the paddle as he would snuff, and sniffed contemptuously at the water treatment. As a last resort he was sent to Cell 13. That night.

HE SAW GLIMMERING SKULLS

And white-robed figures, and saw hell open itself before him and devils ascending and descending into the pit. The next morning Dan was unconscious, but he was cured. He was never reported again for a violation of the rules of the prison, and sat as close to the platform as possible during the Sunday sermons. Iconoclastic guards say that Guard Prittner is responsible for this conversion, and that a dime's worth of phosphorus and 10 cents invested in red fire cured the worst man in the prison. But Prittner says nothing.

Jud Holland, the famous Franklin County "cow killer," went on a rampage recently. He took the water and the paddle, and the suspension treatment, and every other old thing which could be thought of. He laughed at his jailers, and made trouble for them at every opportunity. Then he was ordered to Cell 13. At the door he gave a wild screech of terror and broke away from three guards. He managed to get into the yard, and it took the united efforts of four men to get him back to the cellar. Holland was not kept in the cell overnight, but he has reformed. No more trouble from Jud.

Garland Silvey, of Meigs County, was released on parole this week. Silvey tried to commit suicide in this cell one night. He doesn't talk of what he heard or saw in there, but he has never been reported since. He earned his parole by good conduct.

Charles Smith, a five-year man from Franklin County, made two attempts in one night while in this cell, but was cut down both times.

Richard Proctor, a Montgomery County burglar, and a man of intelligence, entered the cell one night raving with anger and breathing defiance to all. In the morning he was humble and penitent and begged to be taken out. He was left in another night and at midnight was cut down from the same old bar. Proctor has not been reported lately. *Cincinnati [OH] Enquirer* 15 December 1898: p. 3 FRANKLIN COUNTY

NOTE: One wonders why "the same old bar" wasn't just removed to prevent some of these suicides. The "water treatment" involved a ducking tub and a fire hose. The hickory paddles were said to be "sharp-edged." But corporal punishment moved with the times: "The electric battery has superseded the hose and cold water treatment for taming refractory prisoners in the Ohio penitentiary. It is reported to be very efficacious...." *Jersey Journal* [Jersey City, NJ] 16 August 1890: p. 4

Jud Holland, the Franklin County "cow killer," caught in 1892, was compared in the press to Jack the Ripper "the only difference being that Holland's victims were animals instead of human beings." He apparently ripped at least 10 cows and one horse, hiding the cows' sexual organs and other pieces of their flesh in a ruined factory. "The Cow-Chopper Caught/ Jud Holland, a Colored Youth, the Fiend, Who Has Turned Cow Pastures Into Fields of Gore," was one typical headline. The consumptive Garland Silvey was paroled reputedly because he made himself such a nuisance behind bars that the authorities just wanted him gone.

Politicians and bureaucrats haven't changed much in the last century. In this account of ghostly doings in the Statehouse Governor's Office, you can practically hear the Executive Clerk telling his story "off the record," then, backtracking and claiming it's all a joke.

HAUNTED
BY MURDERERS' SPIRITS
AN OLD CUPBOARD IN THE GOVERNOR'S OFFICE
CONTAINS THE PARDON PAPERS OF DOOMED MEN
LOUD RAPS FOLLOW EACH EXECUTION.

Columbus, Ohio. November 23.
Is the Governor's office haunted?
This is the question that is just now agitating the superstitiously inclined about the State-house.

Executive Clerk Bawsell, of the Governor's office, who is ex-officio Secretary of the State Board of Pardons, is authority for the statement that the Executive Chamber is tenanted by at least a dozen ghosts.

According to the Executive Clerk's story it was about five months ago that he first noticed the presence of supernatural beings in the

STATELY OLD ROOMS

Of the Executive Department. In telling the story to a party of friends this afternoon Mr. Bawsell said:

"One night soon after the execution of Jake Harvey, the Dayton man who murdered his mistress, while seated here at this desk, I was startled by a loud knock on the doors of the large cupboard where the applications for pardons and commutations of sentences are kept. I thought it was the wind at first, but investigation proved that it was not. Just what caused the noise I was unable to learn. I thought very little of the affair until the

NIGHT OF THE EXECUTION

Of Craig and McCarthy, the Cincinnati murderers. I was here alone in the office that night, and as far as I was able to tell there was no one else in the whole building excepting the watchman at the treasury vaults and the patrolman in the rotunda. There was no living being here who could have made the noise I heard. About 10 o'clock the knocking in that cupboard began and it was kept up at a lively rate for two hours and a half. Just after the execution of both the murderers was finished there

WAS A PERFECT SHOWER

Of knocks. What caused it I don't know. Of course, I was only joking when I said the place was haunted, for I am not superstitious. If I were the least bit superstitious, however, I would say that the knocking is done by the spirits of the men who have been executed in the penitentiary annex, and whose applications for pardons or commutations of sentences are still stored away in that mysterious old cupboard."
Cincinnati [OH] Enquirer 24 November 1892: p. 1 FRANKLIN COUNTY

NOTE: Inmates Edward McCarthy and Charles Craig were both executed on September 9, 1892. Charles Craig, the first African-American executed in the Penitentiary annex, murdered and decapitated his mistress. Edward McCarthy shot Charles Nederman in a Cincinnati street, then fled from the police, triggering a manhunt. Jake Harvey murdered Maggie Lehman, a prostitute, at Dayton.

HAUNTED
THE SEDAMSVILLE STATION-HOUSE VISITED BY A GHOST

The ghost at the County Jail has not been heard of for some time [5 January 1878], and perhaps the perturbed spirit of Mrs. Mack [see *The Face in the Window*] has at last been mollified, but now comes Sedamsville with a first-class ghost story, and one which seems to be well authenticated by responsible and reliable men. The Police Station-house is an old, rickety, tumble-down shanty, part stone and part frame. The rear portion of it is imbedded in a hill on the north side of the main road to Riverside. Up to within a few months ago the office of the station was on the first floor of the building. Here a certain Lieutenant of the force, who has since been assigned to duty elsewhere, was so wrought up by the steady tramp, tramp of the ghostly visitant, one cold winter's night, that, after hunting around in every crook and cranny of the house to find something that would account for the noise, he gave it up in despair and rushed out of the building and stood for a long time shivering. Being asked by a patrolman why he did not go in to the fire, he said he couldn't stand that d____d racket any longer.

This noise, as if someone was walking, was kept up at intervals until about three months ago, when Lieutenant Brothers, who is now on duty there, moved his office to the story above. His experience while occupying the office has been similar to his predecessor's, and to this day the mystery is as great as ever. Time and again investigations have been made by the officers and Turnkeys, but each time they are baffled.

One night not long since, when Turnkey Guenther was sitting alone, with nothing for company but the cockroaches and gray-backs, with which the old rookery abounds, this old chronic tramp, tramp of unseen feet began. Guenther listened until he could stand the strain no longer. But the worst was to come. Timidly glancing around the lonesome room, his marrow almost froze in his veins when in one corner he beheld a shrouded figure, its gleaming eyeballs starting from their sockets, and a skeleton arm raised as if in warning. It took just a second and a half for the horror-stricken man to leap through the door. After a little while he returned and saw it again standing where he left it. Levelling his revolver at the "thing," he placed his finger on the trigger and just as he pulled it, "it" whisked into nothingness. The ball lodged in the wall close to where the visitor stood.

This seemed to settle his ghostship for a while, but again it has come and just at midnight at the time when churchyards yawn and graves give up their dead, that steady and persistent tramp is heard. Sergeant Norton hears it; Lieutenant Brothers hears it; the Turnkey has seen it, and they cannot explain it away. Like Banquo's ghost, it will not down, but returns nightly to disturb the rest of these men. The bolts on the empty cells, too, have a disagreeable way of moving when no one is near them, and this in connection with the wandering spirit renders the old place anything but a desirable place in which to pass a pleasant evening. Local tradition has it that many years ago the then owner of the house committed suicide in a room from whence these noises seem to come. But whatever be the cause it is a notorious fact that a strange and unearthly spectre has been seen there as described, and that the ceaseless patter of feet can be distinctly heard almost every night. Ask Lieutenant Brothers or his men about it.

Cincinnati [OH] Enquirer 25 February 1878: p. 4 HAMILTON COUNTY

NOTE: "When churchyards yawn" is from *Hamlet*, Act 3 scene 2; Banquo's ghost is a reference to *Macbeth*.

AN OHIO GHOST

Canton, O. Jan 18. Edward E. Howell, an inmate of the county jail, under indictment for grand larceny, aroused the other inmates and officials by shrieks of "Murder! Help!" The officials rushed to the cell and found him prostrated and trembling with nervous excitement. It was some time before he could speak, when he said a ghost had made its appearance in his cell. He gave a minute description of the ghost, which tallied exactly with the clothing and appearance of Geo. McMillen, who was executed here last summer for wife murder, and who occupied Howell's cell. Howell said the ghost suddenly appeared before him with its right hand raised, as if in the act of swearing. Its neck was broken and its head dropping over on one shoulder. The ghost stared at Howell with glassy eyes a short time, and then slowly receded through the walls of the cell. The case is all the more remarkable from the fact that Howell never saw McMillen. He was given another cell, where he kept the other prisoners awake the balance of the night.

Kansas City [MO] Star 22 January 1884: p. 1 STARK COUNTY

The dark environs of the Ohio Penitentiary seemed to fascinate the 19th-century journalist, whether relating tales of the cursed Cell 13 or ghostly re-enactments of tragedies.

DEATH PICTURE IN DARK CELL
HORRIBLE CRIMES COMMITTED NIGHTLY BY
A HAUNTED BLACKSMITH PRISONER
PHANTOM TRAGEDIES
EYES OF CONVICTS SEE MANY GHOSTLY OBJECTS
WHILE ANSWERING FOR SIN

Men who remain long behind the walls that the law decrees shall shut them away from the world because of their sins, become much given to silent thought—not by choice but by necessity—and they become examples of peculiar psychological conditions. From their minds are evolved weird creations of fancy which take the form of tales, sometimes.

Such a man, writing for a paper, says:

"I am a convict. For two years I have cringed behind the gray walls and steel bars of the Ohio Penitentiary. During this time many strange things have happened that are difficult to explain.

"Upon my arrival in the penitentiary I was assigned to double cell 10, block K, range 2, then occupied by a professional house breaker by the name of Cannon. I did not know at that time whether it was because of his hard work every day over a hot ring fire in Hayden's blacksmith shop, or whether it was because of some physical derangement that caused his features to appear so white and drawn, but I afterward learned, and the thought sends a quiver through my frame as I recall it, why the groping form of the blacksmith no longer appeared elastic, and the eyes which once sparkled with merriment turned in their flabby encasements with a dull, careworn expression.

FIRST NIGHT IN PRISON

"It was my first night in the Ohio penitentiary and I had retired early, worn out physically and fatigued mentally. As I climbed to the top bunk I noticed the form of my cell mate on the cot beneath me, sleeping as gently as a child. I quietly arranged myself, turned down the gas, and in a few minutes had passed into oblivion.

"But a little past 12 o'clock I started up wide awake. In the profound silence I had distinctly heard sharp sounds as of a death struggle. I knew the gas had been turned off from below and as I had no matches in my pocket I stooped down and felt with my hand along the lower bunk. It was empty! I was not dreaming. I still heard the same awful sounds, and then, as my eyes wandered in fright toward the grating of the cell door, opposite which a single feeble gas jet flickered and waned I distinctly saw my cell mate and a man who I had never before seen, in deadly combat. I essayed to cry out, but my tongue clove to the roof of my mouth and my lips refused to part, as I sat in my bunk trembling with fear, my eyes protruding from their sockets at the awful sight before me.

FIGHT TO THE DEATH

"My cell mate had the stranger grasped by the throat, and reaching back, drew forth a large knife with a deer's foot handle, the keen blade of which he savagely and repeatedly thrust into the neck of his victim. At last the stranger sank to his knees, weak and trembling from loss of blood, which I saw shimmering in a pool by the grating of the cell door. My cell mate then drew the limp and helpless body to the night bucket and with one tremendous sweep of the dirk severed the head from the body, which rolled from his knee into the uncovered bucket. He then calmly wiped away the blood from his murderous knife, upon the leg of his drawers, and placing the lid upon the bucket and a blanket over the headless trunk, he crawled quietly back to bed.

"I did not sleep any more that night and was up at the first tap of the bell in the morning, expecting to see a gruesome sight. But the cell and its furnishings appeared just as they had before I went to bed; not a trace of blood or disorder could be seen. I looked for the headless body, but there was none.

HAUNTED BY SIGHT

"My cellmate, who had been watching my actions, now knew that I had witnessed the phantom tragedy, and after I had questioned him for some time he broke down and begged me not to mention what I had seen. For two weeks I occupied this cell with the haunted blacksmith and each night I witnessed the same harrowing scene just as I have described it, and then fearing that my mind would suddenly give way under the awful strain, I appealed to be transferred to another cell and the request was granted, but I never mentioned the horrors of the haunted blacksmith.

"In the center of the prison courtyard there is a fountain: it is not very large nor very deep, but the boys call it 'Well's Lake' in compliment to former Deputy Warden Wells. It is rimmed around with concrete curbing, and in the good old summer time three half-grown alligators may be seen lazily basking in the warm sunshine, stretching themselves with careless indifference along the rim at the fountain's edge. Two crescent-shaped flower beds, one on each side of the fountain, afford the saurian a cool resting place when Old Sol gets too spunky.

"One evening in August, 1902, as the shadows began to gather, while walking in the court yard for exercise, I ran upon one of the oldest inmates of the institution, a life man, who had served more than twenty years behind the walls, whose hair and beard were as white as the driven snow.

DROWNED IN FOUNTAIN

"As we walked together along the strip of concrete leading from the deputy warden's office to the guard room gate, we passed the fountain above referred to, and my old friend, leaning heavily on his strong cane, pointed a withered finger at the little body of water, and in a voice trembling from old age and emotion, said:

"'I knowed a convict many years ago who drowned hisself in that fountain, and some o' the boys do tell now as how they have seen his ghost jump into it, but I never seed it o' myself.'

"'Is that so, daddy; tell me about it,' I replied.

"'Wall, it was like this: he was a purty pert feller, sent up from somewhere down nigh Cincinnaty with two years for sumthin' or other. I don't know what now, less'n it was pocket-picking. After he was here nigh on about a year his wife went clean back on him and writ him as how she'd never live with him again. Well, sir, the poor feller climbed into that 'ere fountain and drowned hisself.'

"As the last words escaped the old man's lips, I turned mechanically, and my eyes voluntarily sought the spot, and there, to my horror, I saw, standing upon the very rim of the fountain, the shadowy form of a man, his arms, held high above his head, as in the attitude of diving, his wild eyes glistening in the struggling beams of a distant arc-light, his teeth clinched with determination.

"There was no need to nudge the old man by my side, for he, too, had turned and stood watching the phantom diver with a face as white as marble, his knees chattering beneath him. He only had time to exclaim: 'It is he!' and then—

"Splash!

"The man, or whatever it was, had cast himself forward and into the waters of the fountain.

"With my heart beating wildly I ran swiftly forward, but I saw not a ripple on the face of the still water, and as my eyes pierced the gloom that enshrouded its edges, I could see nothing but three alligators lying at anchor, napping, their slumbers not even so much as having been disturbed by the fateful plunge of the phantom suicide.

"Can such events be put down to the imagination? Remember in this case two persons were witnesses, and my old friend recognized his chum of former years.

"The night guards, who during the solemn watches of the night steal stealthily along the ranges from cell to cell in soft-soled slippers, have nothing to give out for publication, but when approached upon the subject, wink the other eye in a knowing way and reluctantly admit that sometimes queer noises emanate from the caged cells, and frequently as they pass noiselessly by a barred door the fretful mutterings of a restless convict is wafted to their ears through the gratings.

"It sometimes happens that in a single night a convict becomes a raving maniac, awaking with cries and curses the entire cell block. In such cases the night guards are summoned and take the unfortunate fellow away to the insane ward.

"And what has driven him there?

"My friend, if you were his cellmate you would, perhaps, know the reasons, but as you are not, thank God, and go on your way rejoicing."
Kalamazoo [MI] Gazette 16 December 1905: p. 13

NOTE: Yes, the alligators in the pond gave me pause too. It turns out there really *were* alligators at the Ohio State Penitentiary. The first one arrived in a barrel after two guards found the four-foot-long reptile lying in the street. It had escaped from its owner, a saloon-keeper and when the man found that his lost pet was happy in its new home, he let him stay there. A double-murderer from Cleveland, Pat Moran, started feeding the alligator, which quickly grew so tame that it would take food from his hand and follow him around the lawn when he called.

Three more alligators came to the penitentiary when a Columbus man found that the alligators he had ordered from the South averaged five feet long and were so vicious that he was afraid to let them out of their crates. He had heard of Moran's reptile-taming and asked him if he'd care for the alligators. Moran happily accepted and they were added to the fountain. They were wild at first, but by pursuing the same tactics with them that he did with the first "gator" and feeding them every day he finally got them as tame as the other one. He often scratched the reptiles' backs and heads, fondling them like a pet dog. The reptiles gave a bit of trouble in 1910 when Chaplain

Frank Richards wanted to perform a full-immersion baptism in the pond and the alligators objected. They were removed to their winter quarters in the basement of the chapel until multiple prisoners had been baptised. [SOURCES: *The Washington [DC] Times* 31 December 1905, Woman's Magazine Section, p. 11; *The Dispatch* [Columbus, OH] 14 May 1910.] FRANKLIN COUNTY

Given the dark tone of these reports of ghosts in the haunts of crime, I will finish with a spooky mystery in a more light-hearted vein from the Cleveland police station.

SPOOK, BANSHEE OR MURDERER?
CENTRAL STATION POLICE HAVE MYSTERY
WITHIN THEIR OWN WALLS
RIGID INVESTIGATION BEING CONDUCTED BY
BEST OF THE FORCE

There is a deep, dark and impenetrable mystery at Cleveland's central police station, and the best talent of the department is now occupied in an attempt to solve it. It may be murder; it may be ghosts. Which, it remains for the police to learn, and the efforts to unravel the problem will be unceasing until every separate thread lies exposed to the departmental view.

At one end of the first floor corridor in the station is a little side room. Upon the doors are the cabalistic letters "Reporters' Room," and within, upon the floor, are scattered papers and cigar stubs, and things. The chairs and tables are much frequented by the familiars of police headquarters. There are also many cats in the neighborhood of the station; but that, of course, has nothing to do with the present tale.

Late yesterday afternoon, for once in a year, the room was deserted. The doors were closed, and an air of quiet wafted gently about the halls. A squad of policemen entered to report, and breathed deep signs of relief as they noted the deserted atmosphere round about that little room.

"Ain't it great?" said they.

Suddenly came a sound.

"Wo-o-o-w."

Loud and long it wailed. Its cadence floating up the stairway to the court in progress on the second floor.

"What's that," said the squad, halting.

"Wow, Whack, scr-a-a-sh, we-o-o-w."

"It's murder. That's what it is," said the squad with conviction. "Send for Toy Marshal."

The squad was re-enforced by other detachments from the officers' room downstairs and the attachés of the chief's and captains' quarters. With commendable decision a sergeant took charge and deployed his men.

"Guard those doors well," he thundered. "Let no guilty man escape. Hold guns in readiness. Three men deploy and look through the jail windows and find out what you can see."

The jail windows look directly into the little room, and the officers at once deployed.

They returned with blanched faces.

"C-c-cant s-see anything," they gasped. "It's sperrits."

"Whack, zim-m-m me-eow," came from the beleaguered room.

Then up dashed a volunteer. Trained in many a fight, learned in the ways of ghosts and murderers, he rashly promised to storm the room and rescue the unhappy victim of assassin or banshee.

As the now great force of patrolmen stood back, arms to readiness, he stealthily slipped up to the door. Slowly, softly he turned the knob and opened a narrow crack. He looked in. He opened the crack a little wider.

"They ain't nothin' here," said he.

As the officers rushed pell mell into the benewspapered and cigar stubbed apartment, two lithe shadows glided among their feet, unseen, and departed. The room was empty.

Now the police are investigating the mystery. Who was it made that noise? What ghost invaded central station, or what murderer dared pursue his nefarious course within its walls? What did he do with the body?

These questions will have to be answered, for the best talent of the department is at work, and soon the whole nefarious thing will be laid open to public horror. In the meantime, unconnected with the mystery and inconsequent to this story, "Siss," the station cat, has a very sore ear, torn, it is believed, in combat. She is being cared for in the turnkey's room.

Plain Dealer [Cleveland, OH] 29 January 1905: p. 16 CUYAHOGA COUNTY

NOTE: "Toy" Marshall was Toby E. Marshall, formerly Marshal of Lakewood. He was noted for his daredevil spirit and his name was a byword for bravery. He was hailed as a hero for capturing the drunken madman George Wagar who had killed Wagar's own brother, held his family hostage for hours, and nearly killed another police officer. He died aged 46 of heart failure after a sleigh-riding party, on February 15, 1905, just two weeks after this story was published. Undoubtedly this intrepid man would have solved the station house mystery.

4.

The Odditorium:

An Ohio Volcano, Toad in the Rock, and Other Unnatural Wonders

When business is dull with the rural correspondent, he invariably reports a shower of snakes or frogs or discovers a petrified man.

– Washington Post –

In the cabinets of curiosities of the Renaissance or 18th century, you never knew what you might find: a stuffed crocodile, a feather from an angel's wing, or a unicorn's horn. P.T. Barnum updated the concept of the cabinet into the "Odditorium," displaying human and animal freaks as well as stuffed mermaids. Here is a sampling from Ohio's own cabinet of curiosities—bizarre little odds and ends that don't fit neatly into any world view. Charles Fort called these "Damned Data." Step up now and view the Wonders of the Age!

Let's start with the reptile kingdom:

LIZARDS FOUND IN GIRL'S STOMACH

Cleveland, O., Dec. 16. Two live lizards three and a half inches long, several smaller ones, and a number of lizard eggs, were taken from the stomach of Lovel Herman, nineteen, four days before she died, according to Dr. A.J. McIntosh. A post-mortem examination showed that the wall of the stomach had been attacked by the animals, the doctors say. The heart had enlarged to three times its normal size.

For several years she had been ill, complaining that something was clawing at her stomach. Specialists were puzzled until finally Dr. McIntosh, working on the theory that it was a tapeworm, found the lizards.

Miss Herman drank water from a spring in which there were lizards, when she lived at Millersburg, twelve years ago, and it is believed that she swallowed the eggs or the young animals at that time and that they grew while in her body. She craved meat and eggs during the four months of her illness and it is believed she demanded such animal food because the lizards, as well as her body, had to be fed. She ate ravenously, but weighed only eighty pounds.

Incidentally, the health officials refuse to accept the certificate of death based upon the lizard theory, declaring that no such case has been reported since the days of primitive medicine.
Fort Wayne [IN] News 16 December 1910: p. 28 CUYAHOGA COUNTY

For comparison, a young man from Detroit:

Peter Lemen, living in Detroit, two years ago swallowed a small lizard in a glass of water, and it has lived and continued to grow in the man's stomach until it has attained large dimensions.
Athens [OH] Messenger 5 May 1881: p. 1

A Mt. Vernon woman, who no doubt is in opposition to the lizard man of Detroit, claims to have a snake in her stomach. She has tried to coax the reptile from its abode with a pan of milk, but the snake wouldn't pan out.
Athens [OH] Messenger 5 May 1881: p. 1 KNOX COUNTY

COUGHS UP LIVE FROG AND DIES WEEKS LATER DOCTORS PUZZLED OVER STRANGE CASE OF AGED OHIO MAN

Coshocton, Ohio, May 25. Local and other physicians are puzzled over the cause of the death of John Thorn, 67, near Blissfield.

Several weeks before Thorn's death, physicians were told, he coughed up a live frog. The frog, about half an inch long, has been preserved in alcohol.

Naturalists say the animal alleged to have been expelled is not a native of Ohio. Thorn lived near Blissfield forty years.
Daily Alaska Dispatch [Juneau, AK] 26 May 1917: p. 3 COSHOCTON COUNTY

A LIVE FROG IN A WOMAN'S STOMACH

Columbus, Ohio, Aug. 8. The strange phenomenon of a live frog in a human stomach has just developed here. Mrs. Anna Nickel, who lives with her husband in this city, has complained of a peculiar sensation in the stomach, as if something having life was moving about. This continued for six months. A number of prominent physicians in Columbus and elsewhere have been consulted, but none gave the woman relief.

Last evening she complained of a tickling sensation in her throat, and called Dr. Voght, who formed the opinion that the sensation was caused by the presence of an insect. After swallowing a powerful emetic, Mrs. Nickel was relieved by the expulsion of a live frog from her stomach. It was about two inches long, almost white, and the hind legs were missing. The physician gave it as his opinion that the woman, while drinking water, had swallowed the egg, which was hatched by the warmth of the stomach. The frog has been placed in alcohol and forwarded to Professor Youzer, of the American Medical College at St. Louis, with a view of securing a scientific opinion as to the unusual occurrence. *New York [NY] Herald-Tribune* 9 August 1890: p. 3 FRANKLIN COUNTY

NOTE: Reptiles in the stomach were a popular motif both in folklore and in newspaper stories although usually snakes were the creature thought to be causing distress. Typically the victim recalled having drunk from a river or spring, as Miss Herman and Mrs. Nickel did.

In one final, bizarre report, Dr. T.B. Fisher of Marion, Ohio, described the case of a lady who had felt something moving in her stomach for four months. She was ridiculed by her friends as an hysteric, but she silenced them by vomiting a nearly fully grown mouse, which Dr. Fisher kept in a glass jar in his office as a pet. This interesting story is found (alas, without a source) in *A Cabinet of Medical Curiosities* by Dr. Jan Bondeson. Dr. Fisher was a very distinguished Marion doctor. Perhaps he made up the story to account for a fondness for a pet mouse. Or perhaps he was duped by that "hysterical" young lady.

Along with alimentary amphibians and showers of fish (see "The Bloody Hand of Findlay" chapter), the live toad or frog found inside a rock is a perennial Fortean favorite. Let's start with a little background. The 19th century was fascinated by the idea of animals entombed for aeons in rocks. A French scientist performed some experiments to see if such things were possible:

WONDERFUL VITALITY OF TOADS

We have all read of the discovery of toads "in solid stratas of stone," where food and air sufficient to sustain life could not have possibly been had. We have not only read these stories, but the majority of us have put

them down as Mulhatton yarns which were written by someone who did not expect them to be believed. Now comes the scientist, M. Victor Lagroche, who says that he has imprisoned toads in masses of mixed plaster of paris and found them "well, fat and hearty after a lapse of eight years." He argues that if such creatures can live years without air, food or light they "can continue to live on indefinitely."
Delphos [OH] Daily Herald 22 September 1896: p. 3

NOTE: A Mulhatton yarn is a tall tale. The genre is named for a prospector, Joe Mulhatton, who stretched the truth in Arizona around the turn of the 19th century. He was, like the famed Baron Munchausen, a spinner of fantastical tales.

LIVE FROG IN A ROCK

One day last week as Mr. Robert Warwick, who has a contract on the new railroad a little west of Navarre, was assisting some of his men at work in breaking a rock so as to remove it, they found imbedded in this solid sandstone, a LIVE FROG. This frog had a home just about big enough for his body—no larger—where he lived very quietly, who can tell how long? The reptile was brought to town and exhibited in Mr. Estep's store for a short time, where he was placed on the counter, and made efforts to jump, but did not succeed very well, as he had been out of practice for a while. His frogship was taken to Canton to be exhibited to the savants of that place. The Rep. & Rep. makes him out a pretty old fellow—perhaps he was a singer or leaper, or both, before Noah's grand-father was big enough to throw stones at him or his kin. By the time his captors had the frog at Canton he was a corpse. That he was alive when found, and for some time after there is no doubt. It is a strange phenom-enon to find animal life in this condition, but this is not by any means the first case of the kind, as many who have read, even to a limited extent, will remember reading of just such cases in different parts of the world. Frogs have been found alive in the bodies of large trees, where they had existed for centuries. It is also said that bees have been discovered in the hardest kind of rocks, such as are used in constructing mill stones, but these insects were not alive. Such incidents coming to light in various parts of the globe, although unaccounted for to the satisfaction of all, are not such marvels as they once were. Yet they prove to us how exceedingly little we really know of the wonders of creation.
Massillon [OH] Independent 13 December 1871: p. 3 STARK COUNTY

NOTE: The Rep & Rep. was the *Canton Repository* newspaper. Oddly enough, such things are still reported. In 1982 several frogs inside rocks were exposed on New Zealand's North Island by a drilling machine. [*Fortean Times* 40: 7.]

SAYS LIVE TOAD FOUND IN ROCK AT CHANDLERSVILLE
ELSON SUTTON DISPLAYS AMPHIBIAN TO VOUCH FOR HIS STORY

Elson Sutton, of Chandlersville, is proudly displaying a small toad which he claims was found in a pocket inside a large block of sandstone Friday afternoon at Chandlersville.

Sutton said he split the stone which weighed about 300 pounds and out hopped the toad which he caught and placed in a box for display purposes and to prove assertions. Photographs of the pocket in the rock will be secured Saturday as further proof.

The probable age of the toad and how it managed to live inside the rock were left only to conjecture last night. How the toad entered the rock or the rock formed around the toad went unanswered and many theories were advanced for the freak of nature.

According to Sutton, the block of stone had been set in the foundation of a large three-story barn in the rear of his building on the main highway in Chandlersville over 45 years ago by John Fogle, who erected the barn.

The barn was razed to make way for a chicken house. As the stone was too heavy, Sutton split it Friday afternoon along a seam and out hopped the toad.

Zanesville [OH] Times Recorder 30 September 1933: p. 10 MUSKINGUM COUNTY

TOAD IN STONE BRINGS FAME TO SMALL VILLAGE
HUNDREDS OF MOTORISTS VISIT CHANDLERSVILLE
OFFERS FROM MUSEUMS

Finding of a live toad inside a block of sandstone at Chandlersville has brought much publicity to the small town in the southeastern part of Muskingum County and to the finder Elson Sutton who split the stone releasing the toad from his cell.

Several offers have been received by Sutton from museums relative to securing the display rights of the toad and the stone from which it was found.

Alas! The toad lived but 86 hours after gaining his freedom after ages inside the rock. The amphibian succumbed to old age, sunlight or too much air the second day after being found, but he will be preserved for posterity by a taxidermist, Sutton says.

Hundreds of persons have motored to Chandlersville to see the toad, the rock, and Sutton and talk about the strange freak of nature.

Scores of pictures have been taken of the halves of the stone showing the lonely cell in the rock, also of the dead toad and of Sutton.

Some of the views show Sutton holding on his shoulder the sledge-hammer used to shatter the stone and release the prisoner, the lonely toad. Others were taken of Sutton pointing out the long resting place of the toad and others of various scenes around the foundation of the old buildings where the stone was found.

Sutton said Thursday he had received a communication from the Ford Museum at Detroit and sent back an offer of the stuffed toad, both halves of the stone and other big stones of the neighborhood for a new automobile, but had not yet received a reply.

One explanation, probably correct, of how the toad came to be in the stone was offered by a scientist and that was that ages ago the toad hibernated, as is his custom, in a bed of sandy loam and during the winter the stone was formed around the pocket holding the toad, but the toad in moving around to escape, widened a cell inside the block which kept the mass from squeezing out his life. No explanations were given as to how the toad lived through the ages until released from his prison.

The Times Recorder [Zanesville, OH] 6 October 1933: p. 6 MUSKINGUM COUNTY

NOTE: A 1931 article about a Rotarian meeting, published in the *Zanesville Times Recorder*, said that Elson Sutton, "popularly known as 'Human Seal,'" did a balancing act much enjoyed by all. So perhaps he was the type of fellow to play a prank? For much more on entombed reptiles, see "Toads in the Hole," Mark Pilkington, *The Guardian* (January 20, 2005) "Toad in the Hole," Jan Bondeson, *Fortean Times* (June 2007).

What would a cabinet of curiosities be without some two-headed creature, in this case a snake?

The following is from the "Olive," printed in Mansfield, Ohio. This strange animal will convince those who have made so much fuss about the Sea-Serpent that the fertile soil of Ohio can produce as curious animals as their Sea-Serpent: "A black Snake was killed on Saturday the 28th ult. in Plymouth Township, in this county, which was five feet and a half long, and had two heads, one on each end, one of which was somewhat less than the other, but both equally natural. It was killed in an oat field and was seen by a number of persons."
American Advocate [Hallowell, ME] 20 November 1819: p. 2 RICHLAND COUNTY

NOTE: The people making a fuss about the sea-serpent were New Englanders who had seen the Gloucester sea serpent in 1817-1819 at Gloucester Harbor, Massachusetts.

I have written in *Haunted Ohio II* and *Haunted Ohio IV* about Ohio's giant snakes and the Lake Erie mystery beast, South Bay Besse. Lake Erie had many reports about its sea serpents from the 19th century, like this one:

"VICIOUSLY SPARKLING EYES."
THE SEA SERPENT DISCOVERED DISPORTING ITSELF ON LAKE ERIE.

Toledo, Ohio, July 16, 1892. While the schooner *Madeline Dowing*, on its way from Buffalo to this city on Wednesday morning, was passing the Dunning, about one hundred and fifty miles east of here in Lake Erie, Captain Patrick Woods saw, half a mile ahead, the waters of the lake lashed into a foam.

Drawing near, to the surprise of the Captain and all on board, a huge sea serpent, wrestling about in the waters as if fighting with an unseen enemy, was seen. It soon quieted down and lay at full length on the surface of the water.

Captain Woods estimates it to have been about fifty feet in length and not less than four feet in circumference of body. Its head projected from the water about four feet. It was a terrible looking object. It had viciously sparkling eyes and a large head. Fins were plainly seen, seemingly large enough to assist the snake in propelling itself through the water. The body was dark brown in color, which was uniform all along. It would be capable of crushing a yawl boat and its occupants.

As the vessel passed on its course the snake was seen disporting itself on the lake. At the time he saw it the lake was calm and there could have been no mistake in recognizing the object.
New York [NY] Herald 17 July 1892: p. 17. LAKE ERIE

Vintage Lake Erie monster stories must be taken with a jumbo grain of salt. However, this is a marginally more plausible report than some historic accounts of huge serpents leaving silver-dollar-sized scales on the beaches of Lake Erie. Both the captain and ship (actually named the *Madeline T. Dowing*) are real. The Dunning may be the Dunning Light, a lighthouse mentioned in contemporary papers, but which I cannot locate or The Dunning Steam Marble and Granite Manufacturing Company of Erie, Pennsylvania. Incidentally, "South Bay Besse" is named for the Davis Besse Nuclear Power Plant near Port Clinton on Lake Erie.

In 1873 the *Cambridge Jeffersonian* asked the burning question:

IS IT A VOLCANO?

Three miles from Bainbridge, Ross County, is located a hill of considerable altitude known as "Copperas Mountain." Out of the top of this mountain issues a constant stream of smoke, while, on its summit and general surface the vegetation has withered and died, until the whole hill presents a barren, sterile and desolate aspect, blasted as if by a whirlwind of fire. The ground on the top of the hill is so uncomfortably hot that it is almost impossible for a barefooted person to walk there. It is believed by persons who have visited and inspected this *lusus naturae*, that the entire interior of the hill is a mass of ignited combustible matter, and that the fire is and has been spreading with considerable rapidity. The theory presented to account for this strange phenomena, is that on or about the first day of last October, the party to whom the land belongs, was burning brush on the hill side, and that the flames communicated to inflammable matter, probably crude oil, coal, or other combustible substances, contained in the geological formation of the hill, and that the hill being full of such matter, the fire gradually gained headway until the interior has become a mass of molten metal. The quenching of the fire is, of course, impossible from its situation, and how long it will burn, and when, if ever, the fire will reach a point where it can be controlled can only be conjectured. At present there is no danger to be apprehended to property in the vicinity, but there is no telling what shape the thing may eventually take, and there are not wanting those whose imaginative disposition leads them to predict that this is but the beginning of what may turn out to be a young volcano. *The Cambridge [OH] Jeffersonian* 23 January 1873: p. 4 ROSS COUNTY

NOTE: *lusus naturae* is Latin for "a freak of nature"

Twenty-nine years later, Copperas Mountain was again in the news:

HAS OHIO A VOLCANO?
COPPERAS MOUNTAIN IN ROSS COUNTY CAUSING ALARM
SMOKE ISSUES FROM CREVICES IN THE MOUNTAIN SIDE
THE OUTCROPPING SLATE RED HOT
FROM WHICH SULPHUROUS FUMES ARISE
MYSTERIES SCIENCE ONLY CAN EXPLAIN

Washington C.H., Sept. 18. Standing like a sturdy sentinel jealously guarding the picturesque Paint Creek Valley, three miles south of Bainbridge, the garden spot of Southern Ohio, old Copperas Mountain towers above the surrounding hills of Ross County, making them sink into insignificance beside its stately peaks....

But Copperas, like Mt. Pelee, bids fair to prove a treacherous friend. Its stolid, calm exterior, which has stood for centuries, keeping watch and guard over the fertile valley and its busy inhabitants, is now disturbed by internal dissension and the muttering of the approaching storm is heard. Copperas Mountain is on fire.

From the crevices in the slate, which from time to time scales off and falls with a crash into the creek below, may now be seen tiny columns of smoke arising, and closer investigation discloses the outcropping slate red hot. Where the heat is more intense the black slate has turned to a dull brown, and sulphurous fumes arise.

These volcanic symptoms have been noticed before by residents near the mountain, but not until the recent disaster in Martinique has any fear been felt or expressed.

About 20 years ago, according to the stories of the old citizens, Copperas Mountain sent forth smoke and perhaps some flame, which at the time caused a little excitement, but as it died away the people were lulled to peace again, and the incident was gradually forgotten. Several months ago smoke was again noticed on the mountain side, and when some fearless mountaineers laboriously climbed to the spot it was so hot they could stand for a few moments only on the burning slate. About the time of the Pelee eruption some of the natives claim there was an increased activity on Copperas, and on dark nights small flames belched forth, and the smell of sulphur could be distinctly detected in the vicinity.

A great many people have become alarmed at these indications and think there may be some connection with Mt. Pelee, and that perhaps Paint Valley is in danger of a disaster similar to that of the Island of Martinique only on a smaller scale. Others scoff at this and say it is only the outcropping of sulphur and copperas which has become fired by the heat of the sun and that there is no need to fear an eruption.

The sides of the mountain where the smoke has recently been seen is so precipitous that it is almost impossible to make a close investigation unless someone is lowered by means of a rope from the top of the mountain. As the heat is so great, no one has yet been willing to undertake this method of investigation, but it is now possible some action will be taken by scientists to get the actual facts and discover if there are any volcanic symptoms.

Copperas Mountain takes its name from the large deposits of copperas. As the mighty flakes scale off from time to time and fall into the valley the copperas gathers on the exposed places, and can easily be seen. Sulphur springs abound in the vicinity of the mountain...Science alone can discover the secret hidden in its stony breast.

The Newark [OH] Advocate 18 September 1902 ROSS COUNTY

NOTE: Copperas is iron sulfate, also known as iron vitriol. It has a greenish color and was used in inks and dyes, as well as other industrial applications.

As the next article reveals, Science, in the person of geologist Willard Hayes, rather deflatingly solved the mystery.

WILLARD HAYES
SAYS THERE IS NO DANGER AT COPPERAS MOUNTAIN.
ATTENTION OF WASHINGTON

GEOLOGISTS CALLED
TO THE FUMING MOUND IN OHIO

There is no danger of Copperas Mountain, located in Paint Creek Valley, near Bainbridge, Ross County, O., becoming an understudy of Mt. Pelee, according to the geologists of the United States Geological Survey.

The story sent over from Bainbridge yesterday to the effect that the people living in the valley were becoming alarmed over the appearance of the smoke and sulphurous gases at Copperas Mountain was read with interest by the Government geologists. The interest was tinctured heavily with amusement, for it is asserted there is not the slightest possible danger of an eruption. Bainbridge is on the edge of the coal region in Southern Ohio and Copperas Mountain is merely a hill. Very likely coal beds underlie it and their presence, in the opinion of the geologists, explains the smoke and gases.

"If the story is true that smoke and sulphurous gases are issuing from Copperas Mountain it is not difficult to account for them. There doubtless are coal deposits under the mountains and they probably have caught fire. Iron pyrite is usually associated with coal and oxidizes when it comes in contact with the air, forming iron sulphate of copperas. It is usually found impregnated with water from coal mines. Iron pyrites in sufficient quantities may catch fire by spontaneous combustion and ignite the coal. When it burns it forms 'sulphurous' fumes, and I infer from the story that it is this kind of fumes which the people in Paint Creek Valley have seen.

"There is not the remotest chance of a volcanic eruption from Copperas Mountain nor any other seismic disturbances. There are no volcanic mountains in the State of Ohio, and as for their being any connection between Copperas and Pelee, it is wholly impossible."

The Newark [OH] Advocate 19 September 1902: p. 6 ROSS COUNTY

NOTE: Dr. C. Willard Hayes was a distinguished geologist with the United States Geological Survey. Judging from the many times he is mentioned in the newspapers, he seems to have been our go-to scientist, sent all over the world to inspect smoking fumaroles, predict earthquakes, and reassure the public. The 1902 explosion of Mount Pelee, a volcano in the Caribbean, was considered the deadliest volcanic disaster of the 20th century. The eruption and pyroclastic flows killed about 30,000 people and destroyed the town of St. Pierre, Martinique on May 8th. This was extensively covered in the papers and would have been on the minds of the local people, especially as it was reported that fissures emitting sulphurous vapors were seen just days before the Mount Pelee eruption. The Copperas Mountain fire was reported to have burnt out by 1921. Coal fires can burn for centuries. See for example, this page below about the New Straitsville Mine Fire in Perry County: http://www.ohiohistoryhost.org/ohiomemory/archives/216.

A coal fire is probably the best explanation for this Copperas copy-cat in Carrollton:

> Smoke has been issuing from a high hill near Carrollton and the people think it is a volcano.
> *Plain Dealer* [Cleveland, OH] 2 March 1881: p. 1 CARROLL COUNTY

Giant Native American skeletons, usually found in mounds, were a popular theme of the time, as were treasure cave tales. This tale offers the reader a cave, a treasure *and* a giant skeleton. It is difficult to tell from this account whether the men found genuine Adena-Culture artifacts and made up the skeleton story or if the whole thing is a hoax.

FINDLAY CAVE
SKELETON FOUND OF GIANT OF
PREHISTORIC DAYS
ORNAMENTS OF GOLD AND OTHER RELICS
ONCE AN UNDERGROUND RAILROAD STATION

Findlay, O., March 24. A most startling story of discovery in an underground cavern is told by Elmer Bright, a young farmer living east of this city, and his two companions who came to the office of the Waterworks Trustees and made their report of work done for that body. The men have been employed by the board in opening up a cave that has been known to exist in the limestone ridge on the line between this and Seneca County, the entrance to which was closed 32 years ago, by the owner of the land. Legend told of an underground river, and in their search for pure water for Findlay the board ordered the cave opened, with the result that a fortnight ago a stream of the clearest water was discovered running through a large cavern, 70 feet from the top of the ridge. Bright and others have since continued explorations on their own hook.

For several days the three men have been making daily journeys into the cave. Following the stream through a low-ceilinged passageway they came upon a wide drawing room with numerous passages leading from it. One of these led to a wall built by hand. They broke through and the sight that met their eyes froze their blood. The room was 15 or 20 feet square, and in the center on a flat table rock, lay the skeleton of a man of giant stature, to the bones which clung mummified bits of muscle, and over the middle was a covering of animal skins. About the head were placed copper and stone utensils, while at the feet were rude weapons carved of stone.

In substantiation of their statements the men exhibited a small vessel made of copper, the ornament of bizarre shape made of pure gold, as well as a stone hatchet similar to those found in the mounds of Southern Ohio. They say that the other mementos which they have at their homes are stone pottery, stone weapons, a rude stone pipe, pieces of flint and various bits of gold and copper, evidently ornaments. The animal skins that lay over the skeleton crumbled when they endeavored to pick them up, giving evidence of the ages that have passed since this supposed prehistoric chieftain was laid away in the depths of the earth and his tomb sealed with an aboriginal cement.

On their way out of the cavern the men made another discovery which is arousing interest. On the damp and mouldy floor they found a bit of paper evidently torn from a memorandum book. The discoloration of age was upon it, but in pale ink may still be deciphered the words, "James Bare, Oberlin." This is the name of a noted abolitionist and conductor of the underground railway, and his descendants still live in the Ohio college town. The stories of the old settlers tell of many a fugitive slave that slept in the house or barn of Bare in his Oberlin home in the antebellum days. The cave was, it is believed, used as a hiding place for negro slaves.

Newark [OH] Advocate 24 March, 1902: p. 1 HANCOCK COUNTY

One more underground mystery, in a coal mine. Although this is stated in the article as having been first published in the *Wellsville (Ohio) Union*, I have not been able to find the original piece. This article had a very wide circulation so perhaps it was created by an inventive journalist. Or, if such a thing happened, maybe the hieroglyphics were merely simulacra.

A STRANGE DISCOVERY

An extraordinary exhumation has just been made in the Strip Vein Coal Bank of Capt. Lacy, at Hammondsville, Ohio. Mr. James

Parsons and his two sons were engaged in making the bank, when a huge mass of coal fell down, disclosing a large smooth slate wall, upon the surface of which were found, carved in bold relief, several lines of hieroglyphics. Crowds have visited the place since the discovery and many good scholars have tried to decipher the characters, but all have failed. Nobody has been able to tell in what tongue the words were written. How came the mysterious writing in the bowels of the earth where probably no human eye has ever penetrated? By whom and when was it written? There are several lines about three inches apart, the first line containing twenty-five words. Attempts have been made to remove the slate wall, and bring it out, but upon tapping the wall it gave forth a sound that would seem to indicate the existence of a hollow chamber beyond, and the characters would be destroyed in removing it. At last accounts Dr. Hartshorn, of Mount Union College, had been sent for to examine the writing.
Macon [GA] Weekly Telegraph 13 November 1868: p. 4 COLUMBIANA COUNTY

No cabinet of curiosities should be without at least one mystic image of a religious figure, either Jesus or the Virgin Mary. This face of Christ on a whetstone, is unique in the annals of simulacra.

A MUCH VALUED WHETSTONE IN A MUSEUM
THE FACE OF CHRIST APPEARED ON THE STONE
AND SCIENTISTS CANNOT EXPLAIN THE
GREAT MARVEL

Dayton, Ohio. Sept. 28. In the Dayton Public Library Museum one of the greatest curiosities, which attracts more visitors than any relic or heirloom, no matter how highly prized, is the whetstone on which appeared in a moment's time, as if by a miracle, well-defined markings showing a picture of Rafael's face of Christ.

After the whetstone was placed in a sealed box, removed from the touch of human hands, it is said that the lips turned a flesh color, while during the past week, habitués of the museum noted that the lips were parting and that teeth were plainly noticeable.

The stone was donated to the museum some time ago by W.H. Starry, of 830 South Main Street, a real estate dealer, who, while sharpening his knife on Easter Day, 1900, noticed the strange phenomenon. He had been watching the antics of two negro youths in the alley adjacent to the house, while sitting at a window idly sharpening a knife. He had gazed on the stone intently for a long time, and its surface was particularly white.

While his eyes were fixed on the boys in the alley occurred the transformation which startled him to such an extent that he called in his neighbors. It was not long before many persons called to see the curiosity and all sorts of predictions were made by the superstitious.

Mr. Starry decided to turn it over to the museum, and he appeared before a notary to make oath that he in no manner traced the physiognomy.

Tucson [AZ] Daily Citizen 28 September 1904: p. 8 MONTGOMERY COUNTY

NOTE: The image is from *The Transfiguration* by the Italian Renaissance painter Raphael. It was a popular engraving and hung in many a Victorian parlor.

This next "freak of nature" has a whiff of the sideshow attraction about her, especially since I cannot find her mentioned in the Xenia papers.

STRANGE FREAK NATURAL TATTOO
OHIO CHILD IS COVERED WITH LETTERS AND
VERSES OF THE BIBLE
AS IF PAINTED THERE.

A Springfield dispatch to the *St. Louis Globe-Democrat* states that a most wonderful freak of nature has been discovered in Xenia in the person of little Allie Simms, the 3-year old daughter of Charles Simms, Jr. It is doubtful if her like can be found anywhere upon the face of the earth and her condition is one that perhaps will never be satisfactorily explained by science, and it shows to what extent nature will sometimes go out of the ordinary way to mystify mankind.

This little living wonder, who will no doubt go down in history as one of the strangest subjects of the twentieth century, was born in Kentucky and was brought to this city a short time ago. The child is rather small for one of her age, but is considerably above the average 3-year-old child in intelligence. She has a somewhat queer-looking face, with sharp, snappy eyes, and an uncontrollable temper.

On her tongue are to be seen the figures "76" plain enough for anybody to read. Besides these, when she was born, the word "Allie" was also visible on her tongue, and for that reason she was given the name Allie. At the time of her birth the word was so plain that it created a great deal of interest among the doctors. Usually the figures on her tongue are white, but sometimes they turn red. But this is not the strangest part of the story. According to the statement of her father, the child is a sort of periodical chameleon letter press. Once in every 28 days, or about the 29th of each month, regularly, her body becomes entirely covered from head to foot with letters of the English alphabet and Bible verses that can be seen and read by anyone. The letters are about the size of the ordinary newspaper letters, and her father says her whole body presents the appearance of a newspaper, as far as printing is concerned.

The only plausible story advanced for this strange phenomenon is that the impression must have been made in some way through the nervous system by the mother during gestation. The letters and verses are only visible about the 29th of each month, but the figures on her tongue can be seen at all times.

The child was three years old last May. Her mother is dead, and just before coming to Xenia she was put into the children's home at Cincinnati, but as she has such a high temper her father though the managers would not understand her and would punish her too severely, so he brought her here and she is staying with Mrs. Emily Lawrence, in Lawrence Alley.

Riverside [CA] Daily Press 19 September 1903: p. 6 GREENE COUNTY

NOTE: There is no mention of exhibiting the child, so apparently financial gain was not the point if this was a hoax. If this was a real story, it is possible that the child had the condition known as dermographia or "skin-writing," where the skin is so sensitive that touching it produces welts and inflammation, which can look like writing.

Let us finish our tour of the cabinet of curiosities with two mystery animals: a graveyard ghoul and a very curious cat:

FEEDING UPON GRAVES.
A STRANGE BEAST IN OHIO
A FOUL AND FEROCIOUS CREATURE

Fostoria, Ohio, Jan. 22. The strange animal which has been desecrating graves in Perry Township, Wood County, has again been seen.

A gentleman whose veracity is not questioned gives this description of the novel graveyard ghoul: its neck and breast are white, and the rest of the body is black: the tracks of its front feet are about eight inches long and three wide, making impressions in the snow with its claws about twice the length of a man's finger. The tracks made by the hind feet are nearly round, and about the size of a large dog's, except the claws, which are longer and sharper. The animal is about three feet long and eighteen inches high.

It burrows into the ground in the graveyard, and penetrating the coffins therein contained, devours the contents thereof. It travels with such rapidity that all attempts thus far to kill it have proved futile. The man who last saw the animal says it was in the middle of the road, having gone from a farm by literally tearing the fence to pieces. His dog gave chase to the beast, but soon returned scared almost to death.

The people living in the vicinity have frequently heard loud noises which are now supposed to have emanated from this peculiar, unnamed, unknown beast. The animal is said to be slowly working its way toward Toledo.

New York Herald-Tribune 23 January 1884: p. 1 WOOD COUNTY

NOTE: People more knowledgeable than I have suggested that this was a wolverine.

A GREEN CAT
COLUMBUS OHIO OWNS WONDERFUL
IRISH FELINE

"I've never seen a green cat
I never expect to see one;
But one thing I'm sure of,
I'd rather see than be one."

That's about the way one of the good Old Mother Goose rhymes, which was sung years ago, ran.

But—Columbus has a real, live green cat, or, more properly speaking, kitten, or still more properly, it's only a partly green feline. Best of all, this freak of nature was ushered into fresh air and the light of day march 17, when most everyone was wearing the green.

The verdant kitten is the property of Walter Owens, proprietor of a café. Its mother is a common old alley cat, black and white with gray markings. Its father? Well, who knows? The kitten is mostly white, has gray markings, but most of its legs and the top of its ears are a bright real Irish green. The reporter, who inspected the kitten, failed to discover that any deception has been practiced in dyeing the kitten.

Owens has received several fancy offers for his strange pet, one of them coming from an East Side cat fancier, already the owner of nearly thirty different varieties, who says she will give $50 for it. Owens has named the curiosity "Shamrock."

State [Columbia, SC] 7 April 1912: p. 11 FRANKLIN COUNTY

NOTE: The poem is not a Mother Goose rhyme, but paraphrases "The Purple Cow" (1895) by Gelett Burgess.

"I've never seen a purple cow
I never expect to see one;
But one thing I'm sure of,
I'd rather see than be one."

Now, this way to the egress....

5.

Those Who Return:

The Shock of Recognition

It is an ill thing to meet a man you thought dead in the woodland at dusk.

– Robert E. Howard –

Many ghost stories tell of misty, vaguely human figures flitting through a deserted house—what might be called generic ghosts. More startling are the stories where witnesses recognize—sometimes repeatedly—the dead face and figure of a loved one or of a neighbor. It must be particularly unnerving to come face to face with someone you've seen dead, coffined, and buried.

I'LL COME BACK SAID DYING MAN AND HE DID

By Horace Foster

In the beautiful lake district of northern Ohio, not far from Ravenna, stands a haunted house.

It is not an old looking house; the dust undisturbed for years does not lie inch deep on the floors, nor is the paper peeling in great strips from the sweating walls. The doors do not stand agape as though waiting for a householder who never comes, and the wind does not chant weird dirges through the empty rooms.

The house seems modern. Only recently it has been overhauled and made up to date. A frail, delicate woman lives there alone. She is not timid, she says.

Yet the house is haunted. The belated farmer whips up his horses when he nears the place and looks apprehensively about him as he hurries past, as if he feared to see some ghastly thing glide over the silent waters of the lake that lies in the rear of the house.

Strange sounds are heard in that house and strange sights seen there. Heavy footfalls resound through the chambers at dead of night, and unseen hands open window and door. The furnace doors slam—and no one is there. The sound of crashing cymbals breaks upon the still of the night, and at times it seems as though heavy trunks and clinking chains were dragged through the rooms.

The spirit of the former owner of that house haunts it. Drawn by the love of those earthly possessions he found it so hard to leave, he still returns, and, clad in the filmy habiliments with which the spirits of the dead are wont to clothe their vacuity, he returns to haunt the place where he lived.

FARMER HAS SEEN HIM

"I have seen him," says George Blanchard, a farmer who lives in the neighborhood and who knew the man in life. "Mrs. Ida Blocker asked me to come to the house one evening last fall. I came. I remained there with Wallace Bishop, a hired man, as my companion. It was just growing dark, and the shadows seemed to come up from the lake and fill the house. It was one of those still evenings of early fall. The neighbors were at supper and I could hear nothing but the sound of the little waves as they broke on the sand, and the regular breathing of my companion asleep in the kitchen.

"Then I heard another noise. It came from upstairs. Bishop and I were on the alert in an instant. The sound seemed to come from one of the upstairs chambers. We hurried up, but there was no one there, the windows were open and we closed them.

Hardly had we started down the stairs when the noise was repeated; we returned and the windows were open again. The furnace doors clattered; we hurried down there. I saw one of the doors open and closed it. As I closed one, the other would open of itself. There was a slight noise at one side of the furnace. I looked—THERE STOOD THE DEAD MAN! I could feel the hair rise on my head. I did not wait for more."

PROMISED TO COME BACK

The owner of the haunted house died near the last of January. He had been a hard-working man, and had accumulated considerable property. The neighbors respected and feared him. They did not love him. They called him a "hard" man. He was fond of the house he had built, and as he grew older would sit for the long afternoons on the back porch which overlooked the lake and gaze out on its quiet waters as the setting sun turned them into gold.

"This is the prettiest place in the world," he would say, "and if there is a hereafter I will come back."

When he was seized by his last illness and the doctors told him that he could not live, he called his wife to the bedside.

"They tell me that I cannot live much longer," he said. "I have never been a believer in much of anything, but if there is a life after death, I will come back."

He died. The nurse found him one afternoon with his face turned toward the window that looked out onto the lake, and one hand clutching the counterpane on the bed, as though he was loath to leave the world he had loved so well. After that, things settled into their old accustomed way. Pending the settlement of the estate, the widow lived in the house with her twelve-year-old niece. A hired man did the chores.

It was noticed by the neighbors—and what neighbors in the country do not notice is not worth seeing—that no one remained alone in the house. But it was summer time, and everyone was busy caring for boarders from the city, so little public comment was made of the fact.

Pretty soon it was noised about that things were not just right at the old homestead. Passersby at night heard strange noises and saw lights at the windows when they knew that the family was away.

Then the rumor started that the place was haunted, and that its former owner, whom they had seen white and still in his coffin, with the same hard look on his face that they knew so well, was revisiting the scenes of his life.

People asked the widow if it were really so, and she admitted that it was. Her husband had been seen in the house. She had seen him herself, she said.

"WHAT IS IT?"

The district was all agog. Neighbor whispered to neighbor. "What is it?" they said, but no one could find an answer. They spoke of it with bated breath. The more curious would gather about the house after dark, none bold enough to venture in. They would stand at the fence and watch; some of the younger ones would call for the owner to show himself.

One day, it is related, the niece was alone in the kitchen. She had gone to the rear door to throw some apple parings to the chickens. She turned to come in. A scream was heard. "Uncle!" she cried. Her aunt, running in from the front yard, found her swooning on the floor.

The dead man's estate was settled, and the widow, taking her dower, bought a little farm several miles away. The house is inhabited by a woman. She lives there alone. Her husband is employed in the city, and his business is such that he cannot be with her but a few days each month....

"I have heard nothing," she says. "I am not afraid to stay here alone. I can find plenty to keep me busy and when the summer comes my husband will be with me all the time. If anybody has heard or seen strange things here or heard sounds at night, it comes from his own guilty conscience."

Are there still strange happenings in the house?

The neighbors say that there are. Lately, the neighbors say, sounds have been heard there, and the former manifestations have begun anew. Many have heard, but few have seen, and none can explain. Offers have been made to the woman who lives there to keep her company, but she refuses them. She is not afraid.

"STORIES ARE TRUE."

Mrs. Ida Blocker, who lives near the place, and perhaps more than anyone else, knows the history of the haunted house and its former owner, says:

"I do not know who started these stories, but they are true—perfectly true. The noises began shortly after the man's death. At first the people who lived in the house were at a loss to account for them, for the noises did not seem to be localized.

"It was not long after that when there could be no doubt of it. Sounds were heard in the upstairs bedrooms and noises as if people were dragging heavy chains down the stairs. The man himself was seen as well. He appeared dressed in the same worn gray suit that he had worn when alive. He would shake hands with his wife, not with the cold clammy touch of the dead, but the warm grasp of a living hand.

"Sometimes he would speak, but the words were muffled and indistinct. He was merely fulfilling his promise. I have heard him say that he would come back after death and he has. I am glad I do not live in that house and there is not money enough to make me stay there."...

"Yes, I have heard the noises," says Wallace Bishop. "The sounds came from every part of the house. It seemed as if a man was beating tin wash boilers together. I can't explain it—it is beyond me.

"I could always feel when something of that kind was going to happen. I cannot describe what kind of a feeling it was, but I would know beforehand. Toward evening I would begin to be sort of nervous, and I am not a creepy man at all. It was something like the way we feel when a thunderstorm is on the way.

STRANGE FLICKERS OF LIGHT

"After dark was the time when the sounds would be most often heard. There would be little flickers of light through the house, and then the noises would begin, first in the distance as if a carriage was coming up the road; then it would be louder, and they seemed to come from a definite place. At first the family used to run to the room where the noise seemed to come from, but there would be no one there, so they gave it up. They say the noises still keep up, but I don't know."

What is the explanation of it all? Some say that it is the real spirit of the dead man, and some hold that it is a clever trick....

After the stock has been bedded for the night, families who live nearby gather under the center table light and speak of the ghost, and pity the lone woman who lives in the haunted house.
Plain Dealer [Cleveland, OH] 15 March 1908: p. 47 PORTAGE COUNTY

NOTE: Horace Foster may have been mayor of Hudson, Ohio. This story was printed in the newspaper with an elaborate illustration, usually a format reserved for fiction, but parts of this read like a modern paranormal investigation.

Remember the wheelchair in the film *The Woman in White* with George C. Scott?

HAUNTED HOME
OF "OHIO WOOL KING" AGAIN DESERTED
TENANTS CANNOT STAY
BECAUSE OF GHOSTLY VISITS OF MANSION'S
FORMER OWNER
CREDENCE GIVEN UNCANNY STORY

Kenton, Aug. 21. The many friends of David Harpster, the "Wool King of Ohio," will be surprised to learn that his spirit refuses to stay away from the earth, but visits his old home in Harpster, Wyandot County.

The story is that the beautiful Harpster homestead will soon be deserted again. The cause is the reappearance of the ghost of Mr. Harpster.

In 1899 Mr. Harpster died. He was a millionaire stock raiser and wool buyer and for several years was president of the National Wool Growers' Association. He owned farms in Wyandot County and the state of Illinois. His property, in land only, amounted to thousands of acres, while his estimated wealth was over a million dollars. He was laid to rest in the beautiful Oak Hill Cemetery near his home village, and a magnificent marble shaft marks the place where he now lies.

After his death his property was taken possession of by his daughter Mrs. William Bones of New York City. Her husband is a millionaire and they made the old home where she was born and raised, a palace. The grounds were enlarged and beautified and the whole house transformed.

They brought their New York servants with them and the staid old country place became a scene of gaiety and sociability. From all parts of the country, wealthy visitors came and grand balls were given.

This continued for over a year and then, silently, the family moved away. The magnificent rooms and halls were empty and vacant. No reason was given, but soon an uncanny story was whispered among the neighbors. For some time before his death, Mr. Harpster had been an invalid and was moved around in an invalid's chair. The neighbors said that the ghost of Mr. Harpster came and sat in the chair and the inhabitants of the house could plainly hear it move around. This, they say, was the cause of the going away of the gay society that was wont to make merry there.

The house was uninhabited for some time, but, finally, a Mr. Meers of Harpster, a relative of David Harpster, moved into the place. Mr. Meers, it is said, has seen the shade and has decided to move very soon from the place. It is said that he prefers a rented house with no conveniences to the place with the visitor from the other world.

The story of the ghost has a general circulation and while some of the more material people of the section doubt it, it finds ready credence with many others.

The Stark County Democrat [Canton, OH] 22 August 1902: p. 8
WYANDOT COUNTY

ANOTHER GHOST STORY

"I never believed much in ghosts," said old Mrs. Blackburn of Allentown, Allen County, Ohio, "but I tell you, young man, I am certain that I saw one not long ago, and saw it just as plainly as I now see you. One cold winter's night, about the time my husband was appointed land agent here, and before this big house was built, a cattle-buyer was pulled off his horse in the Two-mile Woods just east of this little village, and his throat was cut from ear to ear. He was robbed, of course. The murder caused great excitement at the time and was the talk of the village, and from the Auglaize River to the Indiana line all men of doubtful reputation were arrested, but the right persons were never found, or if found nothing could be proven against them. The dead drover's family offered large sums of money for the arrest of the assassins, but the reward was never claimed.

"This spot on the road that runs through the Two-mile Woods, where the drover was robbed and murdered, was said to be haunted. People refused to go through the woods at night, and we all had a hearty laugh at the experience of old Lawyer Collett of Lima, who walked through this woods one evening just about dark, and, hearing a horse trotting behind him looked around and could see nothing but the vacant road, long and desolate. He resumed his walk. Again the sound of the horse's hoofs fell on his ears, when he took to his heels and ran all the way to Lima. One clear moonlight night in September last my son John and I had been up in Putnam County after peaches. We stayed in Lima with relatives on our way home and had an enjoyable time. It was late when we started for home. You know that it is about five miles from Lima to Allentown. Well, before I knew it we were in the Two-mile Woods. When about halfway through I saw a man in the road. He was standing and had his back toward us. I called John's attention and he said:

"'Mother, I believe that is John Westbay.'

"The man was in his shirtsleeves and was just about such a man as Westbay, rather large and well proportioned. We supposed that, whoever it was, he would hear the noise of our team and get out of the road, but he never stirred. Just as our horse nearly touched him it shied, for he turned and, O Lord, he had a great red gash in his throat. John leaned over toward me (and I don't blame the boy for being scared), and the shying of the horse brought the man, or whatever it was, right in front of the first side wheel of the buggy. The horse jerked forward and both wheels passed through the man's body and never touched him. As far back as we could see he was standing in the road. John was so frightened that the boy slept with his father and me for a month afterward. No amount of money could hire me to go through those woods again at night, and I know many people around here who are just like me on this score. My husband saw something there one night, but refused to say much about it for fear of being laughed at."

Kansas City [MO] Times 30 December 1888: p. 2 ALLEN COUNTY

THE GHOSTLY TOLLKEEPER.
A PHANTOM THAT FRIGHTENS TRAVELERS ON

THE OLD NATIONAL PIKE

There was a good deal of excitement recently over in Belmont County, Ohio, along that portion of the old National Pike extending some four or five miles eastward from St. Clairsville, writes a Wheeling correspondent, over the appearance of an apparition of old Tollkeeper Feltus, who presided at the first gate east of St. Clairsville for nearly a generation, but who died some five years ago, since which time the old toll house has been allowed to fall into ruins. Uly Smith, a traveling salesman, and Henry Johnson, his colored driver, had a thrilling experience with the ghost about 12:30 o'clock yesterday morning, the details of which were related by both gentlemen to your correspondent. They were returning in one of the delivery wagons from a late trip to St. Clairsville, and when nearly opposite the spot where the old toll house stood, the attention of both men was attracted to an object on the left-hand side of the road.

"What's that?" asked Mr. Smith.

"It's a man," said Johnson, whose eyes were a little sharper.

"Oh, I see; it's the tollkeeper," said Smith, who had not been over the road for half a dozen years, and therefore did not know that Feltus, whom he knew quite well, was dead.

Just at this point the off horse ran right over the figure, which, however, was not in the least disturbed, and promptly reappeared at the front wheel of the wagon, standing erect, in Feltus' characteristic attitude, with one arm outstretched to receive the toll.

Mr. Smith said, in explaining what transpired: "I asked him what he was doing out at such a late hour, as Henry had pulled up the horses, but he gave me no answer; the figure just stood there holding out his hand as old man Feltus used to do, and I was as confident that I was talking to him as I am to you this minute. As the rain was pouring down in torrents I asked him why he didn't have a light and not keep us waiting. There was no answer still, and I asked him how much the fare was that I might have enough change, and as he still made no answer I told Henry we didn't have time to waste there in the rain, and to drive on. This aroused Henry, who had his whip aloft, but was paralyzed at the apparition of the old man, whom he knew to be dead, and he drove away only too rapidly, with his hat standing up off his head.

"When I discovered the state of affairs I felt about as scared as Henry did, and I do not care to have another such experience. It is a strange case, and I cannot account for it at all."

Johnson was as confident as Mr. Smith that he saw the ghost of the old man, and he wouldn't put the horses away by himself, he was so scared.

Chicago [IL] Herald 21 June 1890: p. 11 BELMONT COUNTY

NOTE: The tollkeeper was Lambert M. Feltus, father of six children with his wife who rejoiced in the name Zereda. The old National Pike is Route 40.

This next story is interesting for the backstory: the alleged ghost was said to have been one of the world's oldest people. Of course, this was several decades after P.T. Barnum exhibited Joice Heth, George Washington's "161-year-old" former nurse, and Mark Twain satirized the many deaths of the celebrated favorite body-servant of the Father of Our Country, but there was still a fascination with survivors of the Revolutionary War.

AN OHIO GHOST

A special dispatch from Mount Vernon, Ohio, says: A genuine ghost story has just been revealed in our midst, which created considerable excitement and is the all-absorbing topic of conversation among our citizens at this time. A prominent and truthful citizen of this city makes the following statement, and says he has as much nerve as any living man, but has had all he can stand of this kind of nervine. On the night of Feb. 19, at a late hour, while returning home from across the Rhine, he heard a shriek that sounded like the voice of a woman in the direction of an unoccupied house, the late residence of Judge Lane, deceased. Thinking it might be tramps and being determined to investigate the matter he went directly to the house. Reaching there, he claims to have heard a noise within, and to his utmost astonishment and terror he saw that the house was brilliantly lighted and the front door standing wide open, the old Judge, as natural as life, supporting himself on two crutches, his legs being off at the knees. The man took to flight with his ears filled with shrieks and groans as long as he was within hearing distance.

Daily Inter Ocean [Chicago, IL] 12 March 1881: p. 11 KNOX COUNTY

NOTE: "Judge" Lane died February 5, 1881. Here is his obituary:

SAMUEL LANE, CENTENARIAN Samuel Lane, colored, probably the oldest man in the world, died on Tuesday evening at Mount

Vernon, Ohio, aged 123 years. Upon the best obtainable authority, he is believed to have been born in Africa in 1758. He came to this country in 1775, and during the Revolutionary War was body servant of General Mercer. He went to Mount Vernon in 1830, working as hostler, and in 1844 made a speech on the public square in favor of Henry Clay for President. Among his colored brethren he was looked upon as a sort of prophet, and was given the appellation of "Judge," which he retained until his death.

New York Herald 5 February 1881: p. 5

Nervine is a nerve tonic. "Across the Rhine" may be a poetic way to say coming from the "barbaric" country to the city, drawn from the notion of Germanic tribes across the Rhine from Roman territory. I also wonder if it's a euphemism for drinking too much Rhenish wine.

This next story is a variation on the tales of ghosts who cannot rest until their bones are properly buried. In this case, a suicide felt insulted by his placement in the graveyard. Suicides were often not buried in the graveyard at all, but in wasteland, at crossroads, or in the undesirable part of the cemetery to the north of the church because, according to popular lore, Hell lay in the north.

A RESTLESS SPIRIT

Nevada, Ohio, November 16. Early on the morning of November 4 Martin Weidemire, a highly respected German citizen of Crawford County, two and one half miles east of this village was found hanging to the rafters of his barn. He being of such a quiet, inoffensive, jovial disposition that such a thing as his committing suicide was a great surprise, and the family had the sympathy of the community in general. The funeral was set for the following Wednesday, and three of the neighbors commenced to dig a grave in a little graveyard about one mile north of his home. When about half done the minister who was to take charge of the funeral came along and ordered them to stop, as they were in close proximity to others who did not care to have a suicide resting his weary body so near their saintly dust. A second grave was commenced, and when about as near done as the first, another party discovered that the sacred dust of that portion of the graveyard would not submit to such

AN OUTRAGE.

And a third grave was located in the outer edge of the yard, where the body was finally laid to rest. A considerable feeling was manifest at the time and since at the treatment of a poor, unfortunate being, whose mind became unbalanced and saw fit to take his life in his own hands and place himself before his Maker and to be judged by Him.

A movement has been made in the last few days by some of his old neighbors and friends to have his body removed to some other place, as it appears to be his time now to make known his unrest in his much disputed grave, as the following will show: The next evening after his funeral Mr. G. Keisling, an old neighbor, being aroused by some unaccountable noise, went to the door, and, as he says, "there stood Weidemire as plain as I ever saw him." Of course, knowing that he had helped to bury him only the day before, it surprised him, but, being a man of nerve and fearless asked "what was wanted?" Without answering he simply walked toward the outside gate, beckoning him to follow. He again asked him the same question, but received no answer more than

A TROUBLED EXPRESSION

And a motion to follow him. Nervy as he is, Mr. Keisling could not obey the summons, which under any and all circumstances during life he would not have refused his old friend and neighbor, whom he had known so well for the last quarter of a century. Closing the door he seated himself, thinking of what had just occurred, and of the meaning of such a strange visit. A loud rap again called him to the door. Forgetting for a moment his late visitor he obeyed the summons, when a sight met his eye that froze him to the spot. The atmosphere was lighted with a strange light for a distance up and down the road, and a funeral procession exactly like the one attending the funeral of his late neighbor was passing his house, only it was going away from the graveyard instead of toward it. For a few moments his eyes were riveted on the strange scene, and in another moment all had vanished. What did it all mean? That was the question that bothered and troubled this sturdy old farmer until in relating his experience to some of his neighbors, the next day he found that they had seen and heard strange things, and, after consulting with each other, it was determined to remove him at once, hoping in so doing to rest his troubled spirit and relieve his terror-stricken neighbors.
Cincinnati [OH] Enquirer 17 November 1889: p. 16 WYANDOT/ CRAWFORD COUNTY

NOTE: A condensed version appeared in the *Pittsburg [PA] Dispatch* 28 November 1889, giving "Robert Brehmer" as the neighbor visited by the dead man. The phantom funeral is a well-known motif in folklore. That, coupled with the name change, makes this story suspect.

Various religions and cultures have different views about how long after death a spirit lingers on earth: three days, a week, 40 days. A dead man reappearing as a ghost forty years after his death is unprecedented. The late Mr. Woodbeck (possibly Abram Woodbeck, now buried in Delaware's Oak Grove Cemetery) must have been quite the godless local legend for his death to still be recalled so many years later. Or perhaps the memory of that terrible time of cholera fixed his place in Delaware lore.

AFTER FORTY YEARS
THE GHOST OF A GODLESS MAN APPEARS AT HIS OLD HOMESTEAD

Delaware, Ohio, February 9. Down in Concord Township, only a few miles from the spot where the old haunted house stood for so many years inspiring country folk with supernatural awe, another ghost has made its appearance after 40 years. The new apparition is claimed to be genuine and was seen by two responsible farmers, Messrs. Shively and Anson, who live near the Woodgrove Church.

Sunday night, while these two men were returning from church at Bellepoint, near an old cabin they saw approaching them a white horse and cart driven by a man. Naturally they turned out to let the vehicle pass, but instead of passing, the man drew his horse to the left, squarely in front of the two farmers. They halted and then first noticed the peculiar appearance of the horse, the queer, old-fashioned make-up of the cart, and the pale emaciated face of the man, all of which could be plainly seen in a strange, misty light that seemed to surround the figures. One of the farmers shouted to the apparition to move on, but the silent horse and man remained where they stood for a minute and then as silently passed down across the ditch, through a rail fence without splitting a sliver off, down through the orchard of the old cabin premises, and finally vanished into a little mound of earth. Both men could see the ghostly visitor, could even see through it, and see the objects beyond.

The little cabin near where the apparition was seen is at present unoccupied, but owned by W.T. Ropp. Forty years ago, when Delaware was scarcely more than a village, a man named Woodbeck lived in this cabin. He was known as a hard-drinking, very profane and godless man, and one day when he heard that cholera had reached Delaware, he swore with a great oath that he was not afraid of it, nor did he fear man, devil or God. He started immediately for town. He came back a corpse and was buried in the dooryard of the old cabin. Although at different times the old cabin has presented signs of being disturbed by some superhuman hand, not until Sunday night had the ghostly spirit ever shown itself. The fact that a ghost has been seen in the neighborhood has aroused the denizens of the township, and they agree that Woodbeck's uneasy spirit has resurrected itself and is haunting his old home, where in his meanness, he was cut down by the wrathful hand of Providence. *Cincinnati [OH] Enquirer* 10 February 1894: p. 9 DELAWARE COUNTY

Did a tragedy cause a jealous husband's ghost to return? Or was the apparition, as this unsympathetic article suggests, the delusion of an overwrought widow with a guilty conscience?

JOHN M'CURDY'S GHOST.
HIS WIDOW SAYS THE SPECTRE HAUNTS HER IN THE NIGHT TIME.
STRANGE NOISES HEARD ABOUT THE HOUSE WHERE THE GREAT TRAGEDY TOOK PLACE
THE SHUTTERS RATTLE AND ALL KINDS OF OUTLANDISH AND UNEARTHLY SOUNDS DISTURB THE REPOSE OF MRS. MCCURDY

Rumors are now afloat in the northern part of the city that furnish plenty of material for gossip, and that have wrought up the more superstitious element of society to a high pitch of mental excitement. It is said that the ghost of John W. McCurdy, the plasterer, who came to his death by his own hand under such sensational circumstances some months ago, is not content to remain upon the other shore but that he has re-crossed the great Stygian river to harass mortals on earth. As the report goes he makes visits nightly to his old home at the north end of Shorb Street where he carries on in a most weird and soul-racking fashion.

The authority for the rumors is none other than the widow of the deceased, who it will be remembered was the cause of the great tragedy and who escaped death at the hands of her husband only because her head was so hard that the bullet from his revolver flattened out on her skull. She now lives at the house where the trouble occurred with no other person about her but her child and she declares that the place is haunted.

She avers that peculiar and horrible noises abound around the place with no visible cause. The doors creak, rappings are heard, footsteps sound upon the floors and other weird phenomena take place that are sufficient to strike terror into the soul. Not only this, but she declares that she has seen the ghost of her departed husband. The phantom appears at the dead of night, according to her story, and peers through the window, rattles the shutters and otherwise harasses her. Mrs. McCurdy reports that these terrible experiences are almost nightly in occurrence and so wrought up has she become over the matter that it is almost impossible for her to sleep at all.

Whether John McCurdy's ghost does come back to haunt and terrorize his former wife or whether the experiences are simply the result of strong mental action induced by the thoughts of what has gone before and by the surroundings, the *News-Democrat* will not venture to assert, but certain it is that Mrs. McCurdy has been highly wrought up over the affair and there are many of the more superstitious in the neighborhood who would almost rather die than venture in the region of the McCurdy residence on a dark night.

The Stark County Democrat [Canton, OH] 25 August 1892: p. 2 STARK COUNTY

NOTE: Here is the short version of "A Triple Tragedy in an Ohio Town." Canton, April 9.

A terrible triple tragedy was enacted here yesterday and the three victims are all dying from their wounds. Several shots were heard from the house of John McCurdy, on Meyers Avenue. Neighbors quickly entered and found McCurdy, his wife, and Lew Waltenbaugh lying on the floor, bleeding from many wounds. McCurdy has accused his wife of intimacy with Waltenbaugh and shot them both. He then put a bullet in his own head and fell by the side of his victims.

Salem [OH] Daily News 9 April 1892: p. 1

Waltenbaugh was McCurdy's employer and a married father of six. He was said to have been having an affair with Mrs. McCurdy. A detailed account of the entire story can be found in *The Stark County Democrat* [Canton, OH] 14 April 1892: p. 2 and *Cincinnati [OH] Enquirer* 10 April 1892: p. 9.

On the other hand, perhaps Mrs. McCurdy was right to be afraid, not of the dead, but of the living. She had been publically shamed as an unfaithful wife who was responsible for her husband's death. An article from the *Plain Dealer*, which paraphrases the details above, also suggests that some local men considered her fair game:

> "Persons who have visited the locality recently do not take much stock in this [ghost] story, but do claim that Mrs. McCurdy has some reason for being afraid. Three ladies in returning home late at night were almost scared out of their wits by noticing a couple of men hidden in the grass in close proximity to the McCurdy house."

Plain Dealer [Cleveland, OH] 23 August 1892: p. 4 STARK COUNTY

The Medina County Murderess

The photos of Anna and Eva Garrett show two strange, unsmiling women with an odd dignity, like ancient mummies. They both wear little frilled collars, but while Eva looks almost fashionable with her long, elegantly-dressed hair, Anna's wildly spiked coiffure and shifting eyes suggest a haunted being. The newspaper reports of their murder called them "imbeciles" and "unfortunate creatures, to whom a sound mind and clear intellect had been denied." Their father, Alonzo, had married his first cousin, producing several "weak-minded" children, one of whom had died. After his wife's death, he married Mary Heffelfinger, an attractive widow, after only a few weeks' acquaintance. Mary, who had several adult children of her own, complained that she had not been told of the "imbeciles" and would not have married him, had she known that she would have to share a home with the girls whom she claimed had filthy and depraved habits.

There is no doubt that Mrs. Garret was a wicked stepmother. She took away the girls' silk dresses and gave them rags. She banned them from the family dinner table and fed them scraps. They were forced to sleep in a shed or in a room with no bedding and made to do hard labor around the farm barefooted. Several times Mrs. Garrett tried to send them to the county poor house or a lunatic asylum and was heard to say that if the Old Man went back on his promise to send the girls away, there was going to be trouble.

And trouble there was. November 2, 1887, an alarm of fire went up from the Garrett farm. When help arrived, Mrs. Garrett was found moving furniture and household goods outside. What little smoke was visible was issuing from the locked room where Anna and Eva slept. A neighbor, Mr. Dimock, asked Mrs. Garrett where the girls were. She said, "Oh, I'm afraid they are suffocated or burned to death; let us save the things and the house!" "Great Almighty!" said Dimock, "let the house go; we must save the girls!" He kicked in the bedroom door, and, although smoke and flames poured out, helped to drag out the suffocated bodies of the two women. The fire had been confined to their bedroom. Kerosene oil had been spread on the floor, along with dried leaves and crumpled paper. Both girls had bruises and abrasions on their heads. They had died of smoke inhalation. Mr. Garrett was wild with grief over the girls' deaths; Mrs. Garrett scarcely pretended to care.

It was this lack of pretense that seems to have led to her arrest. From the very first, the newspaper reports judged her guilty of murdering her stepdaughters.

Mary Garrett, although her trial was postponed until she had given birth to a son, was convicted October 4, 1888 of arson and premeditated murder (there was some evidence that the furniture had been moved outside hours earlier than the fire) and sentenced to hang. She was sent to the penitentiary in Columbus. The execution was scheduled for January 24, 1889, but the sentence was commuted to life imprisonment in early 1889.

In the "Spooks in the Slammer" chapter, we saw how prisoners were sometimes tormented by visions of the "ghosts" of their victims. Mrs. Garrett, the Medina County Murderess, found herself confronted by not one, but two vengeful spirits.

EVERY NIGHT
THE SPOOKS HAUNT HER
THE DREAD SENSATION OF A CLAMMY
HAND'S TOUCH
A HORRIBLE LAUGH OR A
BLOOD-CURDLING MOAN
ADD TO THE MISERABLE GLOOM OF A
WRETCHED WOMAN
MRS. GARRETT, THE MEDINA COUNTY
MURDERESS, IN AGONY
HER CONSCIENCE ABOUT TO FORCE HER
TO CONFESS
TO THE POISONING AND CREMATION OF TWO
IMBECILES
THE SPIRITS OF THE VICTIMS VISIT HER CELL

EVERY NIGHT
AND STARE WEIRDLY AT HER.

Columbus, Ohio, December 10. The dusky dames in the clean-washed female department of the penitentiary are in a panic of fear, and there is a dread surrounding the place now that keeps down the boisterous laughter in the laundry, and induces the female prisoners to huddle together and never venture alone into the dark corners after nightfall. Each morning, when it has become light enough to justify the boldest in removing the bed clothes from over their heads, there is wonderment as to whether there was a "visitation" the night before, and at the frugal breakfast the scared prisoners question each other in awed tones as to the happenings of the night.

The cause of this state of affairs is a ghost—rather two ghosts.

Strange things have been happening in this pleasant little corner of the penitentiary, which was wont to ring

WITH THE MELLOW LAUGHTER

Of the colored girls who do the laundry work for the institution, or echo to the warblings of the canary birds that are caged there to give the quarters a cheerful tone.

Ghastly knockings, words whispered so as to be heard only by women guilty of dreadful crimes, strange and inexplicable ringings of the entrance bell, sudden awakenings in the night with the sense of a clammy hand on the face or the echo of a horrible laugh or blood-curdling moan have been taken as portents of a terrible vengeance visited upon the guilty by their victims now in the spiritual world. Just outside the enclosure rise the gloomy walls of the dreadful annex, and, since the first visitation, the superstitious female prisoners have discovered strange conditions surrounding that spot of doleful memories.

It all began with the keen remorse of Mrs. Mary Garrett, the Medina County woman, who poisoned her two imbecile step-daughters and

THEN BURNED THE HOUSE

Over their heads to destroy the evidence of her crime. Mrs. Garrett never openly confessed her guilt, but remorse, that keen sting of the conscience, has been goading her on to a complete revelation of the double murder. It has been noticed lately that Mrs. Garrett passes sleepless nights, and emerges from her little cell in the morning with scared, wide open eyes, and haggard face—clear evidence of the hours of communion with the little blue devils of despondency.

For a long time she refused to give any reason for her sleeplessness, but within the past few days has let drop hints which are half confessions of her crime and revelations of the terrible experience through which she is passing. She told another prisoner and finally made the revelation to the matrons and to Captain Kirkendall, of the night watch, that she is

HAUNTED BY THE SPIRITS

Of her murdered step-daughters. They come to her every night, she says, accuse her of the crime of their murder and give her warning of a horrible fate that is to be her punishment.

They sit on her cot, one at the foot, and the other at the head, and, as the ancient mariner did with the tardy guest for the wedding feast, fix her with their lack-luster eyes, and tell her again and again of the agonies they have passed through on account of her crimes. Their cold, clammy hands she feels on her face whenever she is left alone in the dark, and whenever she turns her eyes, she can see the outlines of their faces. The woman is evidently on the verge of insanity, but her superstitious fears and her hallucinations have terrified her fellow prisoners.

This feeling has been intensified by a

MYSTERIOUS, SOFT RINGING

Of the door bell in the middle of the night, when all the prisoners were safely locked in their cells. It comes at just about the hour a few minutes after 2 o'clock, when Mrs. Garrett's great crime was consummated. The female department is shut out from the lawn at the front of the main penitentiary building by a wall, not quite so high as the great wall. In this wall a door, protected by an overhanging perch, has been cut, and all visitors, before being admitted, are scrutinized by the matron through a wicket.

A door-bell is connected with this entrance by an old-fashioned arrangement, consisting of a crank and wire, and every visitor must pull this lever, ringing the bell in the female ward, as a signal, to attract attention within.

One night, shortly after 2 o'clock, this bell rang softly. Most people give it a jerk, Captain Kirkendall alone having the knack of ringing it softly. The matron thinking that

SOMETHING HAD HAPPENED

And that the Captain, who is on duty at night, was seeking admittance, hastened to the door, only to find no one there. The next night, at exactly the same hour, the bell rang again, but no person could be found at the door. A watch was set next night, but the bell rang just the same as before, and the guards could see no ringer.

Captain Kirkendall thought it might be an owl secreted under the head of the porch that disturbed the wire and gave the bell the soft oscillation that is characteristic of his own signal, but Mrs. Garrett says it is a portent, and is intended for her: that the murdered imbecile girls have visited her cell and told her so. The penitentiary officials laugh at the idea, but have not yet explained the repetition of the ringing at exactly the same hour each night.
Cincinnati [OH] Enquirer 11 December 1892: p. 9 FRANKLIN/ MEDINA COUNTY

NOTE: I am not certain why the headlines speak of Mrs. Garrett poisoning the daughters—I have not found that detail in any of the trial testimony. The "dreadful annex" was the building where executions took place at the penitentiary. The ancient mariner alludes to the poem "The Rime of the Ancient Mariner" by Samuel Taylor Coleridge where the mariner fixes the guest with a "glittering eye." Mrs. Garrett was pardoned by Gov. Joseph Foraker at Christmas 1899. Her husband had divorced her long ago; she went to live with a grown daughter. I do not know when she died. She must have died in terror, knowing she was about to meet her victims.

For more information on this horrific case see "Medina's Wickedest Stepmother" in *Women Behaving Badly: Cleveland's Most Ferocious Female Killers*, John Stark Bellamy II, (Cleveland, OH: Gray & Company, 2005) and *Plain Dealer* [Cleveland, OH] 20 May 1888: p. 8.

After this tale of madness and murder, it is pleasant to end the chapter with a story of a happy family relationship; one that lasted well beyond death:

A BRAVE ENGINEER'S GHOSTLY COMPANIONS

Lima, O., February 11. John M. Miller, the brave engineer who lost his life in the railroad collision near Sidney, Ohio, on last Monday was buried on Thursday, the funeral being largely attended, especially by the Masonic Order and the railroad men of this place, the latter having orders from the officials to quit work for the purpose of paying respect to the memory of one of their number who, for twenty years, had never shrunk from any duty, and who died with his hands on the throttle of his engine to save the lives of the passengers on his train. Since his tragic death and burial many stories are told of his eccentricities and superstition, among which are, that he had for years persisted in telling his family and intimate friends that an old fireman, who was killed several years ago and in the same accident in which he himself was crippled, would get on his engine every night he passed the fatal spot, and taking his accustomed seat, would ride with him to the end of the trip. It is also said that he would talk to the phantom just as he used to do when the fireman was alive and well, and that he would never allow anyone else to occupy the seat, always reserving it for his ghostly companion.

A few years ago Miller lost by death a bright little girl, to whom he was greatly attached, and ever afterward she, too, would nightly and daily get on his engine at a certain place on the road, and ride and talk with him until his train neared Dayton, and then disappear. As in the former case, her seat was kept for her in the cab, and no one allowed to occupy it.

At his home a chair was always set up to the table, the crib in which the child had been rocked drawn near, and a plate and food placed on the table, just as when the little girl lived and prattled. It is even said that the father would look at the chair and talk to its supposed occupant just as he used to do during its lifetime, and what seems strange now is that the wife and mother, an intelligent and highly respected lady, entertained and does now, the same superstitious views in regard to the child, and had the utmost faith in all that her husband ever told her about the ghostly visitations on the road.

The dead engineer was a man of more than ordinary intelligence, read much, and was considered by his friends and companions a high-minded, honorable man, and one whose word was as good as his bond. It is certainly true that the railroad officials, for whom he worked so long and faithfully, had the most implicit confidence in him, and looked upon him as one of their safest and best engineers. Yet among those with whom Miller was in most constant companionship, it is said that, entertaining the views he did, and being a professed Spiritualist, if the collision in which he lost his life had occurred through any negligence or fault of his, that the officials of the road would have had to "shoulder" the blame because of having kept so long a man with such known superstitious notions and ideas, and in one of the most dangerous and hazardous positions on the road. The facts, however, that the brave engineer was in nowise to blame for the accident, but, to the contrary, he did all in his power to prevent the awful calamity and save as many lives as possible, even at the sacrifice of his own, proves that the officers of the road appreciated his worth and knew so well "of what kind of stuff" he was made, that they could trust in him at all times and under all circumstances, notwithstanding his queer ideas and unexplainable eccentricities and belief.

But the strangest part of the story remains to be told, and that is that his sudden and terrible death should have taken place at almost the exact spot where his old fireman lost his life and where his disembodied spirit, with that of Miller's child, afterward regularly boarded his engine for their nightly ride.

Cincinnati [OH] Commercial Tribune 12 February 1883: p. 3 ALLEN COUNTY

NOTE: Here is a brief account of the accident that killed Engineer Miller:

Sidney, O., February 5. A terrific collision took place four miles south of Sidney, on the D & M Railroad, between the south-bound passenger and the north-bound local freight. John Miller, of Lima, Ohio, engineer on the passenger train, Clarence Freeman, of Cincinnati, engineer on the freight, and Frank Wheeler, of Cumminsville, baggage master on the passenger train, were killed instantly, and their bodies are now in the possession of the Coroner. Patrick Doolin, of Sidney, Ohio, fireman on the freight, and James Howard, fireman on the passenger, living at Lima, Ohio, were badly injured. There were ten passengers on the train. None of them were seriously hurt. The cause of the collision, as far as known, was the misunderstanding of an order by the conductor of the local freight. The engines are both complete wrecks.

Cleveland [OH] Leader 6 February 1883: p. 3

The *Dayton Journal* wrote this about Mr. Miller's former escapes and his eccentricities.

"He was a peculiar character in many respects, but understood his business and was held in high estimation by his superiors. Twelve years ago his engine was in a collision at Colesville, and again at Anna Station, but both times he escaped with slight injuries. A number of years ago his engine went through a culvert and his fireman was killed, while he again escaped, but this time with a broken leg. Being of a superstitious turn of mind, he always imagined that the spirit of the fireman got on his engine at this culvert every night and rode with him on his old seat to the end of his ride. Miller rarely told this to anyone, but he declared to his friends that when the fireman's spirit did not ride with him he knew that an accident would happen.

6.

Black Cats and Feather Crowns:
Witchery in Ohio

Because a man who believes in ghosts and witches and witchcraft
is two hundred years behind the light of the age he lives in....

– *Ohio Statesman* [Columbus, OH] 10 March 1840: p. 1 –

In my Swiss family anything old-fashioned or outmoded was called
"Dutchy." This comes, of course, from *deutsch*, German, and we hear it
in the phrase "Pennsylvania Dutch." Nineteenth-century papers were quick
to ridicule recent or unassimilated immigrants as superstitious idiots for
their belief in witches and spells. After all, witchcraft was something that
happened a long time ago and far away in some hind-bound Eastern state.
The progressive, well-educated people of the up-and-coming state of Ohio
had no such truck with superstition. Such things were embarrassingly
old-fashioned and foreign: "Dutchy." And yet, stories of witches and their
bewitched prey persisted even into the 1920s.

Fear of witchcraft led to some extraordinarily cruel remedies, as in this
famous 1828 case from Lawrence County.

> The annexed report of a case that came before the court of common
> pleas in this county is from the pen of a legal gentleman of high standing.
> It shows that in our day, the belief in witchcraft has not entirely vanished.
> [The first part of the document has to do with the plaintiff being
> sold an unsound horse.] [The defendant] answered by insisting that
> the horse was in no way diseased, or in unsound health, but that the
> drooping appearance arose from his being bewitched. The defendant
> further stated, that the same witches which were in that horse, had
> been in one or two persons, and some cows, in the same settlement, and
> could only be driven out by a witch doctor, living on the head waters of
> the Little Scioto, in Pike County, or by burning the animal in which
> they were found; that this doctor had some time before been sent for to
> see a young woman who was in a bad way, and on examination found
> her bewitched. He soon expelled [the witches], and also succeeded in
> ascertaining that an old woman not far off was the witch...and she could
> be got rid of only by killing her.

At some subsequent time, when defendant was from home, his wife sent for witness and others, to see and find out what was the matter with her cow, in a lot near the house. They found it frantic, running, and pitching at everything which came near. It was their opinion, after observing it considerably, that it had the canine madness [rabies]. The defendant, however, returned before the witness and others left the lot; he inspected the cow with much attention, and gave it as his opinion that they were mistaken as to the true cause of her conduct,—she was not mad, but bewitched; the same which had been in the horse, had transferred itself to the cow.

By this time the animal, from exhaustion or other cause, had lain down. The defendant then went into the lot, and requested the persons present to assist in putting a rope about her horns, and then make the other end fast to a tree, where he could burn her. They laughed at the man's notion, but finally assisted him, seeing she remained quiet—still having no belief that he really intended burning her.

This being done, the defendant piled up logs, brush and other things around, and finally over the poor cow, and then set fire to them. The defendant continued to add fuel, until she was entirely consumed, and afterwards told the witness he had never seen any creature so hard to die; that she continued to moan after most of the flesh had fallen from her bones, and he felt a pity for her, but die she must; that nothing but the witches in her kept her alive so long, and it was his belief they would be so burnt before getting out, that they never would come back.

Night having set in before the burning was finished, the defendant and his family set up to ascertain if the witches could be seen about the pile of embers. Late at night, someone of the family called the defendant to the window—the house being near the place—and pointed to two witches, hopping around, over and across the pile of embers, and now and then seizing a brand and throwing it into the air, and in a short while disappeared. The next morning, on examination, the defendant saw their tracks through the embers in all directions.

At a subsequent time, he told the same witness and others, that from that time the witches had wholly disappeared from the neighborhood, and would never return—and to burn the animal alive, in which they were found, was the only way to get clear of them: he had been very fearful they would torment his family.

Historical Collections of Ohio, Henry Howe, (Cincinnati, OH: Bradley & Anthony, 1850) p. 291 LAWRENCE COUNTY

I find this next tale of a witchcraft scare in 1897, only a short distance from a major city, terrifying and baffling.

WITCHCRAFT SCARE.
SEVENTEEN FAMILIES AFFLICTED WITH A PECULIAR MALADY
SOME ON THE VERGE OF DEATH
THEY CANNOT SLEEP OR REST AT NIGHT AND KEEP PINING AWAY UNTIL THEY ARE MERE SKELETONS.

Toledo, Jan. 21. Richfield Center, a little village in this county, 17 miles south of here, is in the midst of a genuine witchcraft scare. The little community is composed principally of Germans and are thoroughly convinced that they are being made the victims of some witch or other agent of his satanic majesty. There are 17 families afflicted with the peculiar malady. The thing has been going on for nearly a month and some 30 persons are on the verge of death.

The peculiar malady seizes a whole family at a time from the youngest to the oldest. They cannot sleep or rest at night, and keep pining away until they become mere skeletons. The symptoms in all cases are similar. Several of those afflicted claim that they are being constantly pursued by black cats which make faces and snarl at them. Some of them also claim that certain rooms in their houses are infested with the strange evil spirit, while other rooms are free from its influence.

A.M. Miller came to the city and reported the matter. He is a victim of the strange disease, and had to be carried to and from the carriage which conveyed him, owing to weakness. His wife and four sons are down with the disease and are likely to die.

Richfield Center is located 10 miles from a railroad station. Mr. Miller says that the people firmly believe the whole thing is the work of some witch whom they cannot locate.

Some of the horses, cattle, sheep and swine are victims of the disease.

The people have burned their feather-beds and resorted to other ancient methods in the hope of getting rid of the spell, but they claim they cannot shake it off. Physicians cannot diagnose the malady, but assure the patients that it is due to natural causes, possibly resulting from an unsanitary condition of the village.

Piqua [OH] Daily Call 21 January 1897: p. 3 LUCAS COUNTY

NOTE: This story suggests that the villagers were suffering from poisoning, perhaps ergot (a fungus infecting rye) or white snakeroot plant (which poisoned the milk of the cows who ate it and the people who drank that milk.) There is also the possibility of some neurological disease like mosquito-borne encephalitis. Richfield Center lay in the former Great Black Swamp, noted for its fevers and agues. Drainage of the swamp began in the 1840s, but was not completed until the 1890s. The burning of feather beds was done because witches might hide witch balls or feather crowns (circular formations of feathers) inside the beds, bewitching the persons who lay in them. The witch balls found in the beds are not the blown glass balls commonly known by that name, but pellets made with hair, fingernail clippings, and other materials used in spells. See the stories at the end of this chapter for more on the cursed things found inside feather beds.

This article makes it even plainer that the cows were probably the source of the horror.

DEMON CAT
CAUSING ALL THE SICKNESS AND TROUBLE AT RICHFIELD CENTER, OHIO

Toledo, Ohio, January 21. The inclement weather here to-day has prevented any investigator from driving to the bewitched community of Richfield Center, 22 miles west of Toledo. A farmer named Henry Niemen came to this city, however, and fully corroborated the strange story told last night by Farmer Miller when he came to this city to ask for aid. Everything about the case sounds like a story from the days of Salem witchcraft, the sick now numbering the majority of individuals in 20 families. All claim to have been visited by a demon cat, after which they are simply wasted away by a disease that makes them indifferent to life itself. This cat, by the way, has been hunted with the belief that its death would kill the witch who is making the trouble. All other "witch signs" are said to be present. Many cattle have died, and some that are living give bloody milk, feather wreaths in pillows and beds, and one woman has burned 10 pounds of them which she claims had formed a wreath as hard as stone. The sick claim to be unable to stay in their beds and sleep in the kitchen and living rooms. One man took his entire family to his barn, but were chased back by the demon cat. Miller's relatives, who went back with him to nurse the sick, first visited a priest, who is said to have given them directions for laying the evil spirit.
Cincinnati [OH] Enquirer 22 January 1897: p. 1 LUCAS COUNTY

WITCHCRAFT IN SALEM (OHIO)

Witch trials in Salem! Charges and countercharges of wizardry and familiars! Acceptance of spectral evidence! We know all of the old stories, except that the events in the stories below took place in 1890s Salem, Ohio, not 17th-century Salem, Massachusetts. These charges led to a series of unprecedented church trials, resulting in the expulsion of several church members. The trial was covered extensively in the newspapers and, although they are too long to include, the transcripts provide an enlightening look at the kinds of village feuds and brooding superstition that easily could have led to the hanging of innocent people.

> Great excitement prevails in and about Salem, O. One Jacob Culp is accused of being a wizard and is accordingly shunned by his neighbors. What is worse, his immediate relatives are the most persistent and bitter of all his accusers. It seems there was a shadow of a doubt as to his diabolical powers until Dr. Hoff, a "clairvoyant," of Alliance, O., was consulted. This veritable Dr. Hersog, who is evidently better known in the Black Art regions than in Alliance, pronounced Culp a wizard with a familiar spirit and that settled it. Culp now proposes to prosecute his accusers. It is fitting indeed that this modern witchcraft should break out at Salem.
> *Advance Argus* [Greenville, PA] 25 May 1893: p. 4 COLUMBIANA COUNTY

NOTE: Dr. Hersog was Johann Jakob Herzog, a very orthodox Protestant theologian, author of *The New Schaff-Herzog Encyclopedia of Religious Knowledge*, which includes some references to mythological beings. Perhaps the author is suggesting that Dr. Hoff was as learned as Dr. Herzog in identifying wizards.

BELIEVE IN THE "EVIL EYE."
A TRIAL FOR WITCHCRAFT IN A MODERN TOWN OF SALEM

> The town of Salem, Ohio, was the scene recently of an extraordinary trial, which carries one's thoughts back to the Massachusetts town of the same name that hanged witches in the seventeenth century. Salem has a pretty little Methodist Church, at which farmers worship. For the past two years several families attending the church have been possessed with the idea that they are bewitched. Last summer Howard

Hughes, a well-known farmer, dug a well on his place, but after digging to what he considered a sufficient depth failed to strike water. He was nonplussed for the moment, but, having a half belief in witches, came to the conclusion that his well was bewitched. He went to Alliance to consult with a Doctor Hoff, a septuagenarian, who claims to be a witch doctor. Hoff went back with Hughes, and descending into the well built a fire, and throwing several powders into the blaze went through a powwow performance.

On coming to the surface Dr. Hoff told Hughes that William Culp, a trustee of their church and the wealthiest farmer in the neighborhood, was causing all the trouble with his evil eye and that the well would remain dry until after Culp's death. Hughes told the Breen and Loop families, who also had a weakness for witches, that Culp was the wizard who was bringing all the bad luck on them. From time to time the deluded people kept clear of Culp, but denounced him as an evil man to all who would listen to them. A month ago some cattle belonging to Norman Breen took sick and died and then a relative of Hughes fell and broke his leg. Culp was blamed for all this and the families have been very active in denouncing him as a wizard and dangerous person and advised their friends to keep away from him.

Their belief became so annoying to the pastor of the little church that he concluded to have the superstitious ones expelled and, preferring charges of witchcraft and defamation against them, he organized a church trial, which took place, the presiding elder of the district acting as judge. The trial occupied the whole day and, as a result, Mr. and Mrs. Norman Breen and Howard Hughes were expelled from the fold.
Northern Vindicator [Estherville, IA] 22 February 1894 COLUMBIANA/ STARK COUNTY

NOTE: One of the bitterest enemies of Culp was his sister-in-law, Miss Sadie Loop, who claimed he had murdered his wife, Miss Loop's sister, and his mother-in-law, Miss Loop's mother. She was also expelled from the church for asserting that Culp was a wizard. The powders of Dr. Hoff were standard equipment for a Pennsylvania "Pow-Wow Doctor." Although this is an Algonquian term for a gathering of medicine men, "Pow-Wow" is a primarily German/Pennsylvanian healing tradition using charms, potions, prayers, and folk remedies from *The Long Lost Friend* and other magical books. While this story is a late example of belief in witchcraft, pow-wowing still goes on today in some areas.

This next story, half dire description of lunacy and half Monty Python sketch, comes from the village of Bethel in Clermont County.

There were also living, in the village [of Bethel] at this time a few families not so highly favored in mental ability, and who unfortunately believed in the presence and power of evil spirits and witches. Of this latter class are remembered the Evans and Hildebrand families, the former residing on the lot at present occupied by Dr. McLain, the latter on the Dr. William Ellsberry lot. It appears the Hildebrand family especially imagined itself under the influence of witches, the older daughters, who were young women grown, giving unmistakable evidence that they were possessed by some evil spirits. On the approach of night they would scream, and at times become perfectly frantic from fright of the hideous objects which they professed to see, and which maintained such a spell over them that they were unfitted for their duties. Various devices were resorted to in order to exorcise these spirits.

A large bag of linsey-woolsey was made and held by a member of the family, while the other members went through some ceremony, at the conclusion of which it was supposed the witch had been forced to take refuge in the bag, which was quickly closed, and after being firmly tied was carefully laid on the porch of the house, where it was cut into a thousand pieces with a sharp axe. The fragments were then gathered together and burned; and one would surely supposed that if the witch had perchance escaped death while the bag which confined it was cut into fine shreds, the fire would put an end to its existence.

Not so, however; the influence over the young women remained undispelled, and the witches continued to revel in the Hildebrand house. Soon the spirits assumed a material form, and appeared, as the young women averred, in the person of their neighbour, Nancy Evans; and from this time on it was not long until they believed that Nancy Evans herself was the witch, and that all their troubles had been caused by that unfortunate woman. She was shunned, and all intercourse with the family avoided; but the trouble remained.

At last the justice of the peace was importuned to take the matter in hand, and if the woman, Nancy Evans, were really a witch, expel her from the presence of the afflicted family. The statutes of the Territory had made no provision for a case of this nature, the legislators evidently thinking that witchcraft would not flourish on Ohio soil; so the case had to be disposed of in another way. A tradition prevailed that if a witch were weighed against the Holy Writ, so great would be the overpowering influence of the Bible that the witch would be compelled to tip the beam.

Accordingly, a rude pair of scales was constructed to decide this momentous matter, and all the interested parties having been called, as well as the neighbors, who were to witness the propriety of the proceedings, Nancy Evans was placed on one end of the scales and the Bible on the other, when she was thus adjured: "Nancy Evans, thou art weighed against the Bible, to try thee against all witchcraftry and diabolical practices."

This being done in the name of the law, and with a profound respect for the Word of God, seems to have had a solemn and conclusive effect. Nancy Evans was heavier, very much heavier, than the book, and was thenceforth relieved from all suspicion of being more than a simple old woman, who willingly submitted to this novel process in order to bring peace of mind to her neighbors, whom she sincerely pitied.
History of Clermont County, Ohio, (Philadelphia, PA: L.H. Everts, 1880) pp. 324-325 CLERMONT COUNTY

I've found a number of newspaper reports of persons declared insane or ridiculed because of their fear of witches. Here are two of those stories.

OBEYED THE WITCHES.
A WILL MADE ACCORDING TO IMAGINARY COMMANDS

John D. Bramsche believed in witches.

He thought they would appear to him under certain circumstances.

He did the thing which he thought would cause them to appear, and then made a will disposing of his property in accordance with the directions he imagined they gave.

Those are the causes which led to the filing of a suit in the Common Pleas Court yesterday to set aside the will of the man mentioned.

He died last February, and his will was admitted to probate the following April.

It is alleged that the paper writing is not the will of the deceased, as he was incapacitated mentally from disposing of his property because of age and sickness. He was troubled with delusions about spirits and witches.

One of his beliefs was that his cattle were bewitched; also, that if he would boil a pig for an hour a witch would come from behind the barn foaming at the mouth, and would tell him how to dispose of his property. He did boil the pig, and said that he saw the witch. He then disposed of his property by making a will. It only gave $700 each to William, Lillian and Nettie I. Riemeier, his grandchildren, and their mother. They are not satisfied with that and have filed the suit to set aside the will.

The estate is said to be worth about $500,000.

Cincinnati [OH] Enquirer 18 October 1889: p. 8 HAMILTON COUNTY

BEWITCHED
BY A DIABOLICAL MACHINE THAT MAKES THEIR HEADS BUZZ

J.C. Hartwig and his wife, both old and infirm, appealed to the authorities at Akron, Ohio, Wednesday, to assist them in freeing themselves from a remarkable tribulation. They said they had spent $1,500 to get rid of the spell, but that it had not helped them in the least. They say a neighbor has a diabolical machine which has bewitched them. It has the power of creating a strange buzzing noise in their heads. Every time they relax their watches on his house he starts it going. They have taken turns at night watching his house. They are willing to give anything to break the spell. Every fakir who has been in Akron has carried away a roll of the old folks' money.

The authorities gave them a bottle of anti-witch tonic composed of 99 parts water and 1 of sugar. This they were assured would put an end to the spell. They left for home much relieved. The case is a sad one, as they are squandering their property in a reckless way.

Jackson [MI] Citizen Patriot 30 March 1900: p. 1 SUMMIT COUNTY

NOTE: This story has much in common with modern "mystery hum" cases.

I find the following two stories utterly fascinating, especially the mystical feather crowns and other objects found inside the feather beds. In looking at the folklore of feather crowns, there are two conflicting traditions. I have always associated them with witchcraft or thought of them as an omen of death, but apparently, particularly in Appalachia, they are also a sign that the dead person has gone to Heaven.

I can't help but think that this is a later interpretation, meant to comfort those left behind. After all, if a loved one has died, which is more productive: assuming that the feather crown is a crown of glory or an artifact of witchcraft that must inevitably lead to investigations, trials, and lynch mobs? In these two stories, like the preceding ones, the feather crowns, in the German tradition, mean death.

WITCHCRAFT NOT DEAD.
STRANGE ILLNESS OF A CHILD
AND A STILL STRANGER STORY
WREATHS OF FEATHERS MADE BY
INVISIBLE AGENT
AND THEIR EFFECTS ON MORTALS

Witchcraft, it has been said, is a thing of the past. That statement may be true, but there are still people who have a lurking belief in its mysterious power, as an *Enquirer* reporter, who was wandering about last night in search of news, can testify.

In a way and manner known only to the craft he learned that there was a child lying sick in a certain house on a principal street in the great city, and that from the circumstances connected with the disease the child was believed to be bewitched. Americans, as a class, are not given to entertaining superstitious ideas, and the reporter being one of that class was not at all convinced; but more with the idea of getting an item than for curiosity's sake he allowed himself to be beguiled into visiting the house.

The parents are respectable and well-to-do German people and deserve all sympathy in their present time of trouble. Lying on a bed in the room was the sufferer, a bright little boy of almost seven years of age. The light, blonde hair which lay in curling masses on the pillow framed in a sad, beautiful face drawn with suffering and wasted with disease. The little form was wasted away until it seemed as though existence were no longer possible. The child, so the grief-stricken mother said, was taken ill nine weeks ago. It ate scarcely any thing and seemed to exist principally on water. As to the ailment, she said that they had one physician, but as the child got no better under his treatment they called in a well-known doctor whose opinion is to be relied on, and he said that the child had a slight attack of brain fever, accompanied by spinal meningitis, enough, one would think, to waste a more substantial constitution than that of a child, without assistance from diabolical agents.

In some unknown way strange stories concerning the condition of the sick little one began to circulate about the neighborhood, and

certain well-meaning old German women having put their heads together in solemn conclave decided without a dissenting voice that the
child was bewitched. While the foibles of all people are to be respected,
still the newspaper man was inclined to laugh when the story was told
him of the way in which the work of imposing suffering on an innocent
child had been accomplished by the knights of the broomstick. The old
women above referred to visited the house, and solemnly informed the
mother of their belief, and asked permission to examine the feather bed
on which the child lay. She, while not all imbued with superstitious feelings, but in the vain hope that her child might be restored to health,
consented to the plan. Accordingly, after the boy had been taken from
the bed the ticking was ripped open and there among the feathers they
discovered five unfinished wreaths of feathers, which at once to their
minds, filled as they were with the legends of the fatherland, explained
the reason of the boy's continued illness. A German lady was found,
who in as explicit a manner as possible, explained the wreath mystery,
but before doing so, she expressed her surprise that the reporter had
never seen one, as they were so common.

The wreath begins to form in the bed, and then the person who is
so unfortunate as to repose on that couch is sure to get sick. As long as
the wreath remains in the bed the person continues ill, and if the wreath
is allowed to lay there until the ends of the circle come together just that
minute the patient dies. The only way in which to save life is to remove
the unfinished wreaths from the bed, put on them a copious supply of
salt and burn them in the fire. As long as the circlet stays in the bed in
an unfinished state the patient can neither die nor get well. In support
of her theory the woman said:

"In my life I have seen three. One was as large as a plate. The
feathers are all different colors and lap over each other at the ends just
like the feathers on a bird. The feathers are fastened to a cord, and when
the wreath is finished it is utterly impossible for anyone to break it."
Another wreath that she saw had been found in the bed of a child. The
father once or twice had taken the bed from the crib to use as a pillow,
but he said he was unable to sleep, as he felt all the time as though a
snake were worming about beneath his head.

In regard to the wreaths found in the bed of the child, referred to
in this article, it was said that the old woman took the five wreaths to
an old fortune-teller on Race Street, who is, so to speak, on good terms
with the witches. She kept the feathers, when they should have been

burned, and the woman who told the story to the reporter said that they should have been burned, as then the child would have got well. As it now stands the poor little fellow can neither get well nor die.

Cincinnati [OH] Enquirer 29 May 1881: p. 4 HAMILTON COUNTY

HAVE WE WITCHES AMONG US?

By dint of diligent and persistent search and inquiry, and a promise to reveal no names, we are enabled to present our readers with a choice dish of witch hash for their breakfast.

Some three or four weeks ago it came to light in a limited way that the premises of a well-known successful German barber were bewitched, and a brief mention of the case was prepared for one of the daily papers, but the manuscript fell into his hands, and he destroyed it and begged that the matter be supressed. Now it comes to pass that another quarter of the town is possessed. No. 7 Riddle Street is the place, and a woman living in the rear part of the house is the main afflicted party, and the discoverer of the dread phenomena.

One night last week she determined to examine and see why it was that the feather-bed on which she slept was so uncomfortably rough. She tore an opening in the tick at a point where a big lump presented itself to the touch, and to her horror pulled out the form of a little baby clothed all in feathers. She summoned her female friends without delay, and told them of her frightful discovery with bated breath and trembling limbs. They went with her to the infested bed-room, opened wide the bed-tick, and what was their horror can only be imagined when they found it nearly filled with baby forms, human hands, a human leg from the knee down, and including the foot, a number of rats of sundry sizes, a quantity of balls, and a lot of bouquets all made of or clothed with, feathers sewed together in the most careful and skillful fashion with white silk of a nature so fine as scarcely to be visible to the naked eye.

One of the women present, who is a milliner declared that no human hands could possibly have done the work, so exquisite and perfect is it in all its ways. The woman who slept in the bewitched bed says that she bought the feathers two years ago, made them up into a bed herself, and that nobody else has ever handled them—that is, no human hands. She further vows most solemnly and distinctly that when she bought these feathers there were no chicken feathers in the lot, and now they are all chicken feathers.

The sewing, as we remarked above, was of the most skillful kind possible, the silk being of no more than a gossamer texture, and the perforations of the instrument used in doing the work smaller than those of any needle ever used by mortals here below.

It is to be regretted that ocular demonstration of the truly remarkable phenomena is not to be had, as it would have offered us much pleasure to be able to call the eyes of all our readers to witness, to say go and see for yourselves. But we cannot. One of the women adjured the rest by all that was sacred and holy to destroy the work of the industrious witches and they did it. One by one the feather baby and the human leg and hands and the rats and the balls and the bouquets were solemnly and silently consigned to the flames.

Cincinnati [OH] Enquirer 17 October 1875: p. 5 HAMILTON COUNTY

NOTE: More on feather crowns:
http://carrollscorner.net/FeatherDeathCrowns.htm.
http://www.meta-religion.com/Paranormale/Other/death_crowns.htm
http://archiver.rootsweb.ancestry.com/th/read/MOWASHIN/2004-09/1094925209

7.

The Phantom Coffin:
And Other Ohio Apparitions

Besides if we all became angels why were some of the dead folk he knew still roaming around their familiar places trying to do their old jobs not knowing that they have arms of wind.

– Outa Jantjes, a man from Cape Town, South Africa –

You can tell a lot about an area's history and people from its ghost stories. For example, the South tells tales of haunted plantations and the ghosts of Confederate soldiers. Pennsylvania and West Virginia report ghosts at the sites of coal-mining accidents. States along the east coast relate stories of ghostly pirates and phantom ships. Ohio forms a kind of cross-roads for many ghostly traditions representing the entire spectral spectrum: Appalachian haint stories, Civil War ghosts, the Ohio oil boom, farm, industrial, and railroad disasters; stories of historical characters like Simon Girty and Colonel Crawford; notorious murderers and their victims; Spiritualists, immigrants from many countries, and just plain ghostly folks. It's a history of Ohio—in ghosts.

While Britain has a wealth of stories about ghostly Black Dogs, I have been surprised by how few stories there are of phantom animals in Ohio. This is one of the few examples.

"PHANTOM DOG."
STRANGE IDEA
EXODUS OF QUAKERS OWING TO THE
PHANTOM DOG

A little settlement of Quakers, living near Lewiston, Ohio, immigrated Tuesday to Indiana. The "Phantom Dog" has driven these simple people from Logan County after a sojourn of 50 years.

For years and years "Uncle" Jack McKinnon peddled fish and told the futures of the unsuspecting in Stokes Township. He was always accompanied by a single black dog. When three years ago "Uncle" Jack was found dead in his bed, the canine was also discovered lifeless at the foot of the old man's couch.

"Uncle" Jack was buried by the Quakers. The faithful dog, it is said, was cast into the reservoir.

Recently residents of the vicinity were disturbed by the mournful and continued howling of a dog. Strange stories were whispered about among the superstitious. Citizens of good standing have repeatedly stated that a big black dog prowls nightly among the graves in the Friends' Cemetery. It fills the air with weird and mournful cries. When whistled or called to the animal vanishes.

So the Quakers are moving, after a residence of 50 years in old Logan.

When that mournful and uncanny howl hovers in the still night air the people solemnly say that the "Phantom dog" is out again looking for its old dead master. No one will pass the graveyard day or night, and the residents in the vicinity can stand it no longer.

Jackson [MI] Citizen Patriot 27 April 1900: p. 2 LOGAN COUNTY

Some ghosts seem to ignore the unpleasant fact that they are dead and simply carry on with their daily routine, including going to work. Here are several stories of ghosts who are still on the job.

AN OHIO APPARITION
WRENCH LAY JUST WHERE THE "GHOST" HAD PLACED IT

There is much excitement in the Dunbridge oil field, Bowling Green, O., over an alleged ghost that is said to have been seen on the ill-fated Roller farm, where so many accidents have happened and people been killed. The other night while a thunderstorm was raging, a pumper on that lease declares that he saw the form of C.C. Clark, who was recently killed, with two of his companions, in a boiler explosion. On the very same spot where the boiler exploded another one now stands. About midnight, the pumper says, he was aroused by a terrible crash of thunder and a flash of lightning.

There, not 20 feet away, as natural as life, stood the form of the dead pumper. It sped to the boiler, and, mounting it, placed a large wrench on the safety valve, just as he did on that fatal night when the boiler exploded. He had gone and all was darkness. For a few minutes the pumper was nearly paralyzed with fright, and sweat stood in great drops on his brow; then, taking a lantern, he went to the boiler and, sure enough, he found the wrench hanging on the blow-off. He shut down the engine immediately, blew off the boiler and quit the job.

The pumper is a sober sort of a fellow and a man of good habits, whose word ordinarily would be taken at par. He declares that he had not been drinking nor dreaming, but is certain he saw the ghost of Clark. Workingmen on the adjoining leases are nearly scared out of their wits, and declare that they will quit the ill-fated region, where two horrible explosions happened within a week and no less than a dozen accidents in the past few months. The owners of the lease believe the ghost racket to be the work of some oil speculators, who are trying to make believe the lease is haunted, then will buy it cheap.

Jackson [MI] Citizen Patriot 22 September 1896: p. 3 WOOD COUNTY

NOTE: There was a "gas boom" when major oil and gas reserves were found in Wood County and the surrounding area in the 1880s. By the time of this story, production was beginning to decline.

SAW A "GHOST" IN THE TUNNEL.
CRIB WORKMEN DECLARE THEY ARE HAUNTED BY AN APPARITION
THREE SCARED MEN THROW UP THEIR JOBS AND HURRY FOR SHORE

The fact leaked out yesterday that a supposed apparition in the tunnel at Crib No. 2 threatens to seriously interfere with the progress of the work there. Digging under air pressure recommenced four days ago and already four men have thrown up their jobs and come ashore, either frankly declaring that they had seen the supposed ghost or giving various pretexts to the bosses and confessing to their comrades that they were afraid to again enter the tunnel.

The tunnel foremen and officials of the waterworks department in charge of the tunnel work laugh at the story. They have done their best to kill the absurd superstition by ridicule. The workmen are ready enough to laugh with them over the ghost joke while they are above ground and to vow that no spirit can have power to frighten them, but once in the dimly lighted tunnel with the stories of last summer's horror, in which so many men lost their lives, fresh in their minds, they are more credulous.

Most of the workmen, however, while they admit that there is something queer about the tunnel, say that they will continue to work there in spite of any supernatural influences that may be at work. It has been the weaker men whose nerves are less strong than those of the typical tunnel digger, who have hurried ashore with their baggage during the past week.

J.E. McCarthy, a "skinner" or mule driver, was the first man to see the "ghost." He had been employed for a long time as a waiter at Crib No. 3. He decided at last that he would prefer the job of driving the mule through the shaft at the other crib, as something that would be easier work at better wages.

Last Thursday night he went down to his first shift. The men went behind the air lock to work. McCarthy and the mule waited in the empty tunnel, 3,000 feet from the foot of the shaft. McCarthy is twenty-one years old, a steady workman of good physique and apparently not subject to nervous attacks. He sat composedly in the tunnel watching the rows of electric lights down the long vista of masonry walls and waited for the time to drive the mule car out with the load.

A half hour passed and the elevator man at the top of the shaft was startled by the sudden shriek of the signal whistle for his machine. Such a blast had not been blown on the crib since the fatal night of last summer, when the men hemmed in by the flames tried to signal to the shore for aid. The cage was sent down the shaft at its top speed. The trembling operator waited above expecting a horror but unable to imagine what had gone wrong. When the cage appeared McCarthy was its only occupant. He was pale with fright, and the operator says his hair stood straight up on his head.

'I have seen Plummer Jones," he gasped.

McCarthy had left his mule and run from his station to the foot of the shaft, a good half mile. He insisted on waking Foreman Van Duesen and telling his story to him. The time was 2:30 p.m. [the Foreman was on another shift] and Van Duesen's reception of the ghost story was the most vigorous blessing that such an apparition ever received.

But McCarthy had had enough. He wanted to go ashore at once and if that was not possible to go ashore on the first boat. He said that nothing could induce him to enter that tunnel again. He came ashore the next day on one of the tugs that reached the crib.

Three more workmen came ashore yesterday, who had thrown up their jobs. The workmen on the crib speak of the ghost as the "man with the whiskers" and he is a regular feature in the life there at present. The men have little to enliven their leisure hours and the tunnel "ghost" is

the joke with the least superstitious. The others laugh, but uneasily.
Plain Dealer [Cleveland, OH] 19 January 1902: p. 10 CUYAHOGA
COUNTY

NOTE: A water crib is a structure that protects intake pipes that collect
water from out in a lake to supply a pumping station onshore. Cleveland
began this particular 9-foot tunnel in 1896. It extended over 4 miles into the
lake. Twenty-eight tunnel workers died in five disasters while the structure
was being built.

Plummer Jones died a hero, trying to rescue three men from "that fatal
night of last summer," when a fire at a crib housing the workers killed nine
men. Here is the short version:

CAUGHT: LIKE RATS IN A TRAP. MEN IN A LAKE CRIB WERE BURNED TO DEATH WHILE RESCUERS IN BOATS WERE POWERLESS. TWO DEAD MEN FOUND IN A PRAYERFUL POSTURE. TWELVE BURNED, SUFFOCATED OR DROWNED. ONE OF RELIEF PARTY KILLED, ANOTHER INJURED--NO LIFE PRESERVERS AND PROSECUTIONS MAY FOLLOW.

Five men were burned to death, four were drowned, three, and
possibly four, were suffocated and several injured as the result of a
fire which destroyed a temporary waterworks crib, two miles off the
Cleveland Harbor, early to-day.
Cincinnati [OH] Enquirer 15 Aug 1901: p. 2.

GHOSTLY MOVEMENTS

Mineral Point, Ohio, is just now greatly agitated over the mysterious
doings of a ghost. The story is that his ghostship has taken up his
residence in Holden's fire-brick works. John Swoveland, a gentleman of
truth and veracity, who lives in the village, says that about two weeks
ago the fireman of the works mysteriously disappeared, and has not since
been heard from. A few days after a strange and hideous rattling of
chains was heard in the garret of the molding room, but on investigation
the old chains were found to be hanging and laying in their accustomed
places and not a soul was in sight. Then when the engine room was
destitute of occupants, someone was heard stirring up the fires and

putting on coal, and suddenly the engine would become red hot and the boilers threaten almost to burst. Next, while the workmen were going to dinner, the bricks were scattered all over the floor, and everything in the room thrown into confusion. In investigating the matter, some large flues were taken apart, when such a terrible stench arose that the bricks had to be replaced immediately. The informant states that hundreds of people have visited the spot and heard the noises, but are unable to fathom the mystery.

Jackson [MI] Citizen 1 February 1881: p. 1 TUSCARAWAS COUNTY

While this next tale is told in a stereotypical stage-Cherman dialect, it's a fascinating folkloric story.

GHOSTLY COFFIN MAKER
MYSTERIOUS MIDNIGHT ORDERS FOR COFFINS
A CURIOUS STORY OF JACOB HUMBARGER, A
LANCASTER, O., COFFIN MAKER FIFTY-FOUR
YEARS AGO.

The writer was sitting, a few days ago, in the office of the Hotel Martin, Lancaster, Ohio, conversing with an old resident of that city on various topics relating to the past history of the place when he inquired:

"Did you ever hear the story of Jacob Humbarger, the haunted coffin-maker?"

"Never. Is it out of the ordinary?"

"Yes. It is a curious story, and I hesitate about telling it, for fear people will think I am trying to humbug them with a ghost story."

"I'll accept it as the Gospel."

"As I have already remarked, it is a strange story, and had the effect of making me believe in supernatural manifestations—you will, no doubt, call it superstition. I was a well-grown boy when the things occurred which I am about to relate, and they made such a vivid impression on my mind that they are as fresh to-day as they were over half a century ago.

"Jacob Humbarger was of Pennsylvania Dutch stock, and came here from Lancaster, Pa., three-quarters of a century ago. When I first knew him this city was a village with less than a thousand population. He was a cabinet-maker, and made the rough and substantial furniture in vogue among the pioneers whose sons have since been Congressmen, Governors, Senators, Cabinet Ministers, and Generals.

"He was frugal and industrious, and left some property behind him. In addition to making furniture he made, when occasion demanded it, coffins for the people of all this region. There were no hearses and splendid undertaking establishments in those days. The dead were placed in plain, home-made coffins and carried to the little graveyards in farm wagons or by hand when the distance was not too great, except in rare instances, when there was a little more show and ostentation, and an old-fashioned carriage was used in place of the modern hearse.

"People would come from a distance to Humbarger's shop with the dimensions of a coffin and wait until it was finished and then take it home in a wagon or on horseback, as the case might be.

"One night, or rather one morning, an hour or two before daylight, Humbarger arose, leaving his wife in bed, proceeding to his shop, and lighting a tallow candle, set to work. When Mrs. Humbarger awoke at the usual hour she was surprised to hear Jacob hammering away in his shop, and supposing that he had some job that must needs be finished early in the day, set about preparing breakfast, and when the meal was ready she called her husband:

"'Vall, Chacob, vy for you go of vork so gwick the day?' inquired Frau Humbarger.

"'Vy, Katarine, did you not hear dot man who comes of der coffin by dree o'clock?'

"'Nien, nien, Chacob, you make foolish of me.'

"'I not make foolish, Katarine; dot man come of dree o'clock on der door an say I must haf dot coffin of 10 o'clock, and he gif me the measure on dot vork bench, und I go of work und haf him now half mate.'

"Katarine was incredulous, and Jacob was firm in his asseverations. Certain it was that he had a coffin well under way, and by 10 o'clock it was finished, and Jacob was waiting for his customer while he smoked a pipe.

"Between 10 and 11 o'clock a gentleman appeared at the shop door, and Humbarger greeting him with:

"'You vas a leedle lade, mein frent!'

"'Not very late, considering that I have ridden from near Somerset since half past 7.'

"'Vy for did you go back home after you vake me, uh?'

"'I didn't. I have just got to town.'

"'But you come of mine door last nide, and call me oud of mine bed to make dis coffin.'

"'Oh no, my friend, but it looks as though it would suit my purpose. Let me measure it.'

"The stranger measured it and it was just the size of a coffin he had been sent to procure, and he asked Humbarger if he could have it to take back with him immediately.

"'Dot vas your coffin anyway, since you order him and leaf der measure," promptly responded Mr. Humbarger.

"The price of the coffin was agreed upon, it was paid for, and the farmer took it away in his wagon. Jacob related the circumstances to his wife, who said mischievously,

"'I told you, Chacob, dot no vone voke you up of der nide. You haf been haunted.'

"Humbarger, however, insisted that he had been called out of his house during the night, and that he readily recognized the man who subsequently got the coffin and pretended that he had not ordered it.

"Of course the story soon circulated throughout the village, and the gossips added to it. A month later Humbarger had another nocturnal visit, and a child's coffin was ordered, to be finished in the afternoon. Later in the day a farmer living a few miles west of town called on Humbarger to secure his services, one of his children having died.

"'Oh, yes; I know dot. You come of der nide und told me, und mark der size on dis vork bench.'

"The farmer protested otherwise, but as the coffin was of the exact measurement desired he took it home. Then Mr. Humbarger began to have an indefinable fear that he was haunted.

"The thing was of regular recurrence, and almost everyone who came to Humbarger for a coffin found it ready made to order. The villagers began to fear the coffin-maker, and the coffin-maker avoided the villagers as much as possible. The women and children, and not a few of the men, believed he was in league with Satan, and he suffered a great deal in his trade.

"To those of his neighbors with whom he conversed on this subject— and among them was my father—he said that the orders were delivered in the night by persons whom he immediately recognized when they called for the coffins, and that when they were ordered he found the exact dimensions in chalk-marks on his work-bench the next morning. His wife no longer chaffed him on the subject of the ghostly orders.

"One morning he said to his wife that a coffin had been ordered during the night, but that the man had concealed his face, and he feared that he would not recognize him. He proceeded, however, to make the coffin in accordance with the measurement on his workbench, and at last finished it to his satisfaction.

"I was on pleasant terms with Uncle Jake, as we called him, and happened in the shop just as he was finishing it.

"'Dot man vos somepoddy who vill be buried mit dis coffin,' he remarked. 'I not see who he vas dot order him, but I know it vos for some big man or somepoddy, so I make him of der finest vild cherry und line him of silk und satin. Vy, my poy, I vould not pe ashamed to pe buried of dot coffin minesellvf.'

"A sudden pallor overspread Humbarger's face, he stretched out his hands and fell dead across the coffin he had just finished.

He was buried in it, and the story of Jacob Humbarger was more than a nine-days wonder here in Lancaster fifty-four years ago."
Cincinnati [OH] Post 16 December 1884: p. 3 FAIRFIELD COUNTY

PHANTOM
APPEARS IN BLOODY ROBE
TO FAMILY OCCUPYING HOUSE IN SWELL SUBURB
SAID TO BE THE GHOST OF A MURDERED WOMAN

"You are going to a lot of useless trouble," remarked a gentleman some days ago to a family who were getting their furniture into a house on the hilltops which had been vacant for quite a time.

"Why so?" asked the head of the family, who had congratulated himself upon the cheap rent and good accommodations he had in view.

"You and your family will not live there 30 days. Nobody can live in that house. I don't want to prejudice you against your new lodgings or I would explain."

With this unsatisfactory statement the gentleman walked on, and George T. Landon and family proceeded to put their new home into condition, giving the words of the stranger nothing more than a casual thought. But on the first night of their occupancy Mrs. Landon was awakened about midnight by something that was not a noise, so she says, and standing beside her bed was the ghost of a woman, whose white robes were covered in front with blood. Seized with a paroxysm of fright the woman awakened her husband, but when he opened his eyes the apparition was gone.

NOT A DELUSION.

The next day Mr. Landon endeavored to persuade his wife that owing to exertions incident to their moving she had had a touch of brain fever, and that what she thought she saw was a mere phantasy, and advised her to see a physician. This Mrs. Landon refused to do, affirming that she was well physically, and steadfastly refusing to believe otherwise than that she had seen an unearthly visitor.

The following night Landon himself saw the ghost, he says, and was even more horrified than was his wife. The alleged spiritual guest with its sanguinary front from that night on became a regular visitor to the house and Landon's three children say they saw it pass through the house. The troubled and unhappy ghost when questioned gave back no reply except a sibilant sigh as it dissolved into thin atmosphere.

People living in the vicinity of the house firmly believe that the building is haunted, and insist that a woman was murdered there, and the supposition among them is that it is her spirit returning to the scene of the awful tragedy. There are those who say that a man killed his wife in the house.

Cincinnati [OH] Enquirer 28 February 1902: p. 10 HAMILTON COUNTY

This next story includes the strange combination of a phantom coffin and a ghost who hums a comic song.

IS IT M'GINTY?
ANOTHER GHOST DISCOVERED AT HAMILTON
IT FLITS FROM ROOM TO ROOM, FRIGHTENING THE OCCUPANTS
WHEN IT GETS TIRED IT GOES TO SLEEP IN A VANISHING COFFIN
STRANGE SCENES THAT WERE WITNESSED BY THE RESIDENTS
OF A COTTAGE ON LUDLOW AVENUE

Just at present the residents of Hamilton, Ohio, have a mania for hunting up haunted houses.

The second house with a ghost attachment that has been discovered, and which is worrying the tenants and the man who owns it, is at 540 Ludlow Avenue.

The latest find has all the modern improvements in the way of ghosts. A white form flits in and out, passes its hands over the faces of the sleeping occupants, and when it gets tired, goes to sleep in a nice, white coffin that occupies a prominent position in whatever room the ghost sees fit to put it. It follows the people in the house from room to room, and, when it has had enough sport frightening them almost to death, quietly

WALKS THROUGH A WALL

And goes home to get ready for its next night's scaring expedition. The next appearance of the ghost it has a new programme. It generally flits about humming "Down Went McGinty to the Bottom of the Sea," and many people think that it is "McGinty's ghost" that has moved to Hamilton from the New York docks. At any rate the people are agitated. The story of the haunted house runs as follows:

Some fourteen years ago a family by the name of Gwinn resided in the frame cottage on Ludlow Street, Hamilton. The structure contained four rooms. About the year 1875, a member of the Gwinn family, a young girl, then about fourteen years of age, was stricken with a disease that confined her to her bed for a long time. Some of the most eminent physicians of that day were called to see her and all pronounced it some strange malady, and, in fact, it completely baffled their skill, as none could afford the sufferer any relief. After many days the sufferer became almost

A RAVING MANIAC.

At times, however, she was to a certain degree rational. The parents, on the advice of their family physician, decided to take their child to the insane asylum at Dayton. The girl seemed to know their intention, and begged to be left at home, as she said that she would live only a short time, and desired to die at home. The daughter was taken to the asylum, where she remained for some time without any perceptible benefit. She was then removed to her home and died. Since then some strange things have taken place in the house, and all who have lived in the cottage since the death of the girl have remained but a short time, declaring that the house is haunted, and that the dead

GIRL'S SPIRIT RETURNS ALMOST NIGHTLY.

About three months ago a family by the name of Adrian moved in the house and were there but a short time when they witnessed these strange scenes, the first visitation being one evening after the wife, with her little babe, had retired, and were about to fall asleep. She felt the hand of someone pass over her face. She was much frightened and uttered a shriek, which brought her husband to her side, who was in the adjoining room, but who saw nothing unusual. A few evenings after, the lady was standing before a large mirror arranging her hair when she was startled to see the form of a young girl dressed in white flit past her and vanish. On another occasion she entered the room, leaving the door open, giving her sufficient light to recognize anything in the room, and to her horror saw a

WHITE BURIAL CASKET

In the center of the room. She moved toward it and attempted to lay her hand upon it, but it vanished. She told her husband of her experience, and he partially persuaded her that it was only her imagination. A few evenings after this the husband saw the same thing, and in describing it to his wife she said that it appeared to her in just the same manner. Last Monday the family removed from the house. They say that there are strange noises heard in the same apartment of the house, such as low moans, as if someone was enduring great agony.

Cincinnati [OH] Enquirer 15 December 1889: p. 17 BUTLER COUNTY

NOTE: This is another case of a journalist taking what is, after all, a horrific story of a girl who died in agony and her phantom coffin and making a joke about it. "Down Went McGinty" was a novelty song from 1889 in which the hapless Dan McGinty undergoes a series of accidents ending with his drowning. The last chorus goes like this:

Down went McGinty to the bottom of the sea.
They haven't found him yet, for the water it was wet:
They say that McGinty's ghost haunts the docks at the break of day.
Dressed in his best Sunday clothes.

The other Hamilton ghost stories from the same period are the "Moaning Bridge of Hamilton." (See *The Face in the Window: Haunting Ohio Tales.*) and the ghost of suicide Dick Goddard haunting his family. [*Cincinnati [OH] Enquirer* 24 November 1889: p. 12.]

The antics of the Spiritualists were always good for a journalistic laugh, as in this story from near Sidney:

ASSISTING THE SPIRITS

I well remember the Spirit Rapping craze that swept over the country in the early 50s. I was but a small...boy then and the uncanny subject made me exceedingly careful of the dark...and made me sleep well under cover when in bed. The craze struck Troy with a vengeance, and table tipping grew quite common, that being the medium of communication among spirits in that section. A family named Allen, living in one of our houses near us, gave weekly expositions of ghostly telegraphy to wide-eyed crowds, the man and wife operating the table. My father, who was a profound disbeliever of the craze and a straight-backed Baptist, was greatly annoyed at the ghostly reputation his hitherto quiet property was accumulating and set his head on giving them manifestations of a more material nature for the fun of it, also thinking to drive the mediums out and hoping they would take their immaterial retainers along with them.... My father who was a carpenter, had a number of young men working for him, let them into the secret, and it was their business to be at the séance and rather help things along. Knowing nothing of what was up, on the night in question, I was one of the crowd that filled the sitting room. I had gone there with many misgivings through a great curiosity, but with little courage, it being the first one I attended.

In the center of the room, at a common table, sat the mediums, looking very sedate and mysterious; the crowd was ranged around the room on chairs with some standing in the corners. No talking was going on to break the ghostly silence, and I remember still the feelings of awe which ran over me and up and down my back like cold chills, for it seemed that I could smell the ghosts in the very air. Even those who wanted to cough didn't do it; it was no place for noise. All eyes were fixed on the man and his wife, or the enchanted table which was a rickety old thing, but then I thought the spirits weren't very particular as to the means of communication.

At length, in a low voice, the man asked if anyone desired to communicate with a dead friend. One old lady believer said she would like to talk with the spirit of her husband. Four hands rested on the table – and also all eyes in the room, while nobody breathed. "Is the spirit of Silas Shepherd present?" asked the medium, in a bold tone. Slowly the legs on the opposite side of the table began to leave the floor to fall and give three raps for yes or two raps for no....

Three monstrous raps resounded from under the table, and all hands vacated the haunted room quicker than I could tell it; the effect was so sudden and so startling. The mediums were about as rapid in transit as anyone else; one old lady tried to leave by way of the chimney, going through the fire screen. I saw two men jump through the open window, the sacred table was overturned, and most of the chairs. I wasn't much of a loiterer myself. I think I ran so fast my feet didn't touch the street as I crossed it on my way straight home, imagining all the ghosts of ghostdom were hot after me. To me it was decidedly real, and when I got home I stayed there like a good boy.

My father had slipped around and got under the house in the woodshed, scraping away the accumulated chips sufficiently, and then reaching out he scraped them back to hide his entrance. On his hands and knees he went around the cellar wall and took his place directly under where he knew the table sat. Getting a smooth round rock he wrapped his handkerchief around it to deaden its human sound a little, and when he heard the question, "Is the spirit of Silas Shephard present?" had waited to allow the table legs to rise, and before they could descend, gave the three most monstrous raps that had ever scared a ghost out of its hide or a crowd out of a house.

What of the crowd that had not gone clear home gathered in an excited clump outside on the pavement. Father went to a grate in the wall at the side and heard the conversation. His hands were in the midst of them, swearing they had seen ghosts shooting upward through the ceiling. One man, braver than the most, said he believed a man was under the house, and proposed, if the crowd would follow, to go around and investigate. They circled the house but saw no evidence.

A council of war was then held outside and it was suggested they go in with the mediums and try it over. This was a bold thing to do, but they ventured in. The mediums again seated themselves at the table and asked if the spirit of Jacob Ashworth was present, probably thinking he would be less violent in his demonstrations. Father, being then at his post, waited until the walnut legs had poised before dropping, anticipated the spirit and gave three more resounding licks on the floor above him. In two-thirds of a little jiffy the house was cleared again of mediums and all, and no doubt any ghosts hanging about waiting for their turn.

Another council of war was held outside. From the grating father heard Allen say he'd be damned if they would stay another night in that abominable haunted house, which was seconded by his wife in the most emphatic manner. This was good news to the impromptu spirit under the house.

It might have ended here, but it didn't. A courageous tailor, who was moved also by spirits more material, swore he knew a man was under the house, that he had a pistol and would crawl under and root him out and started for the wood shed again, followed by what remained of the crowd, including our hands. My father at the grate heard his threat and hurried around to the entrance where he posed with both hands ready to grab him by the hair should he venture to crawl under, and make him think he had fallen into the hands of ghosts, or the hands of the ghosts....

When the tailor began to scrape the chips away our hands got his pistol to prevent accidents, promising it to him when he got in. Father was ready for him. When the hole was large enough the doughty tailor laid down, flattened himself but said he guessed he was good for one ghost, and squeezed his head and shoulders under into the inner darkness, and—

With an unearthly howl my father clutched him by the hair. The tailor answered the howl with another of larger calibre, kind of broken up by Help! Murder! Oh Lord! Oh Lord! Let go! Pull me out! Ow Wow! Amid a deal of shouting and laughter he was drawn out by the boots, and without apologies made a bee line around to the street, and on home leaving hat and pistol behind.

Father, having accomplished his mission, then emerged, covered with dirt, dust, ancient cobwebs, and glory, into the hands of his friends, looking like he had had a hard struggle with ghostly combatants himself. The mediums had gone to other quarters for the night, leaving the house alone with not even a ghost in it, and when they heard the explanation of the mystery their anger at my father was exceedingly earthly. Next day their goods were moved, and the house was rented to a family without ghosts. A.W. Bellew in *Sidney Gazette*
The Piqua [OH] Daily Call 29 July 1898: p. 4 SHELBY COUNTY

NOTE: "Spirit rapping" was the practice of holding séances where the spirits rapped out the answers to questions in code "rap three times for yes and two raps for no." Sometimes participants put their hands on a table and the table would rap out the answers. I have not found out who the author A.W. Bellew was although I've found other humorous articles by him.

SIMON GIRTY'S GHOST ABROAD.
SPIRIT OF THE RENEGADE APPEARS TO FRIGHTEN OHIO PEOPLE

Napoleon, O., Aug. 12. Three nights this week the ghost of Simon Girty has made its appearance on Girty Island, seven miles up the river. He appears a solitary figure in a bark canoe, rowing slowly and stealthily in and out of the little inlets of the island. He is dressed in

Indian costume, with a silk handkerchief about his head to conceal the ugly wound which was the cause of his death.

Every five years the ghost comes back, and the form and dress of the old renegade are as well known in the locality today as they were seventy years ago, when he terrorized the early settlers of the country.

Simon Girty was a white man who fell into the hands of the Seneca Indians when a child. He was reared by them, and became more bloodthirsty and cruel than the savages themselves. At the head of a band of outlaw Indians he made his headquarters in the Maumee Valley. He delighted in torturing his prisoners, especially women and children, and his name still conjures up unknown terrors. When hard pressed Girty and his gang would escape to the Island, fortify themselves and defy capture. He it was who led the attack on Col. Crawford and burned the captured men at the stake.

Before his death Girty became blind and suffered excruciatingly from Rheumatism. He continued game to the last, and was literally hacked to pieces when Col. Johnson's men defeated Proctor's force.
Plain Dealer [Cleveland, OH] 27 August 1899: p. 23 HENRY COUNTY

ANOTHER GHOST STORY.
A REGULAR HAIR RAISER FROM LANCASTER.

Lancaster, Ohio, March 2. The dark ages are gone—the days of ignorance, illiteracy, blind credulity and superstition are gone, lost in the dense darkness of the traditional past, crowded into obscuration by progressive truth and education, and a ghost story or a narrative partaking of the supernatural in these enlightened times is material for peculiarity, ridicule, and laughter. However, notwithstanding science, religion and knowledge have forced investigation into every field of research, and have finally driven a host of old, cobwebby fanaticisms, beliefs and myths back into the dead sea of the past...there still lingers in the human mind a leaven of superstition; a belief that behind the veil in the realms of the unseen, there is a power that frequently manifests itself in a very unnatural and direful way. In short, there are lots of those who still believe in ghosts, in the visitations of disembodied spirits, and, as I was recently possessed of a rare bit of history, interesting to these folk, I have concluded to give it them through the columns of the *Commercial*.

The locale is the old Foglesang Road, which leads north from this city, out past the Fairgrounds, and the legendary Mt. Pleasant, where one hundred years ago those hardy scouts, White and McClelland, viewed the savage preparations for war in the barbarous village below; out past the old VanPearse homestead, up the rocky hill and through the oak woods, by the Still-House Hollow, and out through the beautiful reaches of woodland and meadow beyond. The time was more than half a century since when Lancaster was a backwoods hamlet with a howling wilderness all roundabout. Then the Old Foglesang Road was hardly more than a bridle-path, and the rock hill next to impassable on account of its sharp and angular projections, its offsets, deep furrows, crevices and irregularities, and the sturdy old farmers who lived up in that section invariably made their trips to town on horseback.

The Still-House Hollow was a deep, dark, heavily-timbered forbidding ravine, at the head of which, well hidden in the rocks and exuberant vegetation, was an old log still, owned and run by a mysterious specimen of antiquated humanity named Crowley. He was a surly, uncommunicative dog, with scowling visage and repellant aspect and the farmers always gave him and his a wide berth, much preferring to go through the hollow in the broad glare of the sun than after the shades of evening had begun to fall. One night, when the chill November winds were whining and moaning through the leafless oaks, and the first great flakes of winter were descending, a murder was committed in the rocky pass by the Still-House Hollow.

The victim was John Ornsdorf, a recent settler in the vicinity, who came from Licking County, and who was a stock dealer, and in those days a man of money. I say it was murder, but that was never fully demonstrated, yet all the good people of the region were fully agreed upon this point. His horse came home riderless, with empty saddle-bags besmeared with blood and brains and hair. A great crowd visited the spot the next morning, and by the marks on the ground they made out where Ornsdorf had fallen from his horse, just at the brow of the hill, where the rocks began to show themselves from out of the soil. The men discovered, by the bloody trail, where the body had been dragged from the roadside, into the bushes, down the hollow, toward the old log still and up to its very door, which was closed and barred. But the rugged yeomanry who were there were not to be frustrated by bars or bolts, and a few vigorous strokes with an ax acted like the open sesame of the Forty Thieves.

With bated breath they entered the dismal abode of the old benzine-maker, followed the bloody tracks across the main room and into a smaller and rear apartment where there lay, before their eyes, covered and bedabbled with blood, the lifeless corpse of—a yearling steer!

The old farmers stood aghast! What unseemly trick was this? And they gazed in speechless wonder into each other's faces. Search was then made throughout the still, its cramped little cells, dirty, dingy and smoke-begrimed, but nothing was found. Even old Crowley himself had disappeared as thoroughly and completely as if he had been resolved into original elements. The very atmosphere of the shanty smacked of the devil's dominion; the great cracks in the walls looked as if about to open and swallow the intruders, and more than one averred, after well out upon the highway again, that there was a sulphurous smell about the place.

Days grew into months, and months into years, and old Crowley was never heard of again, nor was the mystery of Ornsdorf's murder ever explained. The old log hut still went into rot and decay. The logs tumbled down, and the entrance became choked with briar and bramble. The wolf hid her litter beneath the mouldy floor, and an owl made his habitation in the gruesome garret and finally, under Time's corroding hand, it melted away and disappeared entirely, and a thicket of haw and dogwood sprang up on its site.

The old Fogelsang Road ever after that, to the farmers who went over its rocky way, was a haunted spot, and in the wailing winds of autumn it is asserted the mourning tones of poor Ornsdorf have been heard, and some even declare that the wild shriek he uttered when the death-blow descended has more than once been heard echoing and quavering up and down the dismal defile.

It was many years after before anything was actually seen here and the first man who encountered the unearthly thing that was supposed to haunt the spot was the venerable Jacob Spangler, of Pleasant Township, who can be seen in the city here any Saturday afternoon, and who will verify along with many other good, reliable citizens of that neighborhood, the facts we are recording.

It was in the melancholy November, a clear, moonlit night, not a fitting time for ghost or goblin, when Spangler mounted his horse and started for town in quest of medical aid for a sick member of his family. A cold chill ran up his spine when he remembered he must pass the Still-House Hollow. Now Jake is as courageous as a Numidian lion, and, in those young days a great, strapping big fellow, of prodigious bodily strength, like some of the *quadrumana* we hear of in Central Africa, and he wasn't afraid of the devil himself, but he acknowledges the likeliness of meeting Old Crowley or Ornsdorf on the lonesome road made him feel at least skittish, and he would have much rather have remained at home than make the strip. But there was no help for it, and he rode quietly along, at a gentle canter, cogitating on all the uncanny stories he had ever heard, and thinking particularly of the old whisky maker and the ill-fated Licking settler. Now he glanced furtively on this side, now on that, then watched the great shadowy phantoms stalking athwart the highway as a fleecy cloud floated between earth and moon, when suddenly, as he neared the rocky declivity, the stretch of murky woods through which ran the Still-House Hollow, his horse gave a loud af-frighted snort, then fixed his forefeet, and stood still, quivering in every nerve. Jacob bent forward and looked ahead, and there, standing side-wise in the middle of the narrow highway, was a yearling steer, with glowing eyes and preternatural long hair. Spangler boldly endeavored to urge his horse forward, but he would not budge and he was about to turn and see if he would go the other way, when he felt something seize his leg, and, gazing down, he saw the steer climbing up. He was bereft of the power of motion of sound, and the next moment the long-haired and luminescent bovine had taken a seat behind him with its forelegs resting upon his shoulders, and thus it rode with him until the southern boundary of the woods was reached, when it leaped down and disap-peared into the earth or faded away into thin air. Spangler hurried on to town with feelings easier imagined than described, and an hour later returned with an old physician of this city, long since dead, and again they saw the mystic steer standing by the roadside, near the spot where Ornsdorf had been murdered, but as there were two of them it made no attempt to ride.

For years this strange and incomprehensible creature haunted this spot, and scores of men have seen it and rode with it and to this day there are a number of the older residents of the township who will make affidavit to its existence. For the past ten or fifteen years nothing has been seen of it, the old Foglesang Road has been abandoned and closed up, but there are still those who firmly believe that it can be seen upon any favorable night—those who will never believe but what this thing was a spirit from the other world—was poor Ornsdorf's ghost...
Cincinnati [OH] Commercial Tribune 3 March 1881: p. 8 FAIRFIELD COUNTY

NOTE: I was struck by the weird apparition of a steer with long hair. The notion of a familiar animal changed in some subtle, supernatural way—

with long hair, glowing eyes, sometimes with a human face—is often found in the folklore of the British Isles, as is the chilling action of the animal in climbing up behind the rider. There is a creature called a shug-monkey in England that is known for riding behind late-night horsemen. England is also home to shape-shifting Black Dogs with glowing eyes and long, rough coats. In Muskingum County a similar hybrid entity dubbed "Stumpy, the Man-faced Dog," hitched rides in carriages and frightened travelers. *Quadrumana* is an old scientific term for apes. It means "four-handed ones." Numidian lions were from the northwestern part of Africa and were regarded as unusually fierce. Ornsdorf is also spelled "Ormsdorf." I'm not sure which spelling is correct.

A DRUMMER'S YARN.
STRANGE EXPERIENCE OF A COMMERCIAL TRAVELER IN AN OHIO TOWN
THE SPECTER OF A MURDERED GIRL APPEARS TO HIM
IN THE ROOM WHERE THE CRIME WAS COMMITTED

Steubenville, O., March 9. Last night A. Ashbrook of Philadelphia, Pa., a commercial traveler, stopped at Empire, twelve miles above this city, intending to cross the river to New Cumberland, but there being so much ice in the river he was compelled to remain in Empire. The only hotel was full and he was forced to take quarters in a boarding house kept by Mrs. Hamilton. He was assigned a room, which happened to be the one in which Miss Nancy Weir was murdered about a year ago. There have been rumors that her departed spirit had often reappeared here, but the stories received no credence.

Mr. Ashbrook was not apprised of these ghost stories, however, and knew nothing of the circumstances. Upon retiring he left the lamp burning and, being tired, was soon in slumber. Today he told his experience. He says a dread feeling came over him about midnight, as though some other person was in the room. He opened his eyes and looking in the direction of the lamp saw sitting on a chair a rather attractive woman, wearing a man's white hat and clad in a brown calico dress. Ashbrook asked what was wanted, but received no reply. He then arose and approached the woman and when about to lay his hand upon her the apparition vanished and the lamp was blown out. Thinking that he had had a bad case of nightmare Ashbrook retired again.

This morning he related the facts as told. The singular feature of the case is that Mr. Ashbrook was not acquainted with the murder and his description is almost perfect as to the looks and manner of dress of Nancy Weir when she was killed a year ago.

Plain Dealer [Cleveland, OH] 10 March, 1888: p. 1 JEFFERSON COUNTY

NOTE: Here is an article on the death of the unfortunate Nancy. She was also the mistress of Edward Householder who was indicted for her murder in 1887.

FOUND WITH HER THROAT CUT.
PROBABLE MURDER OF A NOTORIOUS WOMAN AT STEUBENVILLE

Steubenville, O., June 7. About 6 o'clock this evening Nancy Weir, a woman aged about 38 years, was found dead at McCoy's Station, this county, with her throat cut from ear to ear and several stabs on her breast. She had a penknife in her hand. It is not known whether it is a case of suicide or murder, but the general belief is that she was murdered and the knife afterward placed in her hand. The woman is well known from the fact that she was closely connected with the murder of McDonald some years ago at that place, having been mistress of Lewis K. McCoy, the murderer, who was sent to the penitentiary for life, after spending $100,000 in his defense.

Plain Dealer [Cleveland, OH] 8 June 1886: p. 2

Was the guardian spirit of the Camp Sychar spring, a ghostly hermit or the holy ghost of a minister carrying his Bible?

STRANGE
APPARITION OF A MAN
THAT GUARDS THE SPRING AT CAMP SYCHAR
AND VANISHES UPON THE APPROACH
OF HUMANITY
REMARKABLE SIGHT WITNESSED BY

MANY PERSONS
BELIEVED TO BE THE SPECTER OF A HERMIT
OR OF THE MINISTER WHO FOUND THE SPRING

Mt. Vernon, Ohio. November 20. The eastern part of this city and the little Advent village of Academia, situated two miles northeast of the city, are greatly wrought up over the appearance of a ghost at Camp Sychar, the grounds of the Ohio Camp Meeting Association, situated half way between the city and the aforesaid village.

Eight years ago some of the adherents of Methodism began a search for grounds suitable for holding camp meetings where they might assemble and worship God free from the restraint of the outside world. At last they decided upon the present spot, and named it Camp Sychar. It was then a wild and rather inconvenient place, surrounded on all sides by a heavy forest. But what

MOST ATTRACTED THEM

Was the presence of a spring of pure water that trickled out from the hillside unaided by any of the artifices of man. The grounds were improved and a pipe was run from the spring to the roadside, a distance of less than 50 feet and emptied into a large trough that was placed there for the convenience of the public. The qualities of the water soon made the spring famous, until now there is hardly a person for miles that is not familiar with the spring at Camp Sychar.

After the location of the Sychar had been agreed upon there came a few years later another religious sect, the Seventh Day Adventists, who purchased large tracts of land for several miles around, and to the north of the location of Sychar. There a village sprung up, and later an academy was erected. Following this came an electric railway, the owners of which purchased a lovely little spot beyond the village of Academia, which they converted into a park. The railway was then utilized for the triple purpose of connecting the camp grounds, the village and the park.

Several years after the camp grounds had been dedicated, there began to appear strange stories of the actions of a peculiar apparition in and about the spring. It was always described as being tall, gaunt, and clad in the attire of a minister. Under his arm he

INVARIABLY CARRIED A BOOK.

Which was readily supposed to be the Bible. In all the positions in which he has ever been seen he was always described as guarding the spring, as though it were sacred and under divine direction.

The first rumor of the appearance of this spectral sentinel came five or six years ago when a man who had been employed to remain at the grounds and see that they were protected reported the appearance of the ghost. He was so certain of what he had seen that the jeers of those to whom he told of the strange sight failed to make him doubtful, and when later he saw the same spirit return and remain on watch over his charge he became superstitious and refused to remain longer in charge of the camp.

Afterward, when the electric railway had passed by the spring, motormen often saw the strange sight in going by late at night, but always upon the approach of the car the apparition vanished. Any mention of this by the witness among his fellow employees was always greeted with laughter until at last any note of the ghost was scarcely ever made.

Several weeks ago a traveling man named Balfour and a companion, having the night to spend in the city, boarded the cars and went out to the park to while away a few hours before retiring for the night. The regular season at the park closed in September after which time cars ceased to run after 9 o'clock at night. The gentlemen were not aware of this fact, and, after alighting at the entrance, sauntered up into the grounds and did not think of returning until long after the cars had stopped for the night. When they arrived at the entrance they found EVERYTHING IN DARKNESS.

And after waiting until they were convinced that they would be compelled to walk to the city, set out for their return. Being unacquainted with the country they failed to take the regular roadway, but tramped in along the tracks, a much longer and tiresome route.

By the time they had reached Sychar they were thirsty and noticing as they went out that a spring emptied into a trough at the roadside, they turned in to get a drink. They were tired and tramped along in silence. When they had reached the trough Balfour looked over the fence. His heart almost stopped at the sight that met his gaze. Speechlessly he nudged his companion and pointed. There before them was the ghostly sentinel pacing to and fro in front of the spring. Both men stood and looked, being too much taken by surprise to speak. Plainly they could see the figure pace noiselessly back and forth and each time they could see the iron railing surrounding the spring shining through its body. Whenever they looked intently the shadow instantly cleared to an outline, and objects beyond it could be seen as clearly as through murky glass. They stood silently for several minutes watching the weird scene until one of them recovered sufficiently to speak, when the figure vanished like a fog before a midday sun. Returning to the city they told their story substantially as given above.

Many theories are now advanced for the appearance of this specter at so unusual a place. One is that long ago an old hermit lived near the spring and that it was his ghost that has returned to guard the waters. Another is that among the party of Methodists who sought this spot for their meeting grounds was an old minister who was particularly moved in his choice on account of the spring, and that it is his spirit that stands such zealous guard over the spring.

Cincinnati [OH] Enquirer 21 November 1897: p. 17 KNOX COUNTY

NOTE: The camp is named for Sychar/Shechem/Nablus, the location of the Well of Jacob from the Old Testament in the Bible [Genesis 33:18-19; 34:2, etc.] and the well where Jesus asked the Woman of Samaria for a drink. [John 4:5, 6]

This is a peculiar story of an entire family fleeing from angry ghosts. I wonder if the family could have been poisoned by something that caused them to have delusions or hallucinations? But why would they all believe they saw the same thing?

ANGRY GHOSTS
HAVE A TERRIBLE BATTLE BEFORE THE EYES
OF A TERROR-STRICKEN FAMILY

Xenia, Ohio, February 1. On Saturday night a family of seven persons came to this city and took refuge at the home of Archie Valentine, in what is called Barr's Bottom. It was the family of Edward Wallace who have been living in a small log house near the railroad station at Waynesville. When they arrived at Valentine's, who is an acquaintance, the family seemed stricken with terror. It was late at night and their arrival was unexpected. Out of breath and apparently in a frenzy of fear Wallace related the following story.

While he and his family were in a room of his house that evening a ghost suddenly appeared in their presence, blew the lights out, and demanded that they all should desert the house, never to return to it again. On their objecting to this proposition, the ghost took hold of

Cora, the oldest child, and bore her head down on the table and began to beat her. They recognized it as the ghost of Joe Lynch, a man who was murdered near Harveysburg some time ago.

When Miss Wallace began to scream and was nearly dead with fright another ghost entered the room. It was the ghost of Warren Cotton, a relative of the family, who died some years ago, who had come to the rescue of Miss Wallace. He immediately attacked the ghost of Lynch, when a royal battle began.

They yelled like fiends, their eyes gleamed in the darkness, and the very atmosphere seemed charged with electrical sparks. Chairs were broken, windows were broken and the furniture tumbled all over the room. In the confusion of the battle the family fled, leaving all their household goods behind, making their way to this city and declaring they would never return to it again. Mr. Valentine having a small house and a large family hardly knew what to do with his guests. But yesterday evening while they were all in the house together the Wallaces claimed that a spirit was in the house and was warning them to move on. Being impressed that they must do so, they at once arose and departed in the night and darkness without saying where they were going and have not been heard from since.

Cincinnati [OH] Enquirer 2 February 1892: p. 2 WARREN / GREENE COUNTY

NOTE: "In an altercation at Harveysburg, on the 28th ult., Joseph Lynch was shot and fatally wounded by James Buckner." *Perrysburg [OH] Journal* 10 May 1878: p 1.

Waynesville is six miles from Harveysburg—there is no explanation as to why Lynch would visit the Wallaces, since we are not told of any connection, especially so long after his death. I do not know if the Wallaces ever resurfaced.

"Edward Wallace, his wife and five children have disappeared, leaving all their belongings in their house at Barr's Bottoms, near Springfield, O. Before going they told their neighbors that they had been driven from home by the ghost of a murdered man."
Logansport [IN] Pharos Tribune 4 February 1892: p. 1

This next bit of purple prose really does sound like an early 19th-century Gothic novel. It is strange, but is it true?

OLD WARWICK
AROSE IN THE SEETHING FLAMES
AND HIS OLD-TIME WAILING WAS AGAIN HEARD
THE BURNING OF AN OLD LANDMARK BRINGS A
VOICE FROM THE TOMB

Wellston, Ohio, September 11. The terrific storm of rain and lightning which visited this section yesterday, it has just been learned, destroyed an ancient structure which has for many years been one of the most historic landmarks in Jackson County. The story of its ancient structure is so old that it is known to almost every school child in this section of Ohio, and is regarded by those who have heard it as a romance both strange and true.

Nearly a half a century ago, when this settlement was yet in its infancy, and consisted of a desolate wild, broken only by log huts and an occasional charcoal furnace or salt well, a handsome appearing stranger, whose name was afterward learned to be Robert Warwick, supposed to be the son of an English lord, came to Berlin, a few miles south of this city, and began the construction of a large stone mansion which he announced was to be the largest dwelling in Jackson County.

He toiled incessantly day and night, speaking seldom to the workmen whom he had employed and

ALLOWING NO ONE TO KNOW

His history or intentions, and paying his men, uncommon as it was, in British money. Day after day the work progressed, and was the common gossip of the neighborhood. Finally the stonework was completed, and the mansion stood forth, facing the wide highway, like the stately manor house of some wealthy Baron of the middle centuries. Just before the building was ready for occupancy Warwick suddenly ran out of funds, and being too proud to ask his employees to wait for their pay, attempted to complete the building by himself. The exertion proved too much. For months he lay sick, and the new mansion, the pride of his heart, finally passed into the hands of his creditors. The dying man never recovered from the loss. Just a few moments before his death he arose from his bed, and, pacing about the rooms like a madman, he pronounced a horrible curse upon the building and upon those who should ever afterward make it their abode. For years after his death the neighbors

REFUSED TO VENTURE

Near the stately manor, and many claimed that they could see the ghost of "Old Warwick" appear in white at the windows at night. The solitary passer-by at this somber place was overtaken by a tremor at the sight of the gloomy stone structure hidden behind the forest of sighing pines. In later years new families were induced to become occupants, but they one and all made their residence short and eventually suffered some dreadful calamity or misfortune until nearly 15 years ago the building was finally abandoned to decay.

Yesterday it was destroyed by lightning, and it is claimed by those who saw it go down by the anger of the elements that a human voice could be heard crying aloud weird anathemas. Those who heard the voice claim that it was that of "Old Warwick," who departed this life over 30 years ago. Strange and unnatural as this occurrence may seem many of the good people of Berlin are willing to make oath to the assertion that they heard the cries and saw the apparition as it went down to death in the flames.

Cincinnati [OH] Enquirer 12 September 1894: p. 1 JACKSON COUNTY

NOTE: I have not been able to verify that such a person or place existed.

While I included a chapter about the Women in Black in *The Face in the Window*, I could not resist one more story of these sinister specters, this time from Cleveland.

DEATH FOLLOWS
"THE BLACK LADY."
MRS. MARY CORLEY SAYS SHE HAS SEEN A
STRANGE APPARITION.
HER FATHER PASSED AWAY SOON AFTER THE
"GHOST'S" FIRST VISIT
THE FIGURE CAME AGAIN AND HER HUSBAND
LEFT THIS WORLD

Who is "The Black Lady?" That is the question which worries Mrs. Mary Corley, who lives at No. 22 Old River Street.

"The Black Lady" is an omen of death to Mrs. Corley. In short, the "apparition" to which Mrs. Corley gives the above appellation is described as a woman who looks into the window of the Corley home on River Street. The "woman" looks through the window for an instant and then disappears. Twice within a month Mrs. Corley has seen the "apparition." Each time the appearance of the figure was followed by a death. Mrs. Corley's father, Patrick Riley, was a brother of Councilman Riley. Patrick Riley died on September 16, about ten days after Mrs. Corley avers she saw "The Black Lady" looking into her window. Nov. 7, Mrs. Corley again saw the "apparition" at the window. Three days later Mrs. Corley's husband, who was apparently in good health, was taken suddenly sick and died.

Each time Mrs. Corley saw "The Black Lady" she threw up her hands and screamed and she fell into a faint.

Mrs. Corley is unable to explain the strange phenomenon, according to the story she told a friend. The features of the "apparition," or whatever it may be, can be plainly seen by Mrs. Corley, although she cannot remember the face as resembling that of any friend who has died. On each occasion the figure appeared at the same window of her home on Old River Street. The window opens into a sitting room which is now but little used on account of this fact. Mrs. Corley is deathly afraid of "The Black Lady," and would not go into the room alone for the world. The figure is described as being dressed in solid black and always in the same costume. A hood is worn over the head, and her eyes are black and piercing in their intensity. Mrs. Corley says the figure has a sallow complexion, so pronounced as to give the figure a deathlike appearance. The "woman" looks into the window and the moment Mrs. Corley looks in that direction it disappears.

Patrick Riley, who died Sept. 16, left an estate of about $50,000. Last summer he took his daughter, Mrs. Corley, to Europe. They returned early in September. A few days after their return Mrs. Corley claims she saw "The Black Lady" looking into the window. She went to a well-known undertaker who is a friend of the family and told him, it is said, that he would soon be needed by the family.

"Why?" asked the undertaker.

"I've seen 'The Black Lady,'" replied Mrs. Corley.

At that time Patrick Riley was apparently in good health. About a week later he was taken suddenly ill and died in a few days. Nov. 7, Mrs. Corley sent for the undertaker to settle up some business matters.

"I suppose you will be needed again soon," said Mrs. Corley to the undertaker.

In response to a question Mrs. Corley replied: "I have seen 'The Black Lady' again." At that time Mrs. Corley's husband was enjoying good health. Three days later he died.

Mrs. Corley is not naturally superstitious. She is a strong, healthy woman about thirty years of age. She enjoys robust health. A *Plain Dealer* reporter called on Mrs. Corley last evening at the home of her uncle, Councilman M. Riley, on Washington Street. Miss Riley, a daughter of Councilman Riley and a teacher in the Detroit Street School, received the newspaper man, and upon learning his errand immediately declared the family did not want any newspaper notoriety. She also said she nor her family believed that Mrs. Corley saw any apparition at all and that the figure was a creature of Mrs. Corley's imagination.

"It's all due to her nerves," said Miss Riley. "Such things don't bother me, because I never had any nerves."

Mrs. Corley was finally persuaded to come into the room, but she firmly refused to discuss the matter at all. She declared that she did not care to have the matter get into the newspapers. She did not deny that she had seen the figure, which she called "The Black Lady," but she refused to say anything about the matter.

While Mrs. Corley declined to say anything for publication with reference to the "strange apparition," the story has been told to several friends of the family. Mrs. Corley is in deadly fear of the "visitant." On both occasions when she says she saw the woman at the window Mrs. Corley fainted. She never goes into the sitting room alone after night. She does not believe in things supernatural. She declares she saw the face and figure of a woman clearly outlined. Each time she predicted a death in the family would follow. Her prediction came true in both instances.

Plain Dealer [Cleveland, OH] 1 December 1899: p. 10 CUYAHOGA COUNTY

NOTE: There is more than a hint of the Black Widow about this unfortunate woman. Mrs. Corley's remarks to the undertaker seem uncomfortably prescient; begging the question: were autopsies done on her father and husband after their sudden deaths? A $50,000 estate might have been a temptation. On the other hand, the notice of Patrick Riley's will in the *Cleveland Leader* of 28 September, 1899, claims that the estate only consisted of a lot on Old River Street, valued at $1,500 and $2,000 worth of personal property, all of which was inherited by Mrs. Corley.

The visions, which were accompanied by fainting, suggest the possibility of seizures. Thinking supernaturally, perhaps the Black Lady was a banshee.

8.

Letters from the Dead:
Bizarre Ohio Mysteries

Mystery is a resource, like coal or gold, and its preservation is a fine thing
– Tim Cahill –

This chapter is what the Victorians would have called an omnibus, combining several topics in a single chapter. Here are bizarre stories about mysteries that aren't quite ghosts, but which still haunt us.

The Face in the Window's chapter, "Great Balls of Fire," covered a number of puzzling spook lights including the Elmore light, which has been interpreted as a headless motorcyclist's headlamp and the spirit of a suicide. Here are several more stories of these mysterious flickering phantoms, which, unusually, appear in all the colors of the rainbow.

PURPLE LIGHTS PUZZLE FARMERS
STRANGE "HEADLIGHT" DASHES DOWN PIKE AND ILLUMINES THE HIGHWAY

Piqua, Ohio, March 10. Are spooks playing "hob" with farmers in the vicinity of Hetzler's Corners? Or is some practical joker, with a remarkable amount of cleverness, working on the minds of imaginative farmers in that neighborhood?

For some time reports of a strange purple light have been reported in the vicinity and farmers have been wonderfully excited. This talk was all set down to imagination until last night when this phenomenon was noted:

About 7:30 o'clock James Covault, a tenant on the Robert Patterson farm north of Fletcher on the Snodgrass Pike, stepped out into his yard and he saw a purple light which seemed to be burning brightly on the pike about a mile west of his house. He called the other members of the family and they decided that some farmer had painted his lantern a brilliant purple for a novelty.

Suddenly the light began moving rapidly toward the Covault house, advancing by spurts, but at times apparently receding. As it came nearer, almost with the velocity of an electric flash, it assumed the size of a headlight on an automobile. When the end of the lane to the Covault home was reached the light was so bright that the people could plainly see the barn and the cattle in the barnyard.

Here the light halted, and while the family was discussing the nature of the phenomenon it suddenly left the pike and began traveling northward with incredible speed across a field in the direction of C.C. Moore's farm buildings. By the time the purple rays struck the Moore dwelling the light was so brilliant that Mr. Covault says he could see the house and shade trees as plainly as if it had been daylight, although they were over a mile away.

At the Moore house the light suddenly vanished as mysteriously as it came. G.W. Sanders and Mr. H.P. Morgan were other observers of the weird light. Mrs. Sanders thought a building must be burning until she noted the color and quick flashings of the light. She now agrees that she was mistaken, and the entire community is much puzzled.
Fort Worth [TX] Star-Telegram 10 March 1909: p. 7 SHELBY COUNTY

GHOSTS ALONG THE BORDER.
A STRANGE LIGHT HAUNTING THE SCENE OF A LONG-AGO MURDER

Youngstown, O., Jan. 22. Many years ago James Harbush, a wealthy farmer who lived in Ohio, near Vernon, on the Burg Hill and Greenville Road, killed his daughter Mary's sweetheart, Richard Lewis, and buried the body in a meadow. The crime was committed in the presence of the girl. She had gone to fulfill a clandestine engagement with her lover, whom her father was violently opposed to. Harbush had followed and in a fit of anger killed young Lewis. The girl pined away and died. She kept the secret locked in her own breast, and it was buried with her. On his deathbed Harbush confessed his crime.

For several months past the people of that neighborhood have been greatly mystified by the appearance of a strange, brilliant light. It is about twice as large as the flame made by a lantern, and is changeable in hue. At one time it is of a pretty blue tint and at another a bright red, and sometimes a pale yellow. It seemed to rise in the burial ground, glides or floats gently down one hill—always at a uniform distance of about six feet from the ground—up the other hill, and hovers for a few minutes in the locality of the supposed grave of the murdered man. It always returns, however, and disappears in the old Rock Ridge Cemetery.

Mack Doyle and David Stull and other residents of the neighbor-hood have seen the strange light at different times. The superstitious connect it with the murder of Mary's lover. Some are firmly convinced that it is the spirit of the broken-hearted girl, which will never rest until the remains of her dead lover are buried by her side in the cemetery on the hill. Other believers in things supernatural argue with equal firmness that it is the spirit of James Harbush seeking forgiveness for his fearful deed. It is too large for what is commonly known as a will o'-the-wisp, besides midnight stragglers of that species never change colors. To say the least the inhabitants are mystified, as well they might be. A movement has been organized to find out, if possible, what the strange thing really is. Each farmer has provided himself with a large bell, and whoever sees the light first will apprise the neighbors by violently ringing the bell. It will be surrounded and if possible hemmed in, when the virtue of powder and ball in solving the mystery will be tested.
Summit County Beacon [Akron, OH] 4 February 1885: p. 5 TRUMBULL COUNTY

Spook lights are sometimes taken as an omen of death as is suggested in this chilling story from Belmont County. I told of a previous prophetic spook light encounter from Belmont in *The Face in the Window*. The county is full of coal-mines. Could the geography/geology have anything to do with these spook lights?

AN OHIO GHOST

The citizens of Warren Township, Belmont County, are wonder-fully excited over the appearance of a "ghost." The region wherein this so-called spirit has been seen is known as "Hog Sink." About two weeks ago the wife of a citizen of the above named place died. Since that time she has appeared in various forms causing the husband and children to flee in terror at the hour of midnight from their home. A few evenings after her death, the husband states, a ball of fire came down the chim-ney and rested upon the breast of one of the boys for over two minutes. Strange to say, this boy is now very ill, and not expected to recover. A few evenings after the appearance of the ball of fire, the "ghost" mother mysteriously appeared in long, white, flowing robes, and grasping this same boy in her arms carried him to the door and threw him to the ground. She then vanished as mysteriously as she came. The husband

and children fled to the nearest house and cannot be induced to go back. *Wheeling [WV] Register* 6 July 6 1888: p. 4 BELMONT COUNTY

This next story is, frankly, one of the strangest spook light tales I've found. It combines the usual motif of spook lights guarding or leading to treasure with an impressive quick-change-apparition repertoire. Like ball lightning, this spook light seems to react to human interaction. In addition, like the Elmore Light, the Paulding, Michigan Light, and Georgia's Brown Mountain Lights, the light was seen over the course of many years.

THE GOLD GHOST
IT MAY GUARD THE MISER'S POT OF SHINING PIECES
THE PHENOMENAL LIGHT THAT ROAMS O'ER THE WILSON FARM
AT HARRISBURG, STARK COUNTY
IT IS A VERSATILE "LIGHT" WITH A LEANING TOWARD LIGHTNING CHANGES
A MATTER OF FACT ORIGIN
THE PEOPLE IT HAS TACKLED AND THEIR TALK

An uncanny, mysterious light, or rather ball of fire, is an oddity that is seen hovering about a farm near Harrisburg, Stark County, on dark, foggy nights. This ball of fire, it is said, has been seen at various times during the past century. It is a veritable will o' the wisp, ghostly, supernatural and fear inspiring, and many remarkable tales concerning it are told by the country folks around. In short, the "light on Wilson's farm"—as the ball of fire is now called—has been a source of gossip and speculation for years. The "light" wanders to and fro on the farm; it rises high in the air; descends into hollows; tremblingly moves down a small stream of water; suddenly brightens, as quickly fades away; and, so it is said, the "light" pursues and attacks venturesome travelers who attempt to capture it in order to discover its origin.

The land on which this strange light is seen is owned by Solomon P. Wilson, a well-to-do American farmer. Nearly forty years ago it was owned by a German named Knouff. The farm is one and a half miles south of Harrisburg, on the left of the old Harrisburg and Louisville road, as you travel towards Louisville, and consists of about 160 acres of timber and farming land. The soil is rich and the topography of the land gently sloping and rolling. A small stream of water, fed by several springs, flows through the west end of the farm in a sort of swampy hollow. A large barn, a neat farm house and several fine outbuildings and sheds are the buildings upon the land; in fact, Wilson's farm is very much like many others found in the neighboring country. As already noted, many strange stories are told concerning the "light." Several of them are worth repeating.

It is said—and, mark you, these stories are told as they were related to the writer—that a Louisville maiden named Mary Dence was one dark night passing by the old Knouff farm. The maiden was not at all superstitious, and when she caught sight of the strange, pinkish colored ball of fire she cried out: "Whither would you lead me, will o' the wisp?" The "light" immediately came toward her, rested upon the rail fence, then began slowly moving up the small creek. The maiden climbed through the fence and followed the ghostly ball. It darted to and fro, yet traveled always straight ahead, the puzzled girl following. Suddenly the "light" disappeared—faded from her sight. Startled, then horrified, the maiden turned to flee, when missing her footing, she toppled and rolled down a steep hillside and was badly injured upon striking the ground below. She lost consciousness and upon regaining her senses was horrified to see before her bedimmed eyes the phantom ball of fire. Screaming with fright she started on the run for the highway, gained it and sought shelter in a neighboring farm house.

An honest old farmer, Brown by name, was returning toward Louisville from Harrisburg several years ago. With him was his wife. They reached the "Wilson" farm toward 11 o'clock at night—at least, so the story goes—and as it was winter they traveled in a sleigh. The tinkling bells on the horses seemed to attract the "light," for it moved toward the sleigh and rested upon the rear seat. Mrs. Brown was the first to see the mystic apparition and screamed. Brown, attracted by his wife's cries, turned and saw the strange "light." He immediately whipped up the horses, whereupon the "light" changed into a fiery red dog, with glaring eyes, red tongue and awful teeth. Faster and faster went the horses, more and more frightened were Mr. and Mrs. Brown. At last they reached the center of the farm, when the fiery red dog changed suddenly into a ghoulish, blue-colored coffin. It followed the fleeing horses and sleigh; it moved silently, stealthily and quickly. Mr. Brown lashed the horses forward, urging them on and half supported his wife who had fainted. They finally gained the Strasburg Crossing Road in safety, where upon the awful, ghostly coffin faded suddenly away. It was months ere Mr. and Mrs. Brown recovered from their fright.

It is related with declarations of truth that George Beam, a farmer's boy, who lived close by, once upon a time borrowed a horse and wagon from old man Knouff. George attended a ball at Louisville that night and did not return home until after the midnight chimes had rung. The farmer had reached the Knouff farm late at night. Upon reaching the cross roads he saw the mystic ball of fire hovering about the wagon and carriage house on the farm. But he was a brave lad and not at all afraid of the "light" and so he drove toward the barn. Meanwhile the "light" slowly moved toward the door of the carriage house and beckoned the lad to follow. George, evidently controlled by an unseen power, followed. When the "light" went through the carriage house door the lad opened it and passed within. In a corner of the carriage house, moving slowly up and down, was the ghostly "light." Going toward it and glancing toward the last corner, George beheld a large iron kettle overflowing with bright gold pieces. Eagerly he sprang forward to grasp the prize, when there was a hissing noise and the "light" turned into a purple-colored, horrible shaped dragon. Not a sound did the frightful dragon make, but its attitude was one of open defiance and threat. The frightened lad gave but one glance, staggered back to the door, half fell outside and ran screaming toward his home, leaving the unhitched horse standing near the stable door. The next night George was sitting in his room, gazing out a window which overlooked the Knouff farm. Suddenly the strange "light" appeared near a corner of the cross roads fence and beckoned to him. He arose from his seat and leaned far out the window. In the twinkling of an eye the "light" left the fence corner, traveled swiftly toward the Knouff house and ran up the water pipe to an upper window. It still beckoned the lad to follow, but he was so engrossed in watching the strange spectacle that he seemed incapable of walking. Suddenly at the upper window of the Knouff house a weird transformation took place. The "light" changed from a globe form to that of a star. It changed in color from white to green. Again it changed in form and color—this time from a green star to a pink crescent; then to a yellow egg, to a blue headstone, to an iron kettle and then into the form of an old, old gray-haired and white-robed man. The old man raised his right hand and beckoned George to come and secure possession of the kettle of money. But the lad was so startled in viewing the strange spectacle that he heeded not the invitation and in a few moments the old man faded from sight and was seen again no more.

Many years ago, at least a quarter of a century, so it is said, a Harrisburg man named Campbell swore that he would visit the Knouff farm and dare the strange "light" to injure him. That he might feel quite courageous Campbell filled himself with liquor and together with a friend started from Harrisburg at 11 o'clock one dark rainy night for the Knouff farm. The "light" seemed to know the drunken couple were coming for it was waiting for them at the end of the farm nearest Harrisburg. Campbell, reckless with liquor, greeted the "light" with loud curses and taking off his coat dared it to "come on and fight him like a man." Save an uneasy, tremulous dancing the "light" did nothing.

"I dare yez to touch me," was Campbell's challenge to the strange ball of fire. But the "light" started slowly toward the center of the farm.

"Ye coward; ye ___ coward," yelled Campbell, suddenly whipping out a large horse pistol. "Take that, ye spalpeen, will yez?" There was a loud report and in a second, thereafter the strange "light" was at Campbell's side. It had assumed the fiendish garb of a hydra-headed scorpion and ferociously darted at the white-faced, thoroughly frightened Campbell. Then there was a scorching, burning sound and all was still. An hour later Campbell's companion rushed into Bailey's saloon at Harrisburg and told the startled inmates that Campbell had been killed by the "light" on Knouff's farm. But Campbell had not been killed. Several days after the night's adventure related, a wild, half-crazed man, with a badly burned face, was found wandering in the woods near Strasburg. It was Campbell and he was mad.

The foregoing tales are ones that were related to the writer, and it led him to visit the farm and investigate the strange light. It was a bitter cold February day when the writer and a friend started out from Harrisburg to walk to Wilson's farm. At several houses along the Louisville and Harrisville road the country people were interviewed concerning the "light." Almost without exception they agreed that there was a "light" hovering about Wilson's farm, but ascribed to it no ghostly or supernatural powers. Said a farmer' s wife who lives opposite the farm in question: "I've lived here for twenty years and have seen the 'light' many times, and I never seen it leave the creek in the hollow. Yes, I know there are lots of spook stories told about the 'light,' but they are not true. They are told by superstitious persons who are afraid of their own shadows. Wilsons's farm is just as good, if not better, than other farms hereabouts, and you can rest assured all of these spook stories about that ball of fire makes him mad. Why, the 'light' is perfectly harmless—it's nothing more than a will o' wisp, and is caused by the water in the creek being charged with phosphuretted hydrogen gas."

And from all that could be learned of the "light," the farmer's wife's explanation of the phenomenon is correct. At one time there was a graveyard on Wilson's farm. The phosphorus from the buried bones is carried down the small creek of water by the underground springs and as a result on dark, damp, foggy nights an *ignis fatuus* arises. The vain, false fire on Wilson's farm is similar to the ones described in text books on natural philosophy and physical geography. It has a luminous appearance and is generally seen only on foggy damp nights. The "light" is of a pale bluish colored flame and sometimes burns steadily during the greater part of the night. It arises, it is thought, from phosphuretted hydrogen gas, which possesses the power of spontaneous combustion upon coming in contact with dry atmosphere. It can readily be seen that such a harmless apparition is apt to frighten superstitious people who do not understand the nature and origin of the "light" or ball of fire. Mr. Wilson, the proprietor of the farm, is well aware of the "light's" existence, and, it is said, has frequently shot at it in order to observe what effect a bullet will produce on the "light." Mr. Wilson does not care to talk about the "light," for in the past it has injured the sale of his farm.

The will o' wisp is certainly a strange phenomenon and yet, so far as is known, a harmless one. Scientists who love to study nature have a field of observation in Stark County. Perhaps they might capture the *ignis fatuus* on Wilson's farm; perchance they could imprison certain of the spontaneous combustible gases, analyze them and give the result to the world. Certain it is that such a result would prove interesting to scores of people.

The tale connected with the light by the country folk is that an old miser once lived on the Wilson farm and buried upon it a huge pot of gold. That gold his spirit in the form of a fire ball hovers over and protects.

Plain Dealer [Cleveland, OH] 28 February 1889: p. 8 STARK COUNTY

NOTE: A spalpeen is an Irish term for a rascal or worthless person. In this article we see the late 19th century wrestling with trying to be scientific and modern with talk of "phosphuretted hydrogen gas," while fascinated by tales of hydra-headed scorpions and treasure lights.

Even today there are people who claim that they see luminous UFOs flying over or into Lake Erie. But such sights are nothing new; fiery apparitions around the Lake go back a long way as illustrated by these two cases:

OPTICAL ILLUSION ON LAKE ERIE

The Cleveland, Ohio, *Herald* says that a tremendous thunder shower passed over that city on the night of the 3d inst., and adds: "Between three and four o'clock next morning the appearance of a vessel on fire was seen far out on the lake. Some persons thought they could distinguish the sails. During a heavy gust of wind the light disappeared. Such appearances are not unfrequent on the lake, and the more experienced men along the dock think there has been no vessel burnt." *Scientific American*, New Series, Volume 3, Issue 8 (Aug 18, 1860) LAKE ERIE

A MYSTERY ON THE LAKES
THE WIZARD LIGHTS
A CURIOUS PHENOMENON ON LAKE ERIE

I notice in the *Dispatch*, of the 11th inst., the following paragraph:--
"The statement that a vessel was seen burning off Erie on Tuesday night, is corroborated by several persons living on the high lands south of the city, who say they saw it."

On the Tuesday evening mentioned, Oct. 29th, at about 7 o'clock, my attention was called by one of my family to a bright light on the lake, having very much the appearance of a vessel on fire.... I watched the light for some time to ascertain whether there was any perceptible motion.

The lighted object did not move as a real ship would have and the witness concludes that it was nothing more than the "mysterious light," which for many years past, at longer or shorter intervals, has been seen by the inhabitants at this point on the lake shore.

The light has made its appearance generally, if not always, in the fall of the year, and usually in the month of November, and almost always during or immediately after a heavy blow from the southwest. The most brilliant exhibition of the light I have ever seen was during the night of the 24th or 25th, as nearly as I can recollect, of November, 1852. It had been my fortune to witness the burning of the steamer *Erie*, near Silver Creek [a notable disaster when the *City of Erie* burned off Silver Creek,

New York in 1841 and over 250 lives were lost], several years before, and the resemblance which this light bore to that of the burning steamer was so strong that I confidently expected the arrival of the boats from the wreck during the night. Others with myself watched the light for perhaps two hours, and with the aid of a good night-glass obtained what seemed to be a very distinct view of the burning vessel.

The object appeared to be some 200 or more feet in length upon the water, and about as high above the water as an upper cabin steamer, such as was in use upon the Lake twenty years ago. At times the flames would start up in spires or sheets of light, then away from side to side, and then die away, precisely as would be the case with a large fire exposed to a strong wind; and two or three times there was the appearance of a cloud of sparks, as if some portion of the upper works had fallen into the burning mass below. The sky and water were beautifully irradiated by the light during its great brilliancy. The light gradually subsided, with occasional flashes until it disappeared altogether. The light of Tuesday evening, although very brilliant for a time, was not nearly so brilliant nor of so long duration as that of 1852.

I am told that this light was seen by mariners on the lakes as long as fifty years ago, but I am not aware that it has ever been made the subject of philosophical speculation or investigation, or, in fact, has ever obtained the notoriety of a newspaper paragraph before. The only theory approaching plausibility I have heard is that the shifting of the sands caused by the continued and heavy winds of autumn has opened some crevices or seams in the rock of the lake bottom through which gas escapes, and that this gas, owing to some peculiar condition of the atmosphere with which it comes in contact, becomes luminous, or perhaps ignited, and burning with a positive flame. That there are what are called "gas springs" in the water along this portion of the lake shore is a well-known fact, and that highly inflammable gas in large quantities exist at a comparatively shallow depth on the shore, has been sufficiently proved by the boring of wells at different points, as at Erie, Walnut Creek, and Lock Haven, and by natural springs at Westfield and Fredonia.

But whatever the cause, the light is a curious fact, and well worth the attention of those interested in the investigation of the phenomenon of nature.

The Brooklyn [NY] Eagle 12 December 1867: p. 4 LAKE ERIE

We turn from stories of spook lights to the realm of the human—or inhuman. This next mysterious tale is ambiguous as to whether the entity is a deranged or criminal human or a genuine man-beast.

THE PUMA OUTDONE
ROCKPORT AND BEAVERDAM PEOPLE HAVE A
NEW FREAK
TO BE AFRAID OF

Not since the time, several years ago, when Charley Price's famous mythical puma had the natives of the Putnam County swamps dodging their own shadows had a scare been started in northwest Ohio equal to that now in full sway in the vicinity of the village of Rockport and Beaver Dam. The puma will have to take a back seat for the new freak, an account which appeared in the following dispatch from Columbus Grove to the *Enquirer*:

"A strange being, apparently half man, half beast, is seen in the county round about Rockport and Beaver Dam. The creature puts in an appearance at or near farmhouses.

"For some time the farmers in that vicinity have been troubled by nightly visits, apparently from intruders bent on securing money or other valuables. It was the scheme of the prowler to attempt to open a window or fumble at the door locks, then move on to the rear part of the house, and after giving the gates and such outposts a good shake disappears as quickly as he came. The family of Frank Conkleman left their home because of these visits, and while they were gone the strange being was seen.

"The creature is described as resembling a man, although possessed of features coarse and rough, and is said to be covered with hair. The inhabitants of that staid old country vicinity are half crazed with excitement, and the female portion will not venture out after nightfall.

"It is firmly believed that the strange creature is an insane person who has been at large for some time. The being is attired in dress more peculiar to one of the male sex, although scantily clad. A searching party will be organized to capture the fellow, if possible, although his fleetness of foot, and ability at fence jumping almost preclude any idea of so doing."

The Lima [OH] Times-Democrat 14 April 1902: p. 1 ALLEN COUNTY

NOTE: "Charley Price's famous mythical puma" was hunted in the "mammoth Black Swamp puma hunt" in December of 1891. Reports of the puma, which had (naturally) escaped from a circus, were apparently exaggerated. "The author of the fake was a curb stone [untrained] editor from Lima, whose name is Charley." *Lima [OH] Daily Times* 18 January 1892: p. 2

I keep running across strange stories from Columbus Grove: spook lights, hoodoo money, pumas, and odd creatures. Then there is the following tale, which I find baffling. It has elements of classic poltergeist cases, but also strange beings who pelt the family with sticks and stones.

GUARD
PLACED AT ARNOLD HOUSE
TO WATCH FOR ALLEGED SPOOKS
STONES AND STICKS THROWN BY
MYSTERIOUS VISITORS

Columbus Grove, Ohio, October 6. Is the farm residence of George Arnold, a leading prohibition politician of the county, located about two and a half miles north of here on the Ottawa Pike, haunted, and what causes the strange sounds that emanate therefrom? This is the question, which not only Mr. Arnold's folks are trying to solve, but neighbors and citizens of Columbus Grove as well.

One week ago Saturday night the residence was entered and $35 and a revolver were taken from the bookcase in the living room. Mr. Arnold's pension voucher, which was with the money, was found lying on the floor.

Every night since the Arnolds have been troubled by intruders. When they heard strange sounds night after night an investigation was ordered. Upon appearing at the front door they saw what appeared to be a man and woman in a strange little cart in the lane which leads to the house from the road. They had no more than left the shelter of the house when the strange beings threw sticks and rocks at members of the family. It is said that as soon as members of the family leave the house, even though for but a short time, the furniture is turned topsy-turvy and everything is strewn about.

Becoming tired of the strange happenings and perplexed by the embarrassment which his family is compelled to suffer on account of the trouble Mr. Arnold came to town and engaged a number of guards to watch the house. One of these guards is ex-Night Watchman Jacob Sheets. Faithfully has he stood for the past several nights, but as yet has not been able to locate the mysterious sounds nor find any clew to the rock throwers.

Arnold's first wife and several children died within short periods of one another of consumption. He married again, and the children born of the second union assist him in taking care of the farm. The children of the first union who are still living have gone out to make a way in the world.

Most of the strange happenings are said to occur at the house during the absence of the wife. A year or so ago the Arnolds were bothered by mysterious visitors, but after a while they ceased to come.
Cincinnati [OH] Enquirer 7 October 1903: p. 1 PUTNAM COUNTY

I have never been able to trace this next, bizarre story about a mysterious rain of shot in John. W. Lingo's Lebanon hardware store to its original source. I first read about it in *Wild Talents* by Charles Fort, but have not been able to get a copy of the entire original article referenced below, from the extremely rare Spiritualist publication, *Religio-Philosophical Journal*. Lingo, hardware merchant and agricultural implement dealer, had, according to the papers, an extensively checkered career: he taught his dog to answer the telephone, was taken to court after being beaten by Lebanon City Councilman Nathan Woods who caught Lingo in Mrs. Woods' bedroom, and shot a business rival during a field test of a sheaf binder, claiming self-defense. When he was appointed Postmaster of Lebanon in 1887, someone circulated, under cover of darkness, flyers accusing Lingo of "the grossest immorality" and urging the women of Lebanon "for God's sake" to sign petitions for his recall. [*Cincinnati Enquirer* 1 July 1879: p. 1; *Cincinnati Enquirer* 13 June 1884: p. 2; *The United States Mail*, 1887]

In short, John W. Lingo was a man to whom Things Happened. And in 1880, something very strange indeed happened in his hardware store.

Religio-Philosophical Journal, March 6, 1880—copying from the *Cincinnati Inquirer*—That, at Lebanon, Ohio, people of the town were in a state of excitement: that showers of birdshot were falling from the ceiling of John W. Lingo's hardware store. A committee was appointed, and according to its report, the phenomenon was veritable: slow-falling volleys of shot, not of the size of any sold in the store, were appearing from no detectable point of origin. There was another circumstance, and it may have had much to do with the phenomenon: about five years

before, somebody, at night, had entered this store, and had been shot by
Lingo, escaping without being identified.

"Supposed manifestations of a murdered man's ghost."
Religio-philosophical Journal, 28 (n.1; March 6, 1880): pp.4-5. *Wild Talents*,
Charles Fort, edited and annotated by Mr. X, who is tracing each of
Charles Fort's stories to their sources: http://www.resologist.net/
talent12.htm

One of our oldest residents has no hesitancy in pronouncing it a
spiritual manifestation, and says it is a warning sent from the other
world foretelling a direful calamity soon to befall the building or the
proprietor. A séance is soon to be held in the building, in order to test
the mediumistic powers, and if possible unravel the meaning of this
strange phenomenon.
The Cincinnati [OH] Enquirer 25 February 1880: p. 5 WARREN
COUNTY

I have not found any reports that a séance was actually held. This next article
also refers to Lingo having shot a burglar in his hardware store, but that is
another story I haven't found in the papers. Despite the attempt to link this
phenomenon to the ghost of a burglar, it has much more in common with
poltergeist manifestations involving showers of stones. Unfortunately John
W. Lingo is the only person named. If this really was something mysterious
and not a publicity stunt on the part of a man accustomed to notoriety, we
have no hope of finding an adolescent to blame.

Lebanon, Ohio is the scene of a great excitement, caused by a
wonderful phenomenon of showers of ordinary bird-shot falling from
the ceiling of John W. Lingo's hardware store. This strange occurrence
was first noticed by parties who resort to the place each evening to
spend a few hours in social chat. On the first evening quite a number of
persons were in the store when the shot began to fall in different parts
of the room, but principally in the midst of the crowd of persons sitting
about the stove. As the stove was near the hatchway it was thought by
some that some person or contrivance was in the upper portion of the
building which threw or dropped the shot down. Parties were selected
and a thorough search made of the building. All the floors were visited
and every nook and corner ransacked, when the committee returned
and reported no spooks found. Then someone suggested that they
all go to the front end of the store where the ceiling is perfect and no

hatchways to the upper rooms. The shot continued to fall the same as at the back portion of the room. Then it was proposed that all present hold their hands up over their heads, in order that no one could use his hands to throw or drop the shot. Still the shot fell, as usual. Many believe the shot is thrown by the spirit of a burglar who was shot and killed in the store in 1874, while attempting to rob it.

Elkhart [IN] Weekly Review 4 March 1880: p. 2 WARREN COUNTY

As is often the case in poltergeist manifestations, the mysterious events ceased abruptly.

From the shot-filled life of John W. Lingo, we turn to an extremely bizarre case, either of true spirit communication, of misguided kindness, or of heartless cruelty. As Dr. Johnson said, "We shall receive no letters in the grave." Yet for more than twenty years, a Montclova woman was tormented by letters claiming to come from her dead husband.

"OLD TRUEPENNY"
AN OHIO DEAD MAN SEEMS TO IMITATE HAMLET'S FATHER.
HE DOESN'T "REVISIT THE GLIMPSES OF THE MOON" IN PERSON
BUT SENDS GHOSTLY MISSIVES OF ADVICE
A CASE THAT'S PASSING STRANGE

Washington City, Sept. 21. A telegram from Toledo relates the story of a farmer in Montclara [Montclova], Ohio, who died and was buried thirteen years ago, but is still writing to his family. The *Sunday Capital* prints a story quite as remarkable, as follows: "A very remarkable case has come to my attention through a friend in the pension office which furnishes incidents for a novel as powerful as any Dumas or Eugene Sue ever used. In 1864 a lieutenant from an Ohio village was killed in one of the battles in Virginia and his body was sent home, buried with military honors and a handsome monument erected over it by the citizens of the place. Thousands of people paid their tributes of honor to the young hero and looked upon his face as the body lay in the town hall. He left a widow to whom he had been married only a year, and for more than twenty years she has been trying to get a pension; but, although she keeps fresh flowers upon her husband's grave, she cannot prove that he is dead. The records in the adjutant general's office are perfect, and affidavits

can be furnished from thousands of people who saw and recognized his lifeless body, but every few months she receives a letter from him written in a hand as familiar as her own. Two letters never come from the same place; now they are postmarked in Colorado, then in Texas, then in New York. Once she got a note from him dated at Washington. He appears to know what is going on at home, and always alludes to local occurrences with a familiarity that is amazing. He sends messages to old friends and gives her advice about business matters which it seems impossible for a stranger to know. She cannot answer these ghostly missives, because he never gives any clew to his whereabouts, and no detective has ever been able to find him. Her friends believe that the writer is some crank or malicious person who takes this way to annoy her, and the distress the poor woman suffers cannot be measured by any other human experience. Long ago she ceased to open envelopes which came with the familiar address, but sends them sealed to her attorney, who uses every possible means to secure a clew to the identity of the writer. The only circumstances to suggest that it may possibly be her husband are the penmanship and the familiarity the writer shows with the lady's private life, but how he could keep himself posted is another mystery, which cannot be solved. Several times the writer has intimated that he might soon pay her a visit, but the next letter always contains an apology for not having done so. The woman has suffered agony of mind beyond description, and her life has been ruined by this horrible mystery, but of late she has become more resigned, and would neither be surprised or disappointed if her husband should someday walk into her door."
Elkhart [IN] Daily Review 21 September 1885: p. 4 LUCAS COUNTY

NOTE: This story truly is passing strange. I wonder if one of the dead husband's "pards" from his old Civil War unit learned enough about him to impersonate him? The different locations suggest someone either employed by the railroad or a drummer (a traveling salesman) or perhaps just a man with far-flung contacts. But what about the handwriting? "Old Truepenny" is a term taken (again) from Shakespeare's *Hamlet*. It means a true, honest fellow. Dumas is Alexandre Dumas *pere*, who wrote *The Three Musketeers* and *The Count of Monte Cristo*. Eugene Sue was a contemporary of Dumas *pere*, who wrote lurid novels like *The Mysteries of Paris*. Both men had a talent for highly dramatic, sensational plots and would have relished this odd tale.

9.

Glancing Beams of Moonlight:
The Ghostly Women in White

What are these, who are arrayed in white robes? and whence came they?

– Revelation 7: 13 –

Why do ghosts wear white? They have not always done so. The Greeks imagined ghosts with skull faces, wearing black robes. It was somewhere around the beginning of the Middle Ages that ghosts began to appear in white, possibly associated with the custom of burying the newly baptized in their chrism robes or the image of the white robes given to the redeemed in the *Book of Revelation*. From 1666-1680 a series of "Burial in Woollen Acts" were passed by the British Parliament, mandating that the dead should be buried in shrouds of pure English wool, which in its natural state was usually white or cream.

White was the preferred Victorian burial garb color for women and children. Women were often buried in their white nightclothes and white signified the innocence of young children. Stories of ghosts who return wearing the clothes in which they were buried are common. Since the dead were entombed in white clothing or shrouds, it seemed logical that their ghosts should return in white as well. Or is the white garb of ghosts simply a reflection of the pallor of death?

In *The Face in the Window* I wrote of the terrifying Women in Black; now here are their ghostly, pallid counterparts:

GHOST IN AN OHIO FARMHOUSE
A WOMAN'S MYSTERIOUS ACTIONS ARE EXCITING RURAL BUCKEYE COMMUNITY

The members of the family of James Miller, who live near Mount Eaton, O., are terror stricken at the appearance of the ghost of a woman, which, they say, paid them frequent visits lately and has acted in a most unaccountable manner.

The uncanny visitor made its first appearance about a week ago, after all the members of the household except Mr. Miller had gone to bed. He remained up later than usual to take a good night smoke before the fire. As he sat puffing sleepily he says he heard a strange noise behind him, as of someone sobbing. Turning about, he beheld the form of a woman, clothed in white, standing with bowed head and weeping bitterly. Mr. Miller started to his feet in surprise, as he had bolted all the doors leading to the house shortly before.

The woman was a stranger to him, and the manner of her entrance to the house was so mysterious that he asked her how she had got in. At this the figure in white looked up at him with tearful eyes and then walked slowly into the kitchen.

The dazed farmer followed wondering, and by the light that came from the sitting room he says he saw the ghostly visitor place a skillet on the stove and begin to make preparations for a meal. She rattled the dishes in the cupboard and placed two plates on the table.

The rattle of the culinary utensils reached the ears of Mrs. Miller, who was yet awake upstairs and she called down to her husband to learn what was the matter. At the sound of her voice the woman in white slowly faded away.

Mr. Miller immediately aroused all the members of the family and told them what he had seen. They believed he had been dreaming until he showed them the skillet which still stood on the stove. There were no plates on the table, but the white cloth had been unfolded and spread at haphazard. All the doors of the house were locked and a thorough search in the vicinity failed to reveal the whereabouts of the visitor.

The second night after the incident, which was yet unexplained, Andrew Miller, the farmer's son, aged about twenty-three years, who had been to the village for the mail, arrived home after the rest of the family had retired. As he entered the house, he says, the form of a woman stole in after him and stood, with drooping head, before the fire. The young man thought at once of the ghost his father claimed to have seen and determined to investigate.

He accordingly advanced boldly toward the woman in white and laid his hand on her. As he did so she seemed to elude him, and, turning about, he saw her standing in the same drooping posture several feet distant. Another effort to capture her was as futile as the first, and, bent on solving the mystery he entered an adjoining room and producing a loaded shotgun returned. The figure was still standing before the fire, and, taking deliberate aim, he fired.

Simultaneously with the report of the weapon came an awful shriek and as the smoke cleared away, all trace of the ghost had vanished, but the old clock which stood in the corner was shattered by the load of shot which had passed through its case. The shot frightened the members of the family, who had retired, and when the son told them his story of the ghost they were mystified more than ever. The Millers are just now worked up to such a nervous tension that they are afraid to retire at night and have announced their intention of moving.

The appearance of the ghost in the house has revived a long forgotten tale that many years ago an old bachelor who lived there at that time was alleged to have killed a young girl who worked for him. Many are of the belief that the ghost is her returned spirit. The affair has caused much gossip among the neighbors, who have made up watching parties and wait every night within the Miller home for the reappearance of the ghost.

Plain Dealer [Cleveland, OH] 29 April 1900: p. 29 WAYNE COUNTY

Steubenville had a Woman in White scare in 1904, told in a series of very short pieces in the *Steubenville Herald Star*. Although a supposed culprit was captured, at least one sighting occurred about a week after the capture.

The "woman in white" paraded in the lower end of town near the La Belle last night and at least one young man had his hair raised. *Steubenville [OH] Herald Star* 6 October 1904: p. 5 JEFFERSON COUNTY

NOTE: The La Belle was The La Belle Iron Works.

MYSTERIOUS WOMAN

The "woman in white" was about again last night and had a great many people on Sherman Avenue frightened. She made her appearance at about 9 o'clock and Mrs. Burns first saw her and raised the alarm and the whole street was soon out. Many saw her before she disappeared. If some practical joker is doing this he had better take warning as there are several Steubenville people who are aching for a shot at this mysterious person.

Steubenville [OH] Herald Star 11 October 1904: p. 5 JEFFERSON COUNTY

WOMAN IN WHITE
SAID TO HAVE BEEN CAPTURED IN THE

LA BELLE YARDS.

It was reported today that the "woman in white" had been captured and that she turned out to be a brakeman who is employed in the La Belle yards. The report says he was parading about last night enveloped in a sheet and was run down by the yard crew and given a beating.

Nothing of the kind was reported to the police and the name of the joker could not be learned but such an occurrence is said to have taken place.

Steubenville [OH] Herald Star 13 October 1904: p. 1 JEFFERSON COUNTY

TOWN IS HAUNTED BY "WOMAN IN WHITE"

Steubenville, Ohio, October 19. The efforts of the police and many citizens of Steubenville are directed in running down a "woman in white" mystery. The nightly appearance of this white robed creature has created a local sensation.

She was first seen by Charles Pressler, a small boy, who has been sick and nervous since the vision followed him home. At several homes on La Belle Avenue she has appeared and tapped at the windows. She appears frequently to employees about the yards of LaBelle Iron Works.

Several nights ago the wraith was seen by William Schick gliding across the Carnegie Library lawn. All describe her as attired in a white gown resembling a bride's dress with white slippers. The newspapers have printed daily accounts of persons seeing the vision in white, and daily reports are made to police headquarters.

Muskegon [MI] Chronicle 19 October 1904: p. 2 JEFFERSON COUNTY

In January of 1905, *The Steubenville Weekly Herald Star* reported on a spook terrifying the inhabitants of McDonald, Pennsylvania, a town about 25 miles from Steubenville:

MAY BE STEUBENVILLE'S WOMAN IN WHITE ON A VISIT TO PENNSYLVANIA.

The town of McDonald is wrought up over a strange apparition which has been appearing on the streets and frightening the inhabitants. The spectre may be our own "woman in white...."

The story goes on to describe a standard "Woman in Black" apparition, implying that the visiting Woman in White couldn't keep

her gown from becoming sooty in the polluted atmosphere of the Pennsylvania coal country.
The Steubenville [OH] Weekly Herald Star, 27 January 1905: p. 3

This next Woman in White, from Cleveland, was not only seen by several witnesses in the household, she was also observed by a neighbor woman across the alley from her kitchen window.

A VIGOROUS SPOOK.
IT SLAPS A MAN AND GRASPS A WOMAN'S FOOT
A SCARED HOUSEHOLD
THE MEMBERS OF A YARDMASTER'S FAMILY
PANIC STRICKEN
THEY SOLEMNLY DECLARE THAT A GHOST IS
PERAMBULATING ABOUT THEIR PREMISES, DAY
AND NIGHT—WHAT IS THE CAUSE?

There is a badly scared family in a small two-story frame house on the south side of Euclid Avenue near Erie Street. It's ghosts. Charles Liebengood, a yardmaster for the Nickel Plate Railway, lives in the house and he is so sure that something which has been seen at night in one of the rooms is an orthodox spook of the regular hair-lifting, blood-freezing breed, that he is about to move out. Perhaps he may discover, before he goes whether the frightful thing is a flapping lace curtain or flesh and blood on mischief bent, but it is certain that he and his family are now firmly of the belief that they have unwittingly camped down on one of the lids opening out of Old Nick's winter resort. [i.e. Hell.]

Liebengood and his wife are intelligent, and profess that they have, until recently, looked upon ghost stories with ridicule, while he, in addition, has

WITNESSED TOO MANY ACCIDENTS

To railroad men to have weak nerves. When a *Leader* reporter called at the house yesterday afternoon, he found Mrs. Liebengood and her sister-in-law, Miss Sallie Liebengood, performing the work of the house in the shed at the rear of the premises. In response to a question Mrs. Liebengood related the following story: "We have occupied this house since last March. There is not enough money in Cleveland to induce us to live here another week. I won't go in the house in the absence of my husband. I am positive it is haunted. We have all seen the spirit and at different times. My niece, Anna Hogan, who formerly lived with me, was the first to see it. When she opened her eyes one night at a late hour the spirit of a woman stood at the foot of the bed. She saw the eyelashes and saw them move. The spirit was dressed in a long white robe that trailed on the floor and a book was held in the hand. My niece thought it was me and calling me Auntie, wanted to know why I was up at that hour of the night. The form did not speak. This frightened my niece and she screamed at the top of her voice. This awoke me, but before I had time to realize where the screams came from she rushed breathlessly into my room and related her experience. Of course my husband and I laughed and told her that imagination had caused her fear.

ONE NIGHT AFTER THAT

Our little son had a violent attack of the toothache. He and my husband were sleeping in the haunted room. Suddenly, and while he had his back turned to the wall, my husband received a terrific blow on the side of the face with an open hand. He looked up and saw the ghost of the woman standing by the side of the bed. At first he thought it was sister Sallie, who, he surmised, had come in to prevent him from whipping the child. Thinking that the ghost was his sister, he told her to go back to her room for he would whip his child if he wanted to. There was no response. Then a ray of light came through the window. It shone on the face of the phantom, and revealed it in all its ghastliness. Taking the child in his arms my husband jumped out of bed and hastened into my room. He was so frightened he could not speak for some time. The next morning he was hardly able to go to his work. Since then he has not laughed at the stories we told of the ghost. We have seen the phantom several times since that night. One night I saw the figure standing at the foot of the bed. A book was in the out-stretched hand. Before I could crawl out of the bed the spirit grasped me by the foot, but soon released the hold. I hurried out of the room. During the day we can hear the phantom

WALKING ABOUT THE ROOM

And up and down the stairway. It is an uneasy spirit and certainly has some secret to tell. The children have seen it and refuse to go to bed until we take a light and accompany them. They were never afraid of the darkness before." This story was corroborated by Miss Sallie Liebengood and Miss Anna Hogan. A woman, who lives just across the alley at the rear of the alleged haunted house, emphatically asserts that she saw the ghost about 5 o'clock one evening while looking from a window of her kitchen. She firmly believes in ghosts. In fact the whole neighborhood is in a turmoil, and all sorts of stories and conjectures are afloat about the supposed spook. Mr. and Mrs. Liebengood intend to vacate the premises to-day. They say they have been informed by the police that a terrible crime was once committed there.

Whether or not there will be a sequel to this story depends, of course, upon whether by investigation or chance, the real cause of the discomfort to which the occupants of the house have been subjected is discovered.

Cleveland [OH] Leader 3 October 1893: p. 8 CUYAHOGA COUNTY

NOTE: I have not yet found a sequel to this story. The Nickel Plate Railroad was the New York, Chicago & St. Louis Railroad Company, founded in 1881.

Not one, but five Women in White appeared to an "occultist" at Oberlin.

THE GHOSTLY FORMS OF FIVE YOUNG LADIES APPEAR TO AN OBERLIN OCCULTIST IN THE DEAD OF NIGHT
THE STORY OF A HAUNTED HOUSE

Away over in the northwest part of Russia Township, in this county, on what is known as the Gaston Road, stands a modest farm house. Its surroundings are not unlike those of other houses in the neighborhood, and to the casual observer there is nothing unusual about the place. Yet those who reside in that neighborhood pass the house after nightfall with hurrying footsteps and quickening breath, for weird tales have been told of crimes dark and bloody which have been committed there, of ghosts that glide through the glancing beams of moonlight, and of screams and wails which cause one's hair to stand on end and the blood to run cold in the veins. Superstitious people say the house is haunted. Whether this is a fact or not, for thirty years the owner of the place sought in vain for a tenant. Years ago, it is said, a man who laughed at ghosts and made merry over the stories of the nocturnal perambulations of spirits was induced to occupy the house. One night was enough, and the stories he told next day only added to the superstitious awe in which the place was held.

Three years ago Professor Carlos Kenaston, of Oberlin, purchased the property. He cared naught for the yarns about the house being haunted, and he immediately set carpenters and painters at work and the house was soon transformed into a model country residence. The professor and his wife took up their residence there and if ghosts and spirits ever visit the place now their comings and goings are so quietly made as not to disturb the occupants of the house.

The professor has a brother, Mr. Arthur Kenaston, who also resides in Oberlin. The brother is a student of the occult sciences, and thereby hangs a tale, weird and thrilling.

The other day Arthur Kenaston was in Elyria, and while here he called upon Judge Hinman and in the course of a conversation which followed he related the following story.

"For years," said Kenaston, "I have been a believer in occultism, and unconsciously I have become an occultist. Often have I tested my powers in this direction with astonishing results.

"My brother," continued Kenaston, "purchased about three years ago, as you perhaps know, the haunted house on the Gaston Road, northwest of Oberlin. Well, the other night I went to bed wondering if the stories that had been told about the place were true.

"In the middle of the night," he continued "I was awakened by a voice saying, 'Go and See.'"

Kenaston then described how, like Abraham of old, he quietly arose and without waking his wife dressed himself and started upon his lonely midnight journey to the home of his brother, "the haunted house."

"When I arrived there," said Kenaston, "I walked quietly around the house a couple of times and finally sat down upon a ladder which was leaning against the rear of the house. It was a beautiful night. A soft breeze played among the leaves of the trees and the stars shone with an unusual brilliancy. As I sat there, I gradually went into a trance, and suddenly in the starlight I saw the form of a young lady approaching, and behind her came four other female forms. They were all dressed in white, and as they passed before me each one stopped and faced me, and as they did so each in turn raised her right hand with the index finger extended and then throwing back her head she drew her finger across her throat and vanished into the night.

"I no longer have any doubts," said Kenaston "as to whether or not the house is haunted."

Elyria [OH] Reporter 3 July 1901 LORAIN COUNTY

NOTE: Carlos Albert Kenaston was a distinguished agricultural specialist, professor, and engineer who was known for his world-wide travels. I wonder what he, the engineer and scientist, thought about his brother's occult interests?

Our last Woman in White was a stranger in this land. She remains shrouded in mystery to this day.

The French Governess

If in returning you have not saved my life,
then nothing on earth can save me.
Ah! Dear God! To die so young,
when I have sorrowed so long!

– Violetta, Act III, *La Traviata* –

It is like a plot from an opera by Puccini or Verdi: a beautiful young French girl, governess to a wealthy American family meets a Count attached to the Italian Consulate at New York and they fall in love. He is pledged to another and she makes the agonizing decision to end the relationship. She flees to the wilds of Youngstown, Ohio and, after a final, distraught exchange of letters, in despair she throws herself to her death. Only moments after she expires, an unsigned letter from her love arrives, pleading for her to return to him. The curtain falls as the audience weeps.

But this is not an opera; it is a true story.

The headlines in Youngstown and Cleveland were sensational:

A FRENCH GOVERNESS
ENDS HER LIFE BY JUMPING FROM A WINDOW
SHE HAD BEEN IN A YOUNGSTOWN (OHIO) FAMILY
BUT TEN DAYS
BURNING HER LETTERS JUST BEFORE THE ACT
A PROBABLE CASE OF DISAPPOINTED LOVE

SUICIDE AT YOUNGSTOWN
A GOVERNESS JUMPS FROM AN ATTIC WINDOW
AND IS KILLED

HEADLONG FROM A ROOF
A BEAUTIFUL FRENCH GIRL'S TRAGIC SUICIDE
MLLE. GOUDART, A GOVERNESS IN THE FAMILY
OF MR. H.O. BONNELL
TAKES HER OWN LIFE.
THE CAUSE OF THE ACT A PROFOUND MYSTERY

About 7 o'clock Monday morning Mlle. Y. Goudart, employed as a governess in the family of H.O. Bonnell, of Wick Avenue, threw herself from a window in the garret of the house headlong to the ground, with fatal results.

Very little could be learned of Mlle. Goudart's past life. She had only been in this city about ten days. She was engaged by Mr. Bonnell on the recommendation of Mme. Corer, of No. 31 East 17th Street, New York. It is also known that she had been in this country only about three months and that her family live about three hours' ride out of Paris, France, Her father is a judge in a French court. She had told members of Mr. Bonnell's family that she was 23 years of age. That she was highly educated there is no doubt. She had an abundance of jet black hair, beautiful dark eyes and a fair complexion, being a most attractive woman. She possessed pleasing manners and her winning ways soon found for her a warm place in the hearts of all whom she met.

Last Friday she left the house and after being gone nearly all day returned in most dejected spirits, her hair disheveled and her dress soaking wet. She was melancholy. On Saturday she wrote several letters, and seemed to have an air of utter disregard as to her surroundings. She was driven to Dr. Wilcox's office, who examined her and said to a member of the family that her mind was unbalanced and to watch her. On Saturday evening she expressed her intention of returning to New York on Sunday, but was persuaded to give up that idea.

This morning she was called about 6 o'clock by one of the servants. Fifteen minutes later one of the domestics of the household smelt smoke and, upon investigation, found that it came from Mlle. Goudart's sleeping apartment. She went to the door, but was informed that a dress which she was cleaning had been hung too close to the fire. About 20 minutes after this, while the same servant was in the kitchen preparing breakfast, she was startled by the shrill shriek of a woman and a noise outside the house. She ran to a window and saw the form of Mlle. Goudart lying, a shapeless mass, on the flagstone walk that leads alongside the house. About the same time she discovered that there was a fire in the house somewhere. The household was alarmed and the fire department called. Willing hands picked the unfortunate woman from the ground and carried her inside the house. A physician was quickly summoned. She was unconscious and past all human aid, and expired shortly after she had been carried into the house. Upon investigation it was discovered that she had taken some of her clothes into the garret and after stuffing them into a clay chimney crock that she found there, set fire to them and then threw herself head foremost to the ground. She struck on the back of her head, badly shattering her skull and dislocating her neck. The poor woman fell with such force as to actually break a flagstone into four distinct pieces.

The remains were placed in charge of an undertaker and Coroner Booth was also called. The coroner took charge of her personal effects and will investigate the affair. It is supposed now that she met with some disappointment, and it is also believed that she destroyed some letters that she had received from a correspondent in New York City. Several letters were found, however, written in French, and in a man's handwriting that will be translated this afternoon. Among them is a letter received this morning, just a few minutes after she died. She has no known relatives on this side of the water, but it is highly probable that the contents of the letter received this morning will give information as to her identity and the cause of her insanity and suicide.
Youngstown *Telegram* 21 November 1888: p. 5

THE GOUDART SUICIDE
THE BEAUTIFUL GIRL'S ANONYMOUS CORRESPONDENT.
A MYSTERIOUS LETTER THAT CAME A FEW MINUTES AFTER HER DEATH AND THAT MIGHT HAVE DETERRED HER FROM SUICIDE HAD SHE RECEIVED IT.

The all-absorbing topic of conversation for the past 36 hours has been the tragic suicide of the beautiful French girl, Mlle. Goudart, who was employed as a governess in Mr. H. O. Bonnell's household. The facts pertaining to the suicide were published in detail in these columns yesterday and afforded the gossipers a great fund of speculation. Since yesterday it has been learned that one week ago last Thursday, Mlle. Goudart presented herself at the Bonnell residence with a letter of introduction, in which she was highly commended by Mrs. Dick, of No.

1708 Locust Street, Philadelphia. The letter also stated that the writer had brought her from France about three months before; that she was finely educated and that her relations were of the highest. It is known that a man as yet unknown, residing in New York City, had an intimate acquaintance with Mlle. Goudart. During the few days she resided at the Bonnell household she many times spoke of an Italian count in the diplomatic service as a friend. She was in continual correspondence with this unknown man.

Until last Thursday she was merry and took a deep interest in conversation and her duties to the children; on that day she received a letter bearing the New York postmark. A large red seal was used to close the envelope. She opened the letter, perused its contents, and then destroyed it. From that moment she was noticed to act strangely, as though demented. It is highly probable that when she returned to the house on Friday, after several hours' absence, with her dress soaking wet and with disheveled hair, she had endeavored to take her life by drowning.

If the contents of the letter, received on Thursday were only known, much additional light would no doubt be thrown on the matter, for it was the contents of this letter, evidently, that prompted the insane act of self-destruction. A letter was received from the same person and bearing similar seal, with the New York postmark. This letter was received just a few moments after the unfortunate girl breathed her last. It was hastily broken open with the hope of ascertaining the real cause of Mlle. Goudart's strange demeanor and her tragic death. The letter was found to be written in French, with no name signed, or anything in the letter that would lead directly to the identification of the writer. Following is the letter:

"New York, Nov. 17, 1888.

"Your letter is frightful. Not one regret, not one hope, not one reference to yourself. It is so gloomy, so terrifying, that it leaves one to suppose anything, to fear anything. You ask yourself what I can have to tell you. Well, I have but one thing to say, one prayer to make you. Come back here without delay. That which I propose to you is possible. You will find again in a safe and quiet life the calm and serene mind now so gloomy, and in the calm you will find again little by little happiness and possible dream of the future. Come back here you must. I do not know what will become of you if I abandon you to yourself. Your sudden departure from New York when I was just seeing the possibility of offering you a sweet and agreeable home here was a great mistake, but

I am not angry with you and you have still time to repair it. In charity do so. Reflect well on all I said in our last interview.

"Your letter has so upset me that I am not able to understand my impression or sentiments or to collect my ideas. But in one or the other there is no reproach in this cry of distress that I send you. Come back here. It is not in vain that I have promised you my help. My devotion and my feelings toward you will remain unalterable. You will have in me everything that your true feelings recommend. You will always have an honest and a loyal man, a true and devoted friend who will not abandon you, and you will at least have a helper and defender. If he cannot give you any consolation or encouragement you will have a friend who will do all for you. Calm your mind; let a little happiness enter your heart, a smile enliven your face.

"You speak of your father. I shall be happy to do all in my power, but where and how? Your letter says nothing about him. You do not give me the least indication. Ah, poor child! In what moral state are you? Come here at once, I want you; if you have not the means telegraph me. Come, come. You have told me you loved to hear me speak. Come and let us have a little talk, the same as we did that day in my office. Your face bright, your looks animated, caused a profound emotion. But, alas! All that is passed in your horrible resolution. You should take a servant [to accompany you.] The best to you. I await you."

While reading this I wished I had the original French transcription. Perhaps I have an evil imagination, but despite its protestations of honesty and loyalty, the writer sounds to me like a man who has made Mademoiselle a dishonorable proposition, offering not marriage and respectability, but the *bijou* residence of a mistress. A dream of the future, a friend and defender. A sweet and agreeable home. These are not the ardent words of a wedding proposal, but the measured, coded phrases of a diplomat.

The article finished:

The seal on the envelope was made with red wax, about the size of a silver half dollar. There were no words on the impression. It was an octagon figure enclosed by a pointed circle with a plain circle on the outside. It would be recognized at a glance as the stamp of a foreigner. An endeavor is being made to ascertain the identity of this man.
Daily Telegram [Youngstown, OH] 29 November 1888.

The Mahoning County Coroner immediately searched for answers.

THE FRENCH GOVERNESS WAS MLLE. GAUTARD.

Youngstown, Ohio, Nov. 21. A trunk and valise belonging to the beautiful young French governess who committed suicide here on Monday last were broken open to-day by the coroner. Documents found in the trunk show that her name was not Goudart, as was supposed, but Gautard. A duly signed and sealed certificate of birth shows that her full name was Julie Henriette Emma Gautard, and that she was born in Aillant, France, on April 2, 1866. Her father was Jules Gautard, ex-Chief Justice of the Peace of the Canton of Aillant. A diploma of the Academy of Dijon showed that Mlle. Gautard finished her education at that institution on June 5, 1884. The trunk and valise contained a quantity of fine wearing apparel, books, jewelry, etc.
New York Herald-Tribune [New York, NY] 22 November 1888: p. 1

The trunk also contained photos of persons believed to be the girl's parents and siblings.

A photograph of a large, blonde young man was also found. The photograph was taken in London. A few lines in French were written across its face showing it to be a souvenir of friendship. A name was signed, but it was in such a scrawl that it could not be deciphered. The inscription was dated Paris, June 7, 1888.
Daily Telegram [Youngstown, OH] 21 November, 1888

The coroner seems to have concluded his investigation with astounding speed. Within 24 hours, the post-mortem examination was made and the young woman was placed in a plain casket and, after a brief service by a local Protestant clergyman, she was taken to Calvary Cemetery in the dark and buried with no graveside service. The only mourners were Mr. Bonnell and an unnamed Frenchman living in Youngstown.

There were protests in the *Telegram* about the "strange and inhospitable haste with which her remains were treated in this city of Christian civilization....There was nothing in her death that demanded a hasty consignment to mother earth, yet almost within 24 hours from the time life was extinct, the remains were hurried into a grave as though the death had been caused by some pestilential or contagious disease.

Since yesterday cablegrams have been passing between New York and France, informing the parents of the death of their daughter in a foreign land. Their feelings may be imagined on learning of the hasty disposition of the remains of the loved one and that she was consigned to a pauper's grave, before every possible means was exhausted to locate and communicate with relatives."
Youngstown Vindicator 22 November 1888: p. 2 and Youngstown *Telegram* 28 November 1888: p. 2

This hasty burial seems out of keeping with everything else that is known about the Bonnell family and it puzzles me. Perhaps her injuries were so horrific they wanted her buried immediately. They might have felt that her suicide reflected badly on them, as employers, but Mr. Bonnell, who was a kindly man, chose to accompany the body to its grave.

Coroner C.C. Booth rendered a verdict of suicide; some papers added the designation, "while insane," which would allow her to be buried in consecrated soil. Then the Coroner added an odious footnote:

Coroner Booth says he made an examination of the body of Mlle. Gautard and that he is positive in his statement that the girl was chaste. This statement is made in justice to the poor unfortunate, false rumors having gained circulation to the contrary.
Daily Telegram [Youngstown, OH] 21 November 1888

There was an immediate clamor from the community to have the young woman given a more fitting burial. The Youngstown Lodge of Elks led the movement to make the arrangements. Mlle. Gautard's body was unearthed from a very damp grave and embalmed by Drake & Pitts, Undertakers. Hundreds of people filed by her white casket to gaze at the body, dressed in a grey dress found in the young woman's trunk. On the casket was placed a beautiful floral arrangement in the shape of a harp, the gift of the Elks, who knew that she had been a music teacher.

The funeral services were held at St. Columba's Church, then the body was taken to Calvary Cemetery where it was deposited in a vault to await instructions from her family in France.

Although Mlle. Gautard had been in the country for three months, no one seemed to know exactly who she was or the spelling of her last name. There were rumors that she was another missing French governess, a Miss Suzanne Fairweather, who had come from Philadelphia to Columbus, Ohio, and who disappeared on the 9th of November, 1888, supposedly eloping with a priest. (Her badly decomposed body was found in Alum Creek in April of 1889.)

Madame Coyriere, head of a New York agency for music teachers, who had placed Mlle. Gautard with the Bonnell family was shocked to hear of the young woman's death, according to an interview in the *New York Herald*. She added an intriguing detail.

> The Italian Consul, Giovanni Raffo, called a week ago Sunday upon Mme. Coyriere and asked for Miss Gautard's address. He said he had a very important letter for her. It was sent on and soon afterward Mrs. Bonnell wrote to Mme. Coyriere to say that Miss Gautard was acting strangely. Mme. Coyriere thinks that the missive that caused the act was a love letter.
>
> *New York [NY] Herald* 20 November 1888: p. 8

More information came to light when the French Vice-Consul at Philadelphia wrote to Mr. Bonnell:

MLLE. GAUTARD TRIED TO POISON HERSELF IN PHILADELPHIA

Youngstown, November 26. Some additional light regarding the death of Mlle. Gautard has been secured through a letter received to-day by Mr. H.O. Bonnell from the Vice Consul of France in Philadelphia, M. Le Vossiony, who, after speaking of other matters says: "Do you know that when at Mrs. Dick's house, No. 1709 Locust Street, Philadelphia, Mlle. Gautard tried to poison herself with laudanum. So her troubles, whatever they might have been, had commenced long before she entered your house." This letter shows that she was in a state of mind bordering upon insanity when she came here, and explains her conduct and actions just preceding her death.
Cleveland [OH] Leader 27 November 27 1888: p. 2

Mrs. Franklin Dick, the woman who had brought Mlle. Gautard to the United States as music teacher to her children, consistently misspelled her last name and called her "Marie." (Aren't all pretty French girls called Marie?) When inquiries were sent to Mrs. Dick and to the Italian Consul, the replies were, shall we say, diplomatic, saying nothing with the most perfect courtesy.

NO LIGHT FROM MARIE GOUDERT'S
PHILADELPHIA EMPLOYER.

Mlle. Goudert was for a while employed as a governess in the family of Mr. William A. Dick, a banker, of this city. I called upon Mrs. Dick at her residence to-day, and she spoke as follows of the poor girl:

"When I was in Paris this summer I was in need of a governess and advertised in the *Herald's* Paris edition. Among the score of replies I received was one from Mlle. Marie Goudert. I was pleased with the tone of her application and went to see her. She was living in a suburb of the city, where her father was what we call a justice of the peace. I found her family quite decent people, refined and educated. I was pleased with the applicant and her family and I engaged her. I found her a charming girl and took a decided fancy to her. When I came back to America I brought her with me, but after she had been only a short time in this house I was obliged to part with her.

"Why? Oh! Partly from reasons of a private nature and partly because she herself desired to go. There was no quarrel, or nothing disagreeable between us. When I found she was bent on going I gave her the privilege of sending to me for a 'reference' and recommended her to a French employment office in New York city. She went to it and shortly I had an application about her from the Bonnells, of Youngstown. I gave her the strongest recommendations and she was engaged by them. I know of no reason why she should have taken such a rash step. It is true she was despondent at times while with me, and perhaps homesick. She was very pretty, and was about twenty-three years old, I should judge. She always behaved herself in an exemplary manner in my company, and I never heard any tales about her affecting her good name.

"Poor girl, I am sorry for her, and her untimely death has completely unnerved me so much that I have declined to see a dozen reporters who came to ask me to-day about her, but as I got her through the *Herald* I felt, when you were announced, that I ought to tell the *Herald* the little I knew about poor, unfortunate Marie Goudert."

LITTLE KNOWN OF MLLE. GOUDERT BY THE
ITALIAN CONSUL.

The Italian Consul General, who was mentioned in yesterday's *Herald* as having forwarded a letter to Mlle. Goudert, the French governess who threw herself from the roof of the residence of Henry O. Bonnell, at Youngstown, Ohio, Monday, could throw little light on the mystery of the case.

I called at the office of the Consulate yesterday and saw the Consul General. It had been presumed that the letter forwarded to the unfortunate young woman was a love letter. He said that such was not the case, although he was unable to say what the nature of the communication was. All he knew of Mlle. Goudert she had told him herself.

Said he: "Mlle. Goudert came to my office at the same time she applied to Mme. Coyriere and requested me to secure a position for her. It was evident that she was mentally off her balance. She was troubled in spirit and I was so impressed with the nature of doing something to aid her that I urged her to return to her home in France. I insisted on furnishing her a passage. She declined, however, to accept tickets and said she desired to secure employment in this country. Her father, she said, is a judge somewhere in the north of France. I do not recollect the place.

"While I was endeavoring to get a position for her Mme. Coyriere obtained the place to which she but recently went. Now I learn of her death. I am unable to judge of the cause of her suicide."
New York [NY] Herald 21 November 1888: p. 5

There is no mention by Mrs. Dick of any suicide attempt with laudanum. *De mortuis....*"speak no ill of the dead."

"Alas," said Mrs. Dick and the Consul, who knew how to be discreet, "We know nothing about Mademoiselle; Mademoiselle knew no one in New York; had no friends in this country; no, there is no explanation whatever for her death."

I shall be less discreet. "Who is this Count?" asked the *New York Herald*. One possibility is the Count Paolo Emile Thaon di Revel, who is the only Italian Vice Consul of the right time period with this rank. In 1882, Consul-General Raffo gave "a reception and dinner to the Vice-Consul, the Count Thaon de Revel and his bride, at their pleasant apartments." Is it possible that Raffo, who called personally to deliver a letter for Mlle. Goudart, was covering for his associate? Or was there another Count (or a man claiming a title he did not possess to impress a young woman) at the Consulate? And who was the blonde man in the inscribed photograph? We will never know.

At the end of January, 1889, Mlle. Gaudart's casket was taken from the vault and buried in a single Catholic plot at Calvary Cemetery. Her father wrote Probate Judge Wilson to thank the people of Youngstown and the Elks for looking after the burial of his daughter, but regretted that he was not financially able to bear the expense of having the body sent to France. Or did the family not want a daughter whose death hinted of scandal to lie in the family plot?

A suicide so young, so beautiful, so cloaked in mystery must, inevitably, become a ghost. A little over a year after her sensational death, it was said that the ghost of Mlle. Gautard, robed in white, began to walk at the site of her death. In this article, the date of her death has already been forgotten.

THE GHOST WALKS.
YOUNGSTOWN PEOPLE SAY THEY HAVE SEEN MLLE. GAUTARD'S SPOOK

Youngstown, Dec. 8. It is rumored here that the ghost of Mlle. Gautard, the beautiful and cultured French governess who suicided at Henry Bonnell's residence last spring, by throwing herself out of an attic window, has been seen quite often lately on cloudy but moonlit nights walking in the vicinity of the spot where she met her horrible and untimely death. The spector is reported to be clad in white, with her wealth of auburn tresses falling gracefully over her shoulders. She walks with a slow, measured tread, with head bowed and always muttering a prayer or singing a chant which is unrecognizable—probably because it is recited in French. The marble-like form disappears when approached, or when the clouds break away and reveal the moon's bright light. Timid women and children are afraid to pass that way at night and more than one responsible person claims to have seen the French girl's ghost.
Plain Dealer [Cleveland, OH] 9 December 1889: p 1

The site of the Bonnell home is now under the Madison Avenue Expressway, which borders Youngstown State University. The story of the tragic young Frenchwoman seems perfect for a campus legend. But I can find no other stories of her spirit walking.

All who loved her are now dead, but Mlle. Gautard still sleeps at Calvary Cemetery, far from home. There is no stone to mark the final resting place of this beautiful and melancholy young woman who died—for what?
For love?
Or of dashed hopes?

Let us at least give her an epitaph:

> La mort et la beauté sont deux choses profondes.
> Death and beauty are two things profound.
>
> – Victor Hugo –

SOURCES: *Daily Telegram* [Youngstown, OH] 21 November 1888; *Vindicator* [Youngstown, OH] 22 November 1888: p. 2; *Daily Telegram* [Youngstown, OH] 23 November 1888; *Cleveland [OH] Leader* 23 November 1888: p. 2; *Cleveland [OH] Leader* 25 November 1888: p. 2; *New York Herald* [New York, NY] 27 November 1888: p. 7; *Vindicator* [Youngstown, OH] 28 November 1888: p. 5; *Telegram* [Youngstown ,OH] 28 November 1888: p. 2; *Vindicator* [Youngstown, OH] 29 November 1888: p. 7; *Plain Dealer* [Cleveland, OH] 7 January 1889: p. 2; *Plain Dealer* [Cleveland, OH] 26 January 1889: p. 4

10.

The Malice of Inanimate Objects:
A Haunted Telegraph, the Murderer's Clock, and a Hoodoo Chair

Many common objects may be made the vehicles of retribution, and where retribution is not called for, of malice. Be careful how you handle the packet you pick up in the carriage-drive, particularly if it contains nail-pairings and hair. Do not, in any case, bring it into the house. It may not be alone.

– M.R. James –

Possessed possessions are the ghost trend of the moment. There are television shows about demon-infested objects and the people who collect them. Ebay is full of haunted dolls and ghosts in bottles. (One used to have to summon multiple Oxford-educated parsons to conjure a bad spirit into a bottle, but now it can be done in the click of a Paypal button!) Yet haunted objects are nothing new: the people of the past had their doubts about the Ouija board and planchette, were superstitious about letting clocks run down, and it was common knowledge that some objects were simply unlucky, like this hoodoo chair:

EVERYONE AFRAID OF THIS HOODOO CHAIR

There's a "right smart" rocking chair, a "jolly, comfortable" rocking chair—these characteristics are acknowledged by its enemies—standing disconsolated and unoccupied out in Blanchester, Ohio.

No one will accept it and the responsibility of it is driving Edward Hawk, its owner, away from home. It's a hoodooed chair, that's what it is, and all its fine paint and inviting spaciousness cannot cover up the fact.

Why, the very first day it was placed in Edward Hawk's hotel, along with some fifteen or twenty other brand-new chairs, it became a seat of ill omen. William Rockhill, the first man to occupy this rocker, was found dead in it. To be sure, he had long suffered from heart trouble and no one attached any particular importance to the suddenness of his death, nor was the chair given a bad name because of this unfortunate occurrence. No one felt that the chair could rightfully be held responsible for Mr. Rockhill's death. But that was many moons ago, and now Rockhill's sudden decease heads a long list of mishaps in which the chair played an important part—such an important part it looks queer—queer for the chair.

No wonder Mr. Hawk pleads with every new acquaintance to relive him of this unlucky bit of furniture, and it is not very much to be wondered at, either, that no one will avail himself of this opportunity to secure a "fine, comfortable rocking chair free" for here is the record of this strange hoodoo:

> One man found dead in it.
> One man's head cut, body bruised, arm fractured by it.
> One man pitched on his face out of it.
> One man's glasses broken and finger mashed by it.
> One woman thrown out of it.
> One baby found under it.
> One dog knocked senseless by it.
> One man's collar bone broken by it.
> One man pushed down stairs by it.
> Eleven other minor accident caused by it.

"Why don't you chop it up for kindling, Hawks?" is the usual question after this fearful record has been digested and the chair declined with thanks.

CAN'T BE "SMASHED."

"Chop it up for kindling!" snorts Hawk. "Why, I can't smash the blamed thing any more than I can smash the hoodoo. I took it out in the back yard the other day—couldn't get one of the men about the place to touch it—and tried to send it to kingdom come. I was swearing mad at the crazy thing, it was ruining my trade, my disposition, and my appetite. Will you believe it, sir, the very first blow I aimed at its murderous back the ax flew off the handle and hit me such a whack on the shoulder I was lame for a week. I'll acknowledge I was some scared and I gave up trying to turn the chair into fire wood. All foolishness, of course," Hawk continues in a changed voice, remembering that he is trying to get rid of the chair. "You're welcome to it, sir, it's all foolishness about its being hoodooed, and I'm sure it's as comfortable a chair as I ever sat in."

Of course, Hawk's own attitude towards the chair ruins his chances of disposing of it, and this very slim chance is made even slimmer by the attitude of the attendants.

Sun Dent, the porter, describes a wide circle around the chair in cleaning the room and the spot of carpet which it covers goes unswept. Small wonder, for Dent was the first victim of this mysterious hoodoo. It was in August, shortly after the chair arrived, in fact, several mornings after Mr. Rockhill had been found dead in it, that Dent started to carry the chair from the reception room to the porch.

He declares that just as he reached the door the chair gave him a vicious shove, knocked him over, gave him a severe scalp wound and bruised his shoulder. Just how much the chair was responsible for these injuries cannot be ascertained, but the fact remains that the accident happened, and there was nothing about but the chair for Dent to stumble over.

About three weeks after Dent's accident Edward Crossland, a traveling salesman, seated himself in the chair to have his boots shined by Harrison, the hotel's bootblack, when, according to both Crossland and Harrison, the chair, without warning, pitched forward, toppled Crossland out on top of Harrison, knocking the wind out of the latter and fracturing his arm, and giving the former a severe shaking up.

Despite Dent's accident, the chair was considered of good repute until the Harrison-Crossland knockabout. After that strange stories commenced to be whispered about concerning it.

Harrison marked it with a white cross and declared that the chair was bewitched, showing his own wounds and telling of Dent's battered head and Rockhill's death to substantiate his charge. From then on the chair was considered a thing of ill omen, and all the attendants breathed freer when it was removed from the house to the front piazza, where the wayfarers are accustomed to spend restful evenings rocking and smoking and swapping experiences.

It had no sooner made its appearance on the piazza among the other respectable chairs than trouble was in the air. It seems that is just cannot keep its silly legs where they belong, and when Frederic Schwartz, of Cincinnati, settled himself comfortable in it to enjoy an after-dinner cigar and his newspaper, it kicked up its rockers and spilled Schwartz on the floor, giving him a playful bat on the head which laid him unconscious. It also slapped him on the arm, breaking a bone, and punched him on the head, effecting a bad bruise. Examination revealed the white cross and proved the identity of the chair.

HOODOO NOW SETTLES ON CHAIR

After this it was openly stated that the chair was hoodooed and all urged its owner to get rid of it. Hawk is young and has a healthy mind free from superstition, so he ridiculed the idea of a hoodoo and declared that he would keep the chair and live to hear it praised. That was before the antics of this rocker became personal. Less than a week after Schwartz received his spill someone had carried the chair out on the lawn and Mike Brannigan, who was weeding, stumbled over the chair and broke his collar bone. Still Hawk retained his faith in the chair and wondered what made humans so clumsy. The following day Mrs. Clarence Haynes, a patron of the hotel, caught her gown in the chair, fell down four steps, tearing her dress and receiving severe bruises.

A few days later "Bill" Gregory, one of Mr. Hawk's nephews, was trying to play horse with the chair in the lobby, when it turned over on top of him and imprisoned him on the floor. His uncle rushed to his assistance and found the boy unhurt, the heavy portion of the chair having missed him. He was badly frightened, and Hawk, despite his laughing over the superstition, declared that if the chair was going to jump on "Bill" he would break it up.

By that time all of the negroes employed around the hotel had a superstitious dread of the arm rocking chair with the odd tilt to the back and many of the residents of the town came to look at it out of curiosity. So many accidents had been connected with it that several persons declared that while they were not a bit superstitious it was just as well not to take any chances.

A short time after the accident of Mrs. Haynes, Dave Downing, a grocery salesman, weighing about 200 pounds, came to the hotel. He laughed over the story of the hoodoo that surrounded the chair, and that evening he called out: "Sun, bring me that hoodooed chair." "No, sah," said Sun," I ain't gwine to touch dat dar chair."

So Dave brought it himself, and in bringing it he fell over it, down stairs and into the street, hurting himself severely. Still game and trying to laugh, despite his bruises, he carried the chair up the stairs and sat down on it. He was recovering from the bruises and shock incident to his fall and started to lean back, when the chair slid from under him and dropped him to the floor with a thud, his head striking the wall and floor. That was enough for Downing. He acknowledged the hoodoo while he ruefully rubbed his head.

After that Hawk ordered the chair to the garret. That night there was a fire in the garret—and the fire started in the cane seat of the hoodooed chair. Possibly a match had worked into the chair and lighted in some way or a lingering spark from Downing's cigar had fallen into the cane when he fell. The fire was discovered, just in time to prevent a bad blaze in the garret, and the chair was brought downstairs and soaked after which it was given to Riley Andrews, a farmer from Pleasant Plain, who loaded it into his wagon and drove away, declaring he didn't believe in hoodoos and that his wife would be tickled to death to get the chair. Two days later he returned the chair, demanding that Hawk take it back, as his small son had toppled over in it and broke an arm.

CAN'T BREAK IT UP;

Then it was that Hawk took it into the backyard and started to break it up, but as he struck the first blow the head of the ax flew off and fell on his shoulder, so he gave up the attempt. Then Hawk gave it to Will Devers, who was newly married and furnishing his house—but Devers brought it back, declaring that the chair moved around in the dark and threw him down and walked on him.

After that Hawk kept the chair out on the sidewalk, but as everybody in town knew its ill repute it has remained there at intervals ever since. Three times it has been given away and each time it has been brought back with new calamities added to its list. It has come to be an advertisement for the hotel—but, despite that, the proprietor is anxious to give it to anyone who will promise that it will never be returned. He declares that the chair is driving away his friends and patrons and may force him to quit the town to rid himself of it if someone doesn't come to the rescue.

Philadelphia [PA] Inquirer 7 January 1906: p. 2 CLINTON COUNTY

NOTE: Initially this sounded to me like a spoof story, but Mr. Hawk was a very real hotel keeper in Blanchester. Perhaps it was a publicity stunt?

A MUSICAL SPOOK.
PORTSMOUTH IS AGAIN STIRRED UP OVER
A GHOST
WHO PLAYS THE VIOLIN AND GETS DISORDERLY

Portsmouth, Sept. 7. James Hodge, who lives in the Minford Clifford property on Scioto Heights in Nile Township, is responsible for a wild and weird story of uncanny spirits and goblins.

Hodge, who is a prosperous farmer and of more than ordinary intelligence, states that while he does not believe in spirits there have been occurrences at his house that are beyond his ability to explain.

Every night for about two weeks he and his wife were awakened by the music of a violin. For several nights they did not pay much attention to it, except to wonder who was the minstrel abroad at such an unseasonable hour. As Hodge himself was at one time considered to be a violinist the excellent playing of the unknown excited his admiration.

About a week ago they were surprised and alarmed to discover that the music was confined to his house. They made a careful search, and for more than two hours they pursued the music over the house, searching every room for the supposed intruder, but without success. The same scene was repeated the succeeding night. Wednesday night Mr. Hodge who had become exasperated, shouted to the unknown violinist to "Break the ___ thing." Instantly the music sounded louder and with a harsher tone, followed by a resounding crash in the closet in the room the farmer was occupying. He and his wife immediately ran to it, but could find nothing disordered or that would give a clew to the solution of the mystery. But the music had ceased.

Yesterday Mrs. Hodge, in searching a chest in the closet, discovered that Hodge's old violin, which had for years lain undisturbed at the bottom of the box, or chest, was smashed as if struck by an ax. The violin had not been used for so long by the owner that he had forgotten its existence. But he cannot explain the music.

Plain Dealer [Cleveland, OH] 8 September 1895: p. 12 SCIOTO COUNTY

In *The Face in the Window: Haunting Ohio Tales*, the title story told of the strange faces that appeared in window glass around Ohio in the 1870s. Here are two more cases of those mysterious faces in the glass. They follow the exact pattern that this phenomenon exhibited: they developed slowly and cannot be erased.

A QUEER STORY

The *Conneaut Citizen* gives the following account of a phenomenon (or a trick) now visible on a pane of glass at Ashtabula, Ohio:

One of the most singular occurrences we have heard of is the profile of a man upon a window pane on the north side of a house at Ashtabula Harbor, occupied at present by Mr. Charles Lynn. D.B. Geary visited the place on Thursday, for the purpose of gratifying his curiosity, and reports as follows: The outlines of this strange picture were first noticed some six weeks ago, gradually being developed, until on the occasion of his visit, the profile was perfect, and the expression of the eye particularly sharp and clear. Mr. Geary states that while looking at it there seemed to be no escape from the stare: get in what position you will, the eye seems to rest upon you with piercing sharpness.

The profile represents a man of middle age, very heavy, full beard, with turn-down collar. Some days ago Mr. Lynn sold the sash containing this profile to a gentleman for the sum of $25. Upon being removed from its position in the house no trace of the strange picture could be seen, but upon being replaced it was as plain to the eye as before. This marvel is attracting people by hundreds, the road to and from the house being constantly thronged with visitors, anxious to witness the sight. Hon. B.F. Wade and lady are among those who visited the place. Mr. Geary states that all attempts to wash it off have been without the least effect, although the strongest acids have been applied.

Macon [GA] Weekly Telegraph 8 August 1871: p. 1 ASHTABULA COUNTY

NOTE: This is a particularly interesting face in the window story since the face disappeared when the glass was removed. One wonders if this property of the images—a tendency to vanish when moved from their original position—is why none have survived or have been recognized? The Hon. B.F. Wade represented Ohio in the United States Senate.

THE MYSTERIOUS PHOTOGRAPH.

Lawrence, Ohio, has been treated to a first-class sensation lately:

It seems that a curious discovery was made quite lately on the glass of an attic window, in a two-story house in Lawrence of the face of a female, with flowing hair, and partly covering two panes of glass, the face being entirely in one, and the hair flowing into the other pane. The appearance is that of a faded photograph, though everything is perfectly visible. The question is, how came the face on the window? Nobody knows; nobody can give a more rational answer than that it may have been photographed by lightning, unbeknown to the lady who was sitting in front of the window during a thunder storm. When first discovered the face was thought to resemble an elderly lady who had just been buried from the house, and it was immediately worked up into a first class ghost story, and regarded as a wonderful spirit manifestation. But subsequent examinations have failed to discover any resemblance to the departed elderly lady, whose ghost it was supposed to be; and rather inclined people to believe it to be the face and head of a young woman. Thus the mystery remains unsolved. The face and head of a female have

certainly made their appearance on common window glass, and nobody can tell whence they came, nor how the picture was made.
Union [Houston, TX] 13 October 1870: p. 1 STARK COUNTY

The next story of a fiery hand searing the wallpaper during a wake is quite an unusual one. Was the wallpaper glue spontaneous combusting? If so, that does not explain the hand of fire witnesses saw. Was it some form of ball lightning perhaps tracking metals in the ink of the wallpaper? There are stories from Catholic countries about linens scorched by the burning hand of a soul in Purgatory, but we know nothing about the religious beliefs of this family.

SAW A FIERY HAND
WATCHERS IN A CHAMBER OF DEATH VERY MUCH FRIGHTENED

Midway between Mechanicsburg, Ohio, and the neighboring village, Catawba, a something ghostly has been creating a stir. The house is upon the Springfield Pike, and is a neat appearing two-story frame house of modern architecture. It is in the interior of this house that the ghostly scenes are enacted. The last person who occupied the house with his family was a gentleman of the name of Prentiss, but himself and family remained no longer than they could help. A little child of Mr. Prentiss died, and several of the intimate friends of the family were sitting up with the remains. The occasion afforded the first intimation of a ghostly vision about the premises.

It was about 12 o'clock at night, and the occupants of the room sat dozing from their vigil, when with a muffled exclamation, one of the ladies arose from the chair, and, with a trembling hand, pointed toward one of the walls of the room. Seemingly a hand of fire had suddenly appeared upon the wall. The hand first appeared near the ceiling, but did not remain motionless. With the index finger again pressed against the papered wall the hand moved downward until the floor was reached. It then returned to the ceiling and back again, making six perpendicular visits downward and upward, after which it disappeared and was seen no more that night.

What it meant no one could tell or conjecture. Upon examining the wall where the hand had traveled another strange sight was disclosed. Lines, the width of an average adult finger, were upon the wall in the track the fiery finger had pursued, and along each line the wall paper appeared as though seared with a red hot iron. It is not ascertained whether any unaccountable noise occurred during the manoeuvres of the mysterious hand, as the living occupants of the room fled in terror. Although the house is not now occupied, it is supposed that the hand of fire is still at work, as visitors to the house during the day notice additional tracks where it is supposed the hand had traveled and the same seared appearance of the wall paper.

How long the mysterious proceedings will continue is, of course, unknown, but at the present time it appears as though the hand of fire is going to leave its mark upon every inch of paper on the wall.
Repository [Canton, OH] 23 January 1892: p. 11 CHAMPAIGN/CLARK COUNTY

HAUNTED CLOCK
STOPS EVERY MORNING AT THE HOUR WHEN DESPERADO WAS ELECTROCUTED

On Police Inspector Rowe's desk at the Central Police Station stands a pretty Dresden clock. It is quite old, but is an exceedingly pretty piece of bric-a-brac.

"There is something queer about this clock," related the Inspector yesterday. "And there are two men in this department, who, while denying that they are superstitious, keep their eye on that timepiece. I obtained it at the sale of the Ruthven affects. And do you know that ever since I have had it, it always stops a few minutes before 1 o'clock in the morning. That is the hour Ed Ruthven was executed. Ruthven before his death swore that he would wreak vengeance on Patrolman Charles Smith and Sergeant of Detectives Doran for their activity in his capture and prosecution.

"His wife, Lizzie Ruthven, also declared that she would carry out the wish of her husband relative to these two men. She was sent to the penitentiary for a long term for her participation in the crimes of her husband, but escaped and is still at large. I can't explain why the clock always stops at the same place at night, but the fact remains that it does, while during the daytime the hands pass the place on the dial without the least hesitation.

"I have noticed that both Doran and Smith are quite anxious that the clock be kept going, and if I don't wind it myself every morning and start it, one of them will surely do it. They declare that they have no belief in omens or anything of that sort, but they say they want that clock kept going."

Patrolman Smith, at whom Ruthven took careful aim during the fight with the police which preceded Ruthven's escape from the city, cares little about discussing the clock.

"I just want it to keep going," he said. "I feel easier, that is all."

And then growing a little more confidential, Smith told of another little token connected with the capture, trial and conviction of the noted desperado. Ruthven shot and killed Patrolman Shipp, who, with Patrolman Dangler, had surprised him burglarizing a Charles Street residence early one evening.

Inspector Rowe is of the opinion that the majority of men are victims of some sort of superstitious dread.

"I once had a knife," he said, "which had been used by a man who committed suicide in the old Prospect House. It was of excellent steel and took a splendid edge. I liked it and wanted to keep it. When asked to loan a knife, I invariably tendered that one, not forgetting to inform the borrower of its history. It was always returned promptly. On one occasion I forgot to repeat its history to a borrower, and that is the time I lost it. Now tell me why all the rest were anxious to get rid of it as soon as possible, if it was not because they were superstitious?"

Cincinnati [OH] Enquirer 23 March 1904: p. 6 CUYAHOGA COUNTY

NOTE: Edward Ruthven was a burglar who shot Cleveland Police Officer Shipp May 6, 1900, as Shipp chased him down. Ruthven escaped, but was later arrested in Indiana after a desperate struggle with the police. He swore he would kill the Sergeant of Detectives and was confined in a cage during his trial so he could not make good on his threat. He was electrocuted June 28, 1901 at the Ohio Penitentiary. Lizzie Ruthven, who was seen as the brains of the duo in planning their criminal activities, was regarded as more dangerous than her husband. She had also sworn vengeance on the officers who had put her behind bars. With the help of a male convict who was in love with her, she scaled the walls of the Penitentiary and disguised herself as a man. I cannot find that she was ever recaptured.

I wondered about these next two contrasting stories about mysterious music, one perceived as a good omen and the other as a warning, both published in the same Arizona paper in the same year. Journalistic hoaxes or a macabre coincidence? It is difficult to say because the people, locations, and (non-supernatural) situations in both of them are real.

REGARD STRANGE MUSIC AS A GOOD OMEN

Springfield, Ohio, Oct. 11. A phenomenon occurred at the Arcade Hotel between 3 and 4 o'clock this morning. At that time Will Rockfield, son of Landlord H.L. Rockfield, was very ill and his life hung in the balance.

An electrical piano in the café, connected with the hotel, began playing. The café was closed at 11 o'clock and no one had been in there since that hour. The music was heard by the watchers at Rockfield's bedside and they looked at each other in amazement. The clerk was startled. At first he thought a porter had entered the café and started the piano. He went to the door, but found it locked. The piano kept on playing. The clerk unlocked the door and tried to stop the music but failed. Finally the wires connected with the piano were cut.

The phenomenon is regarded as a good omen, as Rockfield's condition is greatly improved.

Tucson [AZ] Daily Citizen 11 October 1907: p. 3 CLARK COUNTY

NOTE: H.L. Rockfield was noted as a hotel manager and was a very rich man, according to the papers, who also reported that his son Will was an invalid.

CHORDS ON A PIANO GIVE DEATH WARNING

Springfield, Ohio, July 9. Despondent because of ill-health Mrs. Margaret Baader, aged 32, of 98 Hubert Avenue, leaped from the fourth story of the City Hospital this morning and sustained injuries which resulted in her death an hour later. She alighted head-foremost on a gravel walk.

A peculiar occurrence, in connection with the death is related by a member of the family. About three weeks ago Mrs. Baader claimed to have heard musical tones coming from the piano at her home, and she became hysterical because she regarded the strange phenomenon as a warning of approaching trouble or death. She summoned her husband home from his work at the shop. On arriving Mr. Baader also claims to have heard the musical tones coming from the piano. He examined the instrument carefully to see whether mice had gotten into it, but could find nothing that would serve as an explanation of the strange occurrence.

On going to the hospital, it is believed that the woman brooded so over the strange "warning," as she termed it, that she was finally driven to suicide.

Tucson [AZ] Daily Citizen 9 July 1907: p. 1 CLARK COUNTY

NOTE: Here is an article from an Ohio paper about Mrs. Baader's suicide.

WOMAN LEAPT FROM HOSPITAL WINDOW.

Springfield, O., July 6. Mrs. Margaret Baader commited suicide by leaping from the fourth story window at the City hospital. Mrs. Baader became despondent, although she was recovering from an operation. She was 32 years old and the wife of A.L. Baader, of the Kelly Road Roller Company.

Repository [Canton, OH] 6 July 1907: p. 5

Ohioans were mentioned as having a particular interest in the "New Planchette" or "talking board."

THE NEW PLANCHETTE.
A MYSTERIOUS TALKING BOARD AND TABLE

"Planchette is simply nowhere," said a Western man at the Fifth Avenue Hotel, "compared with the new scheme for mysterious communication that is being used out in Ohio. I know of whole communities that are wild over the 'talking board,' as some of them call it. I have never heard any name for it. But I have seen and heard some of the most remarkable things about its operations—things that seem to pass all human comprehension or explanation."

"What is the board like?"

"Give me a pencil and I will show you. The first requisite is the operating board. It may be rectangular, about 18 x 20 inches. It is inscribed like this:

"The 'yes' and the 'no' are to start and stop the conversation. The 'good-evening' and 'good-night' are for courtesy. Now a little table three or four inches high is prepared with four legs. Anyone can make the whole apparatus in fifteen minutes with a jack-knife and a marking brush. You take the board in your lap, another person sitting down with you. You each grasp the little table with the thumb and forefinger at each corner next to you. Then the question is asked, 'Are there any communications?' Pretty soon you think the other person is pushing the table. He thinks you are doing the same. But the table moves around to 'yes' or 'no.' Then you go on asking questions and the answers are spelled out by the legs of the table resting on the letters one after the other. Sometimes the table will cover two letters with its feet, and then you hang on and ask that the table will be moved from the wrong letter, which is done. Some remarkable conversations have been carried on until men have become in a measure superstitious about it.

"I know of a gentleman whose family became so interested in playing with the witching thing that he burned it up. The same night he started out of town on a business trip. The members of his family looked for the board and could not find it. They got a servant to make them a new one. Then two of them sat down and asked what had become of the other table. The answer was spelled out, giving a name, 'Jack burned it.'

"There are, of course, any number of nonsensical and irrelevant answers spelled out, but the workers pay little heed to them. If the answers are relevant they talk them over with a superstitious awe. One gentleman of my acquaintance told me that he got a communication about a title to some property from his dead brother, which was of great value to him.

"It is curious, according to those who have worked most with the new mystery, that while two persons are holding the table a third person, sitting in the same room some distance away, may ask the questions without even speaking them aloud, and the answers will show they are intended for him. Again, answers will be returned to the inquiries of one of the persons operating when the other can get no answers at all. In Youngstown, Canton, Warren, Tiffin, Mansfield, Akron, Elyria, and a number of other places in Ohio I heard that there was a perfect craze over the new planchette. Its use and operation have taken the place of card parties. Attempts are made to verify statements that are made about living persons, and in some instances they have succeeded so well as to make the inquirers still more awe-stricken."

Evening Star [Washington DC] 17 April 1886: p. 3

A STRANGE THING

J.A. Long, of Akron, Ohio, told me today of a peculiar thing similar in character to planchette, with which the little manufacturing city in which he lives is bewildered. Its introduction there is something he does not know about, but he has a large family of children, and as the bewitched and mysterious pieces of mechanism made them all so nervous that they could hardly sleep at night, he knows where one particular machine went to. He smashed it up for kindling wood.

"The affair," said Mr. Long, "consisted of a regular board, which may be of any size, but was usually about two feet by eighteen inches, on which were placed all the letters of the alphabet. A little table with three legs on small rollers goes on the top of this board. Two persons sit down with their finger-tips on this table. One of them asks a question to which an answer is desired. Then they await the action of the little table to which their fingers are glued, as it were. It is certainly curious how that table will fly around at times. As the legs point out different letters on the board sentences are formed, which constitute the answer of the question propounded. You would not believe it unless you should operate it yourself, what wonderful and strikingly pertinent answers are made. The whole town has been filled with the machines, but I smashed the one at my house."

Macon [GA] Telegraph 26 February 1886: p. 6 SUMMIT COUNTY

The papers frequently ran stories of the foolish things people did under the influence of the Ouija board or planchette.

A young Ohio couple left home the day of their marriage, a fortnight ago, for Chicago, going by a lake boat, on board of which was a jolly crowd of all sorts of people, with some of whom the young farmer and his wife were quite familiar. On the trip the wife proposed a trial of planchette with a young gallant, and the machine told her that she should accept him. She was by training a free lover, and accepted.

When the boat touched at Milwaukee, they quietly disappeared on shore, and took the cars south. A purse of $1000 she had taken from her husband, and her mother's diamond ring passed into the hands of the gay seducer, who went forward into a smoking car and left with the conductor a note advising her to return to her "hubby."

So much for planchette.

New London [CT] Democrat 30 September 1871: p. 1 LAKE ERIE

NOTE: "Free Love," as the readers of this article would have understood it, was a doctrine that women should be free to choose their partners and not be the property of men in marriage. It was strongly associated with the Spiritualists and the women's rights movement.

GHOSTS
RULE HIS WIFE ENTIRELY,
ACCORDING TO THE STORY OF THE
COLUMBUS ARTIST
WHO SAYS SHE CONSULTS THE "OUIJA" BOARD

Chicago, March 18. Declaring that ghosts rule his wife and that her actions are controlled absolutely by the mysterious powers and commands of a weird "Ouija" board, Artist Franz B. Aulich, of Columbus, Ohio, to-day began action in the Circuit Court to get possession of his six-year-old daughter Marguerite, and to keep her from the influence of her mother.

In his demand for custody of the child Aulich declared that his wife's mind is deranged by her belief in this weird society.

Divorce separated the Aulichs last August when the man, with a studio in the Auditorium Building, was held by the Judge to have been cruel to his wife. Now the woman has been summoned from Columbus, Ohio, where she has been visiting, to make immediate answer to her former husband's charges.

When in Chicago Mrs. Aulich lives at 1170 Washington Boulevard, in a home given her by her husband when they separated last year. Her little daughter has been in her custody since the divorce.

For a few weeks after the divorce decree was entered, according to Aulich, the provision in the decree that he should see his daughter at reasonable times was respected by his former wife. Then the visits of the child to his studio grew fewer in number, and upon the "Ouija" board has been placed the blame for the trouble over the child.

Mrs. Aulich, her husband charges, consults the board in reference to all her transactions, and governs her conduct toward her child and himself by the result indicated by the wavering finger of the mysterious board. The result has been, the man says, entirely to separate him from his child for months.

Cincinnati [OH] Enquirer 19 March 1905: p. 1 FRANKLIN COUNTY

We began this chapter with a malevolent chair and have worked our way through planchette follies. Let us close it with a haunted telegraph with a more benign, but still troubling purpose: to communicate a final message.

A WEIRD EXPERIENCE
A TELEGRAPHER'S REMARKABLE MESSAGE FROM A SPOOK
DOTS AND DASHES OVER AN INSTRUMENT WITH NEITHER WIRES NOR BATTERY
A STORY TOLD BY A MAN WHOSE VERACITY IS VOUCHED FOR
A FRIGHTENED OPERATOR

One of the wildest, weirdest stories of the supernatural that has ever come under the experience of mortal man is told by R.H. Field, the Big Four telegraph operator at South Side station.

Mr. Field is a very intelligent and conscientious man, and he relates his fearful experience with a candor and earnestness that almost make one believe it in spite of its extreme improbability.

"I have been a telegraph operator for twenty-two years. I have told my story to at least a hundred people, and I have never met one yet who would believe that it was an actual fact. I know that it will be a severe test on your credulity, but my experience is Gospel truth. I want you to understand that I have never, and do not now, believe in the supernatural. I have never attended a spiritualistic séance in my life, and am rather inclined to accept the philosophy of Colonel Ingersoll."

Mr. Field was quite reluctant about telling his story for publication, but finally consented to do so. He is an entertaining talker, and related the great event of his life with an ease that showed that he had told it before. "It was several years ago," he began, "when I was much younger than I am now. I was assigned to night duty at a little station called Evansburg, in Pennsylvania, on the New York, Pennsylvania and Ohio railroad. I hadn't been around the world very much, but flattered myself that I had a good deal of mechanical genius. The office was in charge of an old fogy sort of a fellow named Jones. The telegraph instrument got out of adjustment, and I knew something about repairing it. Jones suggested that I take to my home an old-fashioned relay box and fix it up.

"Glad of the opportunity to show what I could do I carried the box to my boarding house one morning and put it on a shelf in an old cupboard and went to bed intending to fix it after my sleep was over. I had been in bed but a few minutes and had not got to sleep when, to my surprise and astonishment, the armature, or what is otherwise known as the lever, on the instrument began ticking. I was perfectly amazed

and thought there must be some mistake. To satisfy myself that I had
not been carried away by my imagination, for the ticking was faint and
subdued, I got out of bed and with fear and trembling opened the cupboard door. I took the instrument in my hand and it continued to work.
I put it on the table, but the sound it made was unintelligible. I turned
the spring so that there would be less resistance, and then, in as clear
and perfect Morse as I ever heard, the invisible person, spirit or whatever it was wrote:

"'Do you get me?'"

I was so overcome that I involuntarily answered, 'Yes,' without
putting it on the instrument. The unknown heard me, for again, in the
beautiful writing, it continued.

"'Thank God, at last! My name is Charles Blake. I am an old timer.
My parents, who reside in Mount Pleasant, Ia., have lost me. They don't
know what my fate has been. I want you to write to my father, Homer
Blake, at Mount Pleasant, Ia., and inform him that I died at Shreveport,
Tex., of yellow fever, on—'. I have forgotten the date, but it was several
years prior to the date of this communication. I was frightened to
death. My hair stood on end. My boarding house was two miles from
the telegraph station, and there was no battery nearer than the station,
and there was no telegraph wire of any kind in that vicinity. I was a little
dubious about the communication, from the other world or somewhere,
I will not undertake to say. Before venturing to write to Homer Blake
as directed I picked up a Western Union tariff book which I had in my
room to see if there was such a town as Mount Pleasant, Ia. I found that
there was such a place, a fact that I did not know before, and that it was
located on the Chicago, Burlington and Quincy railroad.

"To satisfy myself and not be taken in, I wrote a letter to the postmaster at Mount Pleasant and asked him if he knew of anyone in that
vicinity named Homer Blake and to give me what information he could
without telling him what I wanted it for. A few days later I received a
reply, and I have his letter somewhere among my effects, in which he
said that Homer Blake had lived in Mount Pleasant some years before,
but that he had moved away, to what place he did not know. Blake, he
informed me, had two sons, one of whom, Charles, was supposed to be
dead, and the other was a grain merchant in the far west."

"Did you not pursue your investigations further?"

"No, I did not. The truth is I was scared to death. I worked that
wire for eighteen months. Every time I took off the relay it made the
same peculiar noise and worked in a sputtering sort of a way, and to

show that there must have been some hidden or occult force it crossed the other wires. Every once in a while I used to ask Jones if he heard the noise, and he laughed at me. He never believed my story, although the reply from the postmaster at Mount Pleasant somewhat staggered him. I was actually so afraid to take the relay off that my hair used to stand on end, and I never had any further communication with the hidden force that called itself Charles Blake. I shall never forget that experience as long as I live. People look so incredulous and are so apt to believe me a crank when I tell it that I never relate it any more unless I am asked to do so."

Mr. Field lives with his wife at South Side. He is well known in this city and has the reputation of being a truthful and sensible man. There is no doubt in the world that he sincerely thinks that he was talked to on that old instrument without wire or battery, and he declares most solemnly that it could not have been a matter of fancy.

This article first appeared in the *Cincinnati [OH] Enquirer,* 31 July 1892: p. 17. This version appeared in the *Plain Dealer* [Cleveland, OH] 8 September 1892: p. 6 HAMILTON COUNTY

NOTE: Colonel Ingersoll was Robert G. Ingersoll, 19th-century lawyer, orator and agnostic, dubbed "the most noted of American infidels."

11.

A Soul-Freezing Shriek:

Ghostly Noises

One thing I don't like about [spooks] is their rotten taste in music. They always play tambourines...And the spooks are so careless with their instruments. They throw them around the room promiscuously...A well-aimed tambourine can do a lot of damage, even in a perfectly genteel séance.

– Roy K. Moulton –
Repository [Canton, OH] 25 May 1922: p. 4

While the majority of the ghosts of the past are apparitions, a surprising number of hauntings involve only mysterious noises: the groans, moans, and shrieks of the classic chain-rattling spirit, as well as howls, sobs, gurgles, and music. Close your eyes, and listen...

DECLARE GHOST MIDNIGHT GUEST
BIG FOUR EMPLOYEES TERRIFIED BY MOANS AS OF HUMAN IN AGONY OF DEATH
DECLARE "SPOOK" ECHOES CRY OF WORKMAN KILLED NEAR FREIGHT HOUSE

Big Four railroad employees stationed in the vicinity of the Front St. crossing have been getting goose flesh, losing sleep, taking nerve medicine and trembling over terrifying humanlike moans which rend the midnight air every Sunday in that locality.

The uncanny wails, Michael Weir, flagman at Front Street, says have been causing him no end of uneasiness for the past two months. Joe Domley, night watchman at the freight house has been carrying a bigger stick since the moaning, as he calls it, first became apparent and Miss May Murphy, night telephone operator in the freight house declares she has been thrown into hysterics on more than one occasion by the uncanny sounds, which seem to have no permanent place of origin.

Jess Millard and Frank Kennedy of the Lake Shore police say they have tried for weeks to unearth the mystery, which is growing on the nerves of many, but all efforts to locate the genesis of this nocturnal phenomenon have been baffled.

Those who heard the spook-like groans say they resemble those of a human being in the death agony. They bob up first from one place and then another. It appears from the descriptions given to come from the spirit of some restless person, who in life could not stand still long enough to get a check cashed. In fair and foul weather, above the noise of grinding wheels upon heavy rails, it is said, the sound comes regularly and punctually about midnight.

Those who keep accurate track of such things declare the ghost of an ore handler, who was run over and killed at this spot Sunday night, Dec. 6, last, is haunting the place.

Plain Dealer [Cleveland, OH] 14 February 1910: p. 1 CUYAHOGA COUNTY

NOTE: I haven't been able to locate a specific 6 December 1909 accident, but there are newspaper reports of at least two ore handlers being killed in rail accidents in the second half of 1909.

Many hauntings consist exclusively of rappings and footsteps. Often these are ascribed to a murder victim, but it is unusual to have traces of a murder actually unearthed at the time of the manifestations.

LIVELY SPOOK.
CINCINNATI HAS A GHOST
A GHASTLY FIND

Cincinnati, Aug. 31. There is much excitement at No. 373 West Eighth Street, this city. The place is a fashionable boarding house, kept by a worthy and respected woman, who is much disturbed over the ghostly revelations. For some time the boarders have been much disturbed by inexplicable noises. Sudden and mysterious reports, as of a small explosion; knocks, rappings and other sounds. A vacant room gave out sounds as if someone walked with heavy stride back and forth across its carpetless widths. Investigation was fruitless of results.

Beneath the house the entire length is a cellar. It is never used, but the door is often found open. As no one ever goes into the cellar the wonder is who opens it. For several days workingmen have been about the house laying new pavements in the rear and repairing a brick wall. One of them, wanting some sand, went into the cellar, where some had been dumped on the muddy floor. In the dark he pushed his spade into the earth and found something not sand or mud. It was a bone. Further investigation by two young women boarders in the house, who braved the horrors of the situation, revealed the skeleton of a woman fairly well preserved except the hip bones. On the limbs some flesh still clung. There was nothing else. Not a clew to the crime of some past day. A more thorough search will be made today.

Plain Dealer [Cleveland, OH] 1 September 1895: p. 2 HAMILTON COUNTY

Was it spooks or dance-mad youngsters?

SPOOKS? OHIO CITY WILL INVESTIGATE LORAIN COUNCIL TO HUNT FOR VIOLIN GHOST AND OTHER MUSICAL GOBLINS

Lorain, Sept. 25. Musical spooks! Sh-h-h-h! The ghost of the violin, jazz skeletons, piano goblins, saxophone blues—they're all here—and they've worried Lorain residents so for the past week that a list of names went to city council petitioning that worthy body to conduct an investigation.

The mystery centers in the Century Park Dance Pavilion at the outskirts of the city.

The hall, standing majestically on the banks of Lake Erie, was, at one time, perhaps the most popular summer resort dancing rendezvous between Cleveland and Cedar Point.

But in the middle of the summer a state building inspector came and ordered the place closed. The floor was unsafe, he said, and in danger of collapse under the strain of a big crowd. The city safety director complied with the order.

The spirits of many a popular dance tune refused to die with the building inspector's edict.

In the still hours of the night, nearby residents assert, frequently can be heard the mystic moan of a saxophone, the tattoo of the drum, the sharp tone of a violin and the shuffling of feet.

But the hall, sitting off in a little grove, back nearly a hundred yards from the only thoroughfare in its vicinity, at such times is black as night.

The doors, one night for instance, were locked. There were no lights—no signs of life, but still came the strains of "Oh, By Jingo." And the mysterious shuffle of feet.

It would all happen, Edgar-Allan-Poe-like, around the hob-goblin hour of 12. In the daytime superstitious persons would pay the hall a visit.

They would find, as usual, no signs of life. The cobwebs still cobbed and "for rent" was on the door—merely that and nothing more

And then, again would come, again, the midnight music and the nocturnal dancers.

And now council has been asked to investigate.

Some night, councilmen won't tell the exact date, the city lawmakers will pay the place a visit.

Practically all of the councilmen have expressed themselves as unbelievers in ghosts and spooks

One councilman, who resides near the dance hall, blames a crowd of young people. He says they were disheartened when their dancing place was abolished.

"They are holding dances of their own, I believe you will find," he told other members of council.

Plain Dealer [Cleveland, OH] 26 September 1920: p. 45 LORAIN COUNTY

NOTE: I fully expected to find a sequel telling of the discovery of those young people holding their own dances, but it never appeared. "Oh, By Jingo" was a Tin-pan Alley hit just after the First World War.

Was there ever an old tavern *without* the ghost of a traveler murdered for his money and thrown down a well? However, this story has an unusual twist in a skeptical doctor seeing a dance going on upstairs and insisting on joining the party.

THE HAUNTED HOTEL
STRANGE SIGHTS AND SOUNDS IN AN OLD TAVERN
IN A NORTHERN OHIO COUNTY
A TRAVELER MURDERED FOR HIS MONEY
RETURNS IN GHOSTLY FORM AND MAKES
A DISTURBANCE

Toledo, O., Nov. 15. Not far from this city on a road passing through a well-improved part of the country stands a quaint, solitary and untenanted house with two wings known through all that part of the country as

"THE HAUNTED HOUSE"

The story is told that about fifty years ago when the hotel was kept by a Mr. Goster, a man stopped there with a large amount of money. He was known to have gone there but he was

NEVER SEEN AFTERWARDS

His horse was found loose in the road the next morning, but the man was never seen again. It was said afterward a young man caught Goster burying a corpse in the cellar of the house, but was bribed for $1,000 to say nothing about it. Goster afterwards died, it is said,

IN GREAT AGONY,

Trying to explain something but was unable to speak.

In 1837 or 1838 an advertisement appeared in a western paper inquiring for information concerning a man who started on a horseback journey to the west from Connecticut in 1835 or 1836. His name the writer withholds for reasons before mentioned. The notice stated that he had a large sum of money on his person with which to purchase land. He was heard from frequently until he left Cleveland, O., after which time no intelligence of him had been received. The description of the man corresponded with that of the well-dressed traveler who came to a sudden halt at the wayside inn. This dissipated every doubt concerning Goster's guilt, but nothing was done to bring the murderer to justice on account of his children, nor was the advertisement answered.

THE HAUNTED HOUSE

If the subsequent history, weird and unnatural, of the old deserted tavern were left out, the story would be very incomplete. If there is any such thing as a "haunted house" the old inn on the ridge is one. It is certainly haunted by traditional horror if not by ghosts. There are countless absurd and unfounded romances about the old tavern extant, but none but those from credible authority which have been accepted even by scoffers at supernatural occurrences will be given. Ever since the cloud lowered over the inn extraordinary and unaccountable noises have been heard and sights seen about it. The sound of a muffled hammer striking on the lid of an empty box or coffin has been heard about the house for fifty years. Music of incomparable sweetness has traveled from room to room at dead of night for half a century. There is one door in the building, that to the room the traveler is supposed to have met his death in, which has not been closed two minutes since the dark night in the fall of 1835. It will fly open as often as it is shut, regardless of any obstructions placed to resist it.

DEEP, AGONIZING GROANS

Have been heard at night emanating from various parts of the house for one and a half generations. A young lady then teaching school in the district nearest the tavern and whose reputation for veracity is absolutely unimpeachable went to Goster's to board. She had heard the ghostly tales told of the tavern, but being a woman of strong mind, they did not in the least intimidate her. In two days she left. At first she refused to converse on the subject of her experience in the hotel, but being besieged with questions as to what induced her to leave she found it necessary to make some disclosures to satisfy public curiosity. As if there for investigation, she requested to be assigned to the dreaded room. She said to a friend:

"I slept in the haunted tavern two nights. I shut and bolted the door to my room again and again, only to see it spring open without a touch from any visible agent. I heard a hollow thumping at short intervals throughout the night, which seemed to come from the cellar and travel upstairs until it reached the hall, receding in the same direction it came. The thumping was accompanied by deep, forced groans like the dying throes of a man throttled to death. I also heard sounds resembling the moving of chairs in the rooms off the hall. As to the origin of the frightful noises and the cause of the strange opening of the door, I express no opinion, but it is generally believed to be performed by the spirit of a man supposed to have been murdered in the room I occupied."

THE GHOSTLY DANCE.

There lived in the vicinity a physician who was a decided unbeliever in spirits of any description. He was a plain, blunt man, whose word was entirely trustworthy. He had covered the weird tales of the wayside inn with ridicule and done his best to falsify them. "I have gone past the tavern in the darkest of nights," he frequently said, "and never seen anything ghostly, although I have often invoked the spirits to come forth." One day he came to a neighbor in a sober and perplexed mood, and being asked the cause of his glum aspect, said: "What I tell you now, Mr. L___, is on my word as a man. Last night, which you remember was dark and stormy, as I was coming up the road on horseback, I saw the ballroom in Goster's hall lit up. The light streamed out of the windows, illuminating the yard and road. On closer observation I saw the forms of dancers flitting gaily about the room. 'A ball is in progress at Goster's; I will drop in,' I said to myself, spurring up my horse. As I approached the tavern the light shone brighter, and I heard the notes of the violin and flute and caught an occasional accent of the caller's voice. All was going merry as a marriage bell. I hitched my horse and lifted the door latch. Strange enough the barroom was dark and the door locked. I then tried the back doors but that too was fastened. By this time I was not a little vexed, and lifting my whip stock, I hammered lustily on the panel. Mr. Goster appeared in his nightclothes. 'You're a pretty landlord to be in bed when your house is full of merry company,' I said in a rallying voice. 'Let me go upstairs.' 'Don't know what you mean, doc,' he replied. 'There is no one in the house but the family, and we all sleep downstairs. Are you, too, trying to give my house a bad reputation? I did not think that of you.' Perplexed and out of patience I seized the lamp and said dictatorially, 'Follow me; we shall soon see.' He obeyed and I led the way up the dark and lonely stairs to the ballroom. I opened the door, but never was there a room more dark and silent, and never a more nonplussed man than myself. We descended. When I rode away the brilliancy and revelry had departed from the ballroom and all was as gloomy as we had left it." The doctor was ever afterward conservative on such subjects and never again repudiated the stories of the "haunted house on the ridge."

MYSTERIOUS SOUNDS.

When Goster died his wife built a fine dwelling about twenty rods from the tavern and moved into it, abandoning the hotel business and the hotel itself, although the latter was a very good and comfortable house. The place was rented, but the tenant did not inhabit the house three weeks. His rest was disturbed by the proverbial groans, pounding and music, and he declared that he would not live in the house for the whole farm. Another family took possession, but its occupancy was of short duration. Then it was offered free of charge to anyone who would dwell there. Three different families, considering themselves ghost-proof, moved in—among them a burly butcher, who "was not afraid of the devil himself"—but none of them remained three weeks. They all complained of the unnatural interventions and noises as reported. It was finally shut up entirely and has not been inhabited for many years.

The melancholy old inn is generally avoided after dark. Few pass it at night except with nervous step and a cold shudder. It is true that many of the spookish demonstrations could be explained by certain young [pranksters] bent on having fun at the expense of the superstitious, and it is said on good authority that a musician proficient in the art of ventriloquism, both vocal and instrumental, frequented the place for mischievous purposes. But in the mind of the public these facetious agents do not account for the extraordinary witchery of the "haunted house," and it is believed to this day that if the cellar and the well in the back yard were dried up the bones of the missing traveler would be found and the weird spell broken.

Plain Dealer [Cleveland, OH] 16 November 1885: p. 3 LUCAS COUNTY

The ghost hunters at the Hardin County Armory took painstaking precautions to trap their ghost—to no avail.

BUSY GHOST IN OHIO
HARDIN COUNTY ARMORY THE SCENE OF ITS OPERATIONS
SPOOK OPENS DOORS, WALKS THROUGH THE BIG HALL
WITHOUT LEAVING A MARK BEHIND HIM, AND LAUGHS AT WATCHERS

There are uncanny doings in the Hardin County Armory at Kenton, Ohio, and according to common report, the handsome structure is haunted. The Armory is used by Company I, Second Regiment, O.N.G. [Ohio National Guard] and the offices of the Hardin County Surveyor and Probate Judge are on the first floor. The building is lighted by electricity. The uncanny demonstrations consist of unearthly laughs, sounds as though heavy boxes were being dragged across the floor, and a number of similar demonstrations including a mysterious opening of locked doors.

A few evenings ago a party, consisting of William B. Strope, First Lieutenant, Company I, Corp. Ned F. Stevenson, William Alt, William Watson, Lucien Brown, and the *Chicago Inter Ocean* correspondent, made an investigation. In order to more easily detect any attempt at practical joking, the rope, by which the large arc lights which illuminate the drill floor are turned on and off, was carried up into the gallery, where the watchers took their station, leaving the drill floor vacant. By these means the arc light could be flashed on in a second, and every nook and cranny of the old floor lighted up brightly. Previous to turning out the lights the whole floor was gone over from cellar to roof, and every door and window tightly locked.

The watchers then retired to a small room off the gallery and waited. There was nothing doing until almost midnight. Suddenly one of the party said: "Look at that door!" Although it had been tightly latched, it was slowly swinging open as though some unseen force was pushing it. One of the party arose and, closing the door, stationed one man on the outside, while he saw that it was locked from the inside and the key removed. He had no more than taken his seat until it opened as before. This time it was allowed to swing all the way open, and as it struck the wall, out of the darkness of the drill floor came a laugh that can be described no other way than "nerve chilling." The man who held the rope that lighted the lamps gave a quick jerk. In his haste, both arcs and incandescents were thrown on, and with their brilliancy the laughter ceased. There was nothing whatever on the door. Although the nerves of the watchers were somewhat shaken, the lights were again turned out.

The lights were allowed to remain on for a few minutes and French chalk was spread all over the door. In spite of this, as soon as the examination was made the chalk was undisturbed by any footprints.

At this point another inspection was made of the locks on the doors and windows. There was no possible way for anyone in the building to escape. The party then went together and explored the whole building once more. Even a coal pile was turned over in the cellar, but nothing whatever could be found. While the party was downstairs the footsteps and other noises above them on the drill floor could be heard, but the chalk was again undisturbed.

The watch was continued until one o'clock in the morning in the storeroom. The noises continued at intervals and the door refused to stay shut unless there was a heavy box against it. As the party left the building the laughs re-echoed through the empty halls.

The spooky demonstrations began to be noticed last fall. The county engineer and a force of his men were at work late one night when they heard a noise in the main part of the building. Thinking that someone had broken in and was trespassing, they made a search but found nothing.

Washington [DC] Bee 24 May 1902: p. 6 HARDIN COUNTY

It is disturbing how often a ghost is a crying baby. I have seen and heard a number of them myself (for example, "A Ball at Columbian House" in *Haunted Ohio III*) and they are heartbreaking. This is a story from the 1914 *Dayton Daily News* ghost story contest. Does the child cry for its murdered father?

THE CRY OF A BABY

Several years ago when I was a small child, my father and mother lived in the country a few miles from town. This farm house had been known for many years as the haunted house, and that no one could live in it.

One day as Mother and I were sitting in the kitchen we heard a baby crying which frightened us so much we could not speak. After a while Mother asked me to go into the next room and see if there was a baby in there. On going in the room and looking around, I heard the same cry again, but could see nothing, so I returned to the kitchen and began my work.

Mother was sitting at the kitchen table and as the weather was very hot, she had taken off her shoes and stockings and was sitting with her feet under the table. All at once I heard someone say something to someone, so I looked around and under the table I saw a small baby playing at the feet of my mother. I started toward the little one but before I could get to it, the baby had disappeared.

When Father came in both of us told him of what we had seen and he only made fun of us. But Mother and myself had become so frightened that we said we were not going to stay at the place that night. But Father very brave decided he would stay during the night and see if he could see or hear anything. So he did, and about midnight Father was aroused from his sleep, by hearing music in the kitchen and the sound of voices talking, the sound of a baby crying. But Father had become so frightened that he could not move. After he had listened a while he heard at the foot of his bed two women talking in a very low conversation. The women, from what Father could hear, were talking over some trouble and seemed to grow angry at each other.

After a while the women went to the kitchen where the music had been heard, and when the two had entered the kitchen, Father heard the reports of a revolver and the cry of a woman. It is said that in this house there was a man killed, he was killed in the kitchen where the sound of music was heard. This man was the father of the baby that myself and Mother had heard crying in the morning. The father of this child is buried on the same farm, but no one had ever been able to find where he is laid. G.M.T.

Dayton [OH] Daily News 2 February 1914 MONTGOMERY COUNTY

This following story is an odd one; it combines several elements: the classic rappings of the poltergeist, a disembodied (and profane) voice (as heard in the mysterious Tennessee Bell Witch case), and, once again, a hidden treasure. This motif is often found in ghost and poltergeist cases and I associate it with Trickster spirits—the searchers are taunted and given clues and detailed rituals or instructions for getting the treasure, but they never find it.

A WICKED GHOST
EXCITING THE PEOPLE AT DELAWARE, OHIO
PROFANE IN HIS LANGUAGE AND PERSISTENT IN HIS RACKETS
THE SPIRIT CLAIMS TO BE FROM THE REGIONS OF THE DAMNED
AND HAS BEEN THERE FIFTY-EIGHT YEARS

Delaware, Ohio, November 1. For several days past this city has been considerably worked up over a so-called spiritual manifestation which has been presenting itself at the residence of some of our best citizens. The house where the spirit presents itself is a two-story frame house on Spring Street, and is occupied by the families of Dr. Main and Mr. Tom Crickard. The neighborhood is one of the best in our city. The families who occupy the house are among the best in this place, and up to the time of this demonstration had been the most decidedly sceptical on the question of Spiritualism.

The so-called ghost has been troubling them for several weeks, but they have kept quiet on the subject, fearing that the public would scoff at them and set them down for cranks. Several friends, however, having called, and the voice having talked to them from the walls, and having excited their curiosity, the matter has finally leaked out, and the neighborhood has become greatly worked up over the matter.

An *Enquirer* representative visited the house for the purpose of investigating the affair, and during a stay of half an hour, and despite repeated solicitations, was unable to get but one reply from the spirit. After several solicitations the spirit finally replied: "I am here," in a coarse, masculine voice. At the time we were there only ladies were present, and as there is no cellar in the house no one could have been concealed. A thorough search failed to reveal the source from which it came. The reporters were unable to get further replies from the spirit, but reliable parties state that the voice has said that it died fifty-eight years ago, and is now in hell. The voice is very profane, and says that although he is an imp of the devil, his parents were good people and are now in heaven. He claims that some $20,000 are buried under the house which is now on the site, although he says when he died it was occupied by a log-cabin.

The parties who occupy the house are greatly excited over the affair, and say they are unable to rest any time at all or to do any of their work, for as soon as they do so the spirits set up a rapping and use the most profane language ever heard. An investigation will be immediately set on foot to ascertain whether the causes are supernatural or otherwise. Whatever the cause may be, the interested parties are greatly excited, and the outcome of the investigation will be closely watched by all who are in possession of the facts in the case.

Cincinnati [OH] Enquirer 3 November 1884: p. 1 DELAWARE COUNTY

NOTE: This account seems like it should have been followed up with an exposure of a clever ventriloquist or spiteful adolescent, but I have not been able to find an end to the story.

A CONNEAUT GHOST STORY.
A SPRIGHTLY SPECTER THAT CARRIES A LIGHTED LANTERN UNDER ITS CLOAK

Conneaut, Feb. 3. Conneaut has a ghost, a real, bona fide ghost, and, though many persons came into contact with it at different times and places during the last fall and the forepart of the winter, its midnight wanderings and ghastly, frightful figure have not given our citizens much concern or furnished a topic of general conversation until now. It is a sprightly ghost from all accounts and looks after its bodily comforts and intellectual development quite as carefully as we of the flesh do, for it changes its habiliments as the season demands and frequently is seen perusing some book of science or ethics. Its abode is a large boat house on the bank of the river, a few rods above the Lake Shore arches, where its midnight orgies may be heard and whence it issues in search of ghostly prey or to frighten the belated traveler whom it chances to meet.

Near the spot where the boat house stands, twenty-four years ago, a handsome and clever young man of the name of Woodward, stepped into a small skiff to row himself across the river. While unfastening the skiff he fell down in a fit and drowned in less than three feet of water. Ever since persons in quest of pond lilies and those who by chance or of necessity came in proximity to the place, fancied they saw a disturbance in the water or heard weird, uncanny sounds which emanated from the interior of the boat house. Until last fall the ghost never ventured forth nor indeed had it ever been seen, though many stories in proof of its existence had been related; but now almost nightly someone meets it walking either along the railroad track, or silently ascending the steep bluff between the city and the river flats. On cold nights it carries a large lantern partly concealed by a coarse woolen cape; its head is thrown back, eyes partly closed and its respiration is accompanied with a gurgling sound as if it were attempting to expel water from the nasal passages.

Plain Dealer [Cleveland, OH] 4 February 1891: p. 5 ASHTABULA COUNTY

A musical Christmas ghost from Portsmouth. I wish the story had mentioned what kind of tunes the "spirit" played as the men disassembled the instrument.

"SPIRITS" PLAY ON ORGAN SAY HILLTOP RESIDENTS

Hill-Top residents are all agog, and the more superstitiously inclined are greatly agitated over the mysterious automatic playing of an old family organ at the home of Charles C. Terrell, of No. 1401 High Street.

Mr. Terrell, who is a carpenter employed with Contractor Henry Cook, and at present working on the new Brunner building, had just started to light the candles on the Christmas tree at his home for the pleasure of his children on Christmas night, when suddenly the organ began playing, though no one was touching the keys. Mr. Terrell laughed, as he suspected somebody was playing a trick on him. The music continued and he called in his wife. She urged him to go outside and investigate, but he concluded to rather lay low so as not to give any satisfaction to the supposed practical jokers. Finally Mrs. Terrell became so insistent that to please her he did go out and walked all around the house. There was no sign of any person and the next door neighbors were gone.

"It must be right in this room," said Mrs. Terrell. The husband himself began taking a more serious view of it, and he went to the home of Milton H. Monroe and wife. They were entertaining some company, but going to the kitchen door he related the strange occurrence to Mrs. Monroe, who is a warm friend of the family. She accompanied him home and after listening to the music for a few minutes, hurried back and invited Mrs. Haney and daughter, who were her guests, to go with her to the Terrell home. Mr. Monroe was the last to come. The organ continued playing louder and louder.

Both Mr. Terrell and Mr. Monroe pressed down and lifted up the various keys without creating the slightest sound, but the music from the other unknown source continued. Mr. Monroe then sat down and began pumping the organ and it played, but as soon as he removed his feet and allowed the air to go out his music stopped, while the other continued. The men present then moved the organ to the middle of the floor and took apart the front and back, but the music continued unabated. In all it had played twenty-five minutes. Some of the women present were crying, fearing that the music was an omen of something dreadful to happen. On Thursday evening the organ again began playing Mr. Terrell hurriedly summoned Mr. and Mrs. Charles Lewis and other neighbors, but it ceased playing in about five minutes. All told eight different persons have heard the organ play besides Mr. Terrell and his immediate family, and none can offer any explanation for it.

Portsmouth [OH] Daily Times 28 December 1912: p. 9 SCIOTO COUNTY

The next story has a ghost that was seen as well as heard and the spook (or was it an animal?), had an unusually large vocal range.

GHOST STORY
TWO YOUNG WOMEN NEARLY FRIGHTENED TO DEATH
BY A WEIRD VISITOR AT HOMEWORTH

For some time past a ghost has made its appearance frequently to different persons living at or near Homeworth. Last Saturday night was the last visitation of this weird guest as a result of which two estimable young ladies of that place received a scare from which they are not likely to recover for some time. It seems that this ghost is of a very uncanny nature and well-fitted, judging from the looks of the thing, whatever it may be, to play the title role among the many spirits in ghostdom. The large bridge near the east end of Homeworth is a favorite haunt of the apparition, from which it suddenly springs and through terror, inspired by the horrifying appearance of the spectre, all persons are put to flight. Some linger to take a second look at this thing, when, phantom-like, it flits from place to place, but it is safe to add that a second look is more than sufficient for the most courageous human being to withstand, and they beat a hasty retreat.

This ghost is described along the lines that would fill the most fanciful ideas ever conjured up on such a subject. The shriek emitted by the spectre, just as it vanishes into the air above, is the most awe-inspiring cry mortal being ever attempted to describe. Beginning in a low wail, like the cry of a love-sick cat, it swells in cadences until it reaches a soul-freezing shriek, then breaks off abruptly into the moans and sobs of a dying babe. A large and well-armed party has been organized, and the matter will be investigated, as people living in that neighborhood are worked up to a pitch of frenzy through the excitement occasioned by the repeated appearance of the apparition.

The Stark County Democrat [Canton, OH] 21 January 1897: p. 7
COLUMBIANA COUNTY

This is a strange tale combining a threatening ghost with the satirical "emptying of a jug" and "rats as large as cows."

FLAT ROCK NEWS

About ten or twelve years ago, Frederick Harpster planted about 40 rods of willow which was to serve as a fence. The willows have grown from 20 to 30 feet high, but as a fence they are a failure, and Isaac Horner has taken a contract to dig them out some time during the coming winter.

Last Friday evening about 7 o'clock, David Rushton, Howard Diehl and Allen Belden saw a man standing near the willow fence, saying quite audibly, "death to the one who attempts to destroy these willows." They, supposing that someone was trying to play a trick on them, at once determined to make a rush upon him. When within about four feet of the object it suddenly vanished. It is not necessary to say how those brave men ran for life and how that by the sudden rising of Belden's hair his cap flew off and he ran home bare headed, making good time. Since then it has come to light that spooks have been seen at that place for a number of years. Frank Harpster has repeatedly heard the emptying of a jug; Jacob Brindle saw a man without a head; Bill Betler heard the rattling of chains, and rats as large as cows have been seen.

I have not yet heard what Mr. Horner will do. He is not in a hurry to go to the other world, and prefers to remain here yet a while.
Tiffin [OH] Tribune 4 November 1875: p. 3 SENECA COUNTY

This chapter has rung many changes on the theme of ghostly noises. Now hear the bells, bells, bells, bells haunting the Tedrick farm in Adams County:

BETSY!
IS THAT YOU?
IN THE NAME OF THE FATHER SPEAK!!

There is a disposition in the less enterprising press to censure the publication of the facts and doings about the goblin-haunted grounds near Winchester. It is alleged that the publication encourages superstitious beliefs. The *Jeffersonian* is of the opinion that the pranks, and odd doings of men ought to be reported as well as some other things—particularly when a whole countryside is excited. Now crowds, many of whom come from twenty miles distant, and some from farther away, go to Reuben Tedrick's house and grounds to see and hear of the mysterious bell-ringing. Whilst the *Jeffersonian* reports the actual state of apparent facts, it hopes that no superstitious beliefs will be founded or encouraged by them.

The Mysterious Bell Ringing is still heard, daily, nightly, and hourly; at the house, in the fields, by all the members of the family—so they say. No one who sees them doubts them. Either from imagination, some trick upon them, or other reasons, they do hear. There are old antagonisms in the community about the farm upon which Mr. Tedrick lives. He had before the death of Mrs. Elizabeth Cramer, an adjoining farm. There were occasional quarrels between them, which went so far as to induce the old lady to declare that after her death, Mr. Tedrick, whom she suspected of wanting it, should never own it in peace. "If in my power," she said, "I will come back," and again, "I will haunt you after I am gone." A daughter who died a few years before the old lady also declared at her death that she "Would come back and see him." They were German people and had earnestness in these statements. From these declarations the superstitious and the spiritualist of the community built a belief that old Mrs. Cramer's and her daughter's spirits are back haunting and following the family now occupying the old homestead, near which their bones and those of a half dozen more lie in the adjoining graveyard.

Mr. Reuben Tedrick has some of this belief if the report of his recent doings are true. It is said that at midnight when graves yawn, he arose and went to the fence of the graveyard and there, with the soil of the place creeping up between his toes, his night shirt waving as a flag of truce to the ghosts, with chattering teeth cried out, "Betsy! Is that you? In the name of the Father! Speak!" There was no answer. The grim tombstones were silent and the graves had no voice. One man has been heard to say that besides the hearing of the eternal clanging of the bells, there has been seen a bright light to rise from the ground near the house and going by it, at last fixed itself upon the top of old Mrs. Cramer's gravestone where it burned brightly for some time.

The story about the burial of old Mrs. Cramer alive has no other foundation except that there is assurance that at her burial there were no certain evidences of her death, and some who were present at the funeral firmly believed that the old lady was not dead, yet the persons from whom the statements in this article come, say that the usual test of death by a looking glass was tried. Rev. Tannehill preached the funeral sermon, witnessed the test of death: but on consideration now, is not positive of the fact. She was sick but a few hours and from full health went to the grave. Her daughters are fully assured that she was dead before burial.

It has been said that others besides the family have heard the bell ringing. Miss Yingling, a daughter of Rev. Yingling of Winchester was of the belief that she heard it, and that following the sound, she was led from the house to the old lady's grave. Argument from her father and others has convinced her that she might have been affected by the stories, and by imagination. Wm. Parker, H. Dugan, Wm. Powers and others are reported to have heard it.

Mrs. John B. Hixon, a daughter of old Mrs. Cramer, is firmly of the belief that the spirit of her mother and of her sister Elizabeth have come back to haunt the place, being without rest whilst Reuben Tedrick lives upon it. She thinks the bell-ringing a proof of it, for the placing of a farm bell near the house was the first act of ownership by the present proprietor. Mr. Hixon, her husband, believes in spirited manifestations, and showed our reporter a copy of the *Advance and Review*, a journal "devoted to the interests of modern spiritualism," in which is an account of the materialization of Lucille Western, and an army officer who came back to sing the "Star Spangled Banner" for the company.

These are the latest stories afloat. No wonder, exaggerated as they are, that crowds come on Sundays and weekdays, in the night time, too, to hear and see. The fences on the farm are being thrown down, the crops are being trampled, and the household must be in the direst distress.

Cambridge [OH] Jeffersonian 16 June 1881: p. 3 ADAMS COUNTY

NOTE: Mass hallucination? Mass tinnitus? Some variant on a "mystery hum?" The suggestion that Mrs. Cramer haunts because she was buried alive adds an extra chill to the story. The "usual test of death by a looking glass" is holding a mirror to the person's nose and mouth to see if it mists with a breath. Lucille Western was an actress, most remembered for her role in the melodrama, *East Lynne*. She died in 1877 and was a popular ghost to call up at Spiritualist séances. See *New York Herald* 4 January 1891: p. 23. I am bitterly disappointed that I can't find the dead officer who sang the National Anthem.

12.

The Headless Horror:
Poor, Pitiful Pearl Bryan

In came Pearl Bryan's sister
And falling to her knees,
Begging of Scott Jackson:
"My sister's head, O please!"

But Jackson was so stubborn,
A naughty word he said;
When you meet Pearl in Heaven
You'll find her missing head.

– Anonymous ballad –

Many writers have told the story of the horrific murder of Pearl Bryan. I will only briefly recap the details. Ever a ghoul for a sensation, I am more interested in uncovering the paranormal aspects surrounding a case that shocked the nation and even echoed into the Great Beyond.

It was the old, sad story: Boy meets Girl; Boy seduces Girl; Boy decapitates Girl when she insists he make an Honest Woman of her.

The newspapers of the time depicted the tragedy's protagonists in terms of the stock characters of melodrama: Pearl Bryan, a girl pure as the driven snow, led astray by the mustache-twirling fiend, Scott Jackson; Alonzo Walling, the villain's sidekick; Pearl's Aged Parents; Will Wood, who was first believed to be the villain who ruined Pearl, but became the Boy Who Loved Her From Afar by the time the curtain fell.

Pearl Bryan was the youngest of a family of well-to-do, respectable Indiana farmers and their twelve children. She was pretty, indulged by her parents and siblings, vivacious, and popular. While many men were smitten by her, she did not seem interested in any of them, until, through her cousin, Will Wood, who was half in love with her himself, she met Scott Jackson. As the papers reported, he was a young man of a family of the very best, but a criminal with vicious habits, a whited sepulcher. He was fair-haired, with violet-blue eyes, a handsome, affable, pleasing man of fine form and features, yet "a villain of the deepest dye, a very demon in human shape."

Pearl's parents trusted their daughter and believed Jackson to be a gentleman. The couple spent much time together, alone. When Pearl found that she was pregnant, she was afraid to tell her parents. Instead she confided in her cousin Will, who contacted Scott Jackson to see if he could arrange for Pearl to go to Cincinnati for an abortion or "criminal operation," as it was called.

Alonzo Walling was Jackson's roommate in Cincinnati. He was characterized in the papers as a simple country boy from Mt. Carmel, Indiana, the support of his sickly mother who sacrificed to send him to dental college, where Walling fell under Jackson's sinister influence. He was to either perform or procure the criminal operation. Pearl Bryan went to Cincinnati on the train, telling her parents that she was going to see some friends in Indianapolis. She may have believed that she and Jackson were going to marry. The young woman was seen in the company of Jackson and Walling at a saloon, where one of the men slipped something into her drink. Then all three climbed into a hired surrey and drove off towards the bridge to Kentucky. It was the last ride of Pearl Bryan's life.

On the morning of February 1, 1896, John Hewlin, a farm hand, found the headless body of a woman on the Kentucky farm of John B. Lock, near the end of the Fort Thomas electric car line, just over the river from Cincinnati. The body was lying on its stomach in a pool of blood, with arms outstretched. Her hands were cut to the bone by defensive wounds. The head had vanished.

An autopsy revealed that the woman was about five months pregnant. The coroner determined that her head had been cut off while she was alive. There seemed no way to identify her. There was nothing distinctive about her clothes, except for her shoes, which were unusually small and narrow and bore a label from Louis & Hayes, Greencastle, Ind.

The police were baffled until a Mr. Poock, a Newport shoe dealer, and the hero of this melodrama, came forward. Mr. Poock had noticed manufacturing details that suggested the shoes had been made in Portsmouth, Ohio. The manufacturer informed the police that they had shipped a dozen pairs in that style to a store in Greencastle, Indiana.

On the following Monday Cincinnati Detectives Crim and McDermott took the train to Greencastle and worked their way through a list of shoe buyers, finding all accounted for, except Pearl Bryan. Pearl's mother wept as she identified the shoes and clothing of her dead daughter. "Did they find her head?" was the pitiful question from her elderly father. "We don't want her grave pointed at as the grave of a headless woman."

Scott Jackson had been a welcome caller at the Bryan's Greencastle home. Mrs. Bryan told the police that he was the only person that Pearl knew in Cincinnati. Other sources whispered of Jackson's intimacy with Pearl and that he had known she was pregnant. Jackson and his roommate Alonzo Walling were arrested, but each denied any involvement and blamed the other.

To break the stalemate, in a scene strangely reminiscent of the old custom of making an accused murderer touch the body of the victim to see if it would bleed, Police Chief Deitsch brought Jackson and Walling to see Pearl's body. But the men did not crack.

AT THE CASKET
WALLING AND JACKSON ACCUSE EACH OTHER OF THE MURDER

In all the strange and curious situations which have marked the windings of this mysterious case, there was none so weird and pathetic as that which took place in Epply's undertaking establishment, on Ninth Street, opposite the City Hall, one afternoon. The body of Pearl Bryan had been brought from the Newport Morgue to this city in readiness to be shipped to the home which the girl had left, full of life and vigorous youth, such a short time before.

Chief Deitsch considered that it would be a good plan to confront Jackson and Walling with the mute evidence of their crime, hoping that, if guilty, they might break down and confess. A light snow was falling when the two prisoners were taken across the street from the Central Police Station to Epply's. When all was in readiness they were ushered into the room where the casket reposed.

The scene was painfully impressive. The mutilated body was attired in the costume which Pearl had worn when she graduated. To the east of the casket, in a chair, sat Mrs. Stanley, the sister of the dead girl, dressed in mourning. On her right stood Mayor Caldwell, on her left her brother Fred, and on his left, Chief of Police Deitsch. When the prisoners were brought in Jackson was placed on the opposite side of the casket near its head so near in fact that had the girl been alive she could have reached out her hand and touched him. Walling was placed near the foot of the casket. Jackson looked at the body for a full minute, then shaking his head from side to side, he gave vent to a series of audible sighs. For a few minutes not a word was said, until Mayor Caldwell announced:

"This is all that is left of poor Pearl Bryan."

There was another short period of silence, broken by Chief Deitsch: "Do you recognize the body before you?" he asked, addressing Jackson.

"I suppose it is that of Pearl Bryan," came the reply.

"What makes you think so?"

"I see her relatives here."

"Did you murder this poor girl?"

"No, sir, I did not."

'Who did?"

"I have every reason to believe that Mr. Walling did."

"Do you recognize the body?" asked the Colonel, turning to Walling.

"No, I do not, but I suppose it is Pearl Bryan's."

"Did you murder her?"

"No, sir."

"Who did?"

"I believe that Jackson killed her."

All this time Mrs. Stanley wept quietly while Fred glared steadily at Scott Jackson, never removing his eyes for an instant. There was another minute of silence after the last response, and then the prisoners were taken back to their cells.

Cincinnati [OH] Enquirer 19 April 1896: p. 17 HAMILTON COUNTY

It was said that Pearl's sister went down on her knees and begged Jackson to tell her where the head was. It was said that he replied, "'I can't tell you anything about it."

Almost immediately, the paranormal circus began. The authorities were besieged by Spiritualists, psychics, and stage mind-readers, all eager to find Pearl Bryan's head and solve the case. Perhaps the most colorful of the mind-readers was Nathoo, High Caste Brahmin and Conjurer, who, for the length of his engagement at the New Museum, was featured in daily puff pieces in the *Enquirer* with such headlines as:

UNCANNY
RITES OF A HINDOO
NATHOO, HIGH CASTE BRAHMIN AND CONJURER
VISITS THE SCENE OF THE PEARL BRYAN MURDER
AND CONDUCTS A MOST PECULIAR CEREMONY

HE WILL TRY TO LOCATE THE MISSING HEAD

Yesterday there was conducted a ceremony which has never before been performed in this portion of the globe. It furnishes a story the like of which no paper has ever before published.

Nathoo, the high-cast Brahmin and Hindoo conjurer, went to the spot near Ft. Thomas where the body of Pearl Bryan was found and went through the mystic rites of his religion, which gave him a clew which he thinks will lead to the discovery of the missing head.

Just how far his wonderful powers can lead him time will tell, but he speaks earnestly and positively when he said that the head was where it could be found and that one ambition of his life was to locate it. In a day or two he will complete the work which was begun yesterday.
Cincinnati [OH] Enquirer 1 March 1896: p. 8 HAMILTON COUNTY

A MIND READER
THINKS HE MIGHT HELP TO FIND THE
MISSING HEAD

Chief Deitsch yesterday afternoon received a letter from Kokomo, Ind., which is self-explanatory. It is given below:

Kokomo, Ind., February 10, 1896.

"Philip Deitsch, Chief of Police, Cincinnati, Ohio—Dear Sir: If you have not yet succeeded in locating the hiding place of the head of Pearl Bryan we think we can materially assist you. If you are confident that either Jackson or Walling knows where the missing head is, and if you can get them into the subject, the secret may be discovered by bringing them in contact with Paul Alexander Johnstone, the noted mind reader....All we ask to make the experiment is a guarantee of expenses on the trip and in case of success a suitable reward....Very truly yours. Frederick K. George, Manager, Paul A. Johnstone."

"Are you going to send for Johnstone?" Colonel Deitsch was asked, after he had finished reading the letter.

"Why, certainly not," he replied. "I don't believe in that nonsense..."
Cincinnati [OH] Enquirer 11 February 1896: p. 8 HAMILTON COUNTY

The location of Pearl Bryan's head became a national obsession. The search spawned multiple "discoveries" of her head, even years after the murder. At least six skulls were uncovered, as well as a decomposed head found in Columbus, which was later identified as the head of prostitute Josie Joiner.

226 THE HEADLESS HORROR

Tipsters sent the police as far afield as Chicago to search and a madman in Maine was questioned about his claim to have buried Pearl's head in an Ohio River sandbar. A Spiritualist medium was one of the first to announce that she had gotten some answers from the victim herself.

A SPIRITUALIST
SAYS WALLING KILLED MISS BRYAN AND JACKSON
DISPOSED OF THE HEAD.

Lexington, Ky., February 9. A Lexington woman, who claims to have Spiritualistic powers, is giving nightly séances in her home at No. 176 North Limestone Street. Her name is Annie Lewis. She is an Albino of small stature, 68 years of age and spent several years of her life as a snake charmer in the Forepaugh show. Discovering that she possessed what she terms "medium powers" she quit the show business and settled in Lexington to delve into the mysteries of the spirit world. Learning that she had invited a number of persons to be present during a "conversation with the spirit of Pearl Bryan" this evening, an *Enquirer* correspondent visited the place and was told that the séance was just over, and that it had been very successful. Mrs. Lewis had called up the spirit of the unfortunate girl, and had asked her many questions. The spirit had said that Walling killed Pearl Bryan, and that Jackson carried her head away. Her head was in a water-closet on the Kentucky side of the Ohio River. No answer came to the question as to why or where the crime was committed.
Cincinnati [OH] Enquirer 10 February 1896: p. 5

Entertainment venues were quick to exploit the sensation. An anonymous booklet was quickly published about the murder called *The Mysterious Murder of Pearl Bryan* or *The Headless Horror*. Songs and ballads by the dozen were written about the tragedy:

Heck and Avery's New Museum will assuredly do a big business next week. The announcement is made that one of the new special attractions will be a troupe of Bedouins. Another great feature will be Prof. Bror Sundeen, the wonderful Swedish mind reader. He is said to be the best the world has ever known. He will accomplish the most wonderful things while here. It is said that he will, during his engagement, make an effort to discover the location of Pearl Bryan's missing

head. Calamity Jane will remain another week. The horse and coupe owned by Chester Mullen and said to have carried Pearl Bryan to her death, will also remain on exhibition. A new series of living pictures will be presented illustrating the Ft. Thomas tragedy. Today and tomorrow will be the only days on which visitors to the Museum can secure a copy of the touching song entitled "Pearl Bryan's Fate," which Mr. Charles S. Knight is singing in the theatre.
Cincinnati [OH] Enquirer 22 February 1896: p. 6. HAMILTON COUNTY

Reporters were allowed free access to the prisoners at the Cincinnati jail, possibly because the authorities were hoping one of the men would let slip some incriminating detail. An *Enquirer* writer, who spent the day with Jackson, described how Jackson first wrote to his mother telling her he was an innocent victim of circumstance and asking her to pray for him. Next he wrote his attorney, Woodmansee, "requesting him to write to a certain young woman of Louisville, asking her if Walling did not ruin her in his room at Carlisle and John Streets." Then he prepared a statement of his actions from "Monday, January 27 until the day of his arrest. This he read to the reporter as he finished, page by page." Several times he asked the reporter if he thought the public would believe it. As Jackson worked he hummed popular tunes, joked, and laughed. "Jailer Kushman and Chief Deputy Heine remarked that he was the coldest-blooded fellow ever locked up in jail." *Cincinnati [OH] Enquirer* 10 February 1896: p. 8 HAMILTON COUNTY

Jackson's brazen question about the plausibility of his statement was bad enough. But it is the following casual scene that most chilled my blood.

Pearl Bryan's hat was found just a short ways out of Newport along with a bloody handkerchief, identified by Walling as Jackson's. Jackson was handed the hat. "Jackson took the hat, adjusted the ribbons, turned it around for fully a minute, then said: "I can't say that that is her hat...I think the hat she wore was a smaller one." Jackson again took the hat in his hands and began to adjust the ribbon bows, at the same time saying: "I have seen my sister do this work and I understand it a little."
Cincinnati [OH] Enquirer 10 February 1896 pg. 8 HAMILTON COUNTY

While the evidence listed by the police was mostly circumstantial, it was damning. Jackson and Walling were the last persons to have seen Pearl Bryan alive and Jackson had ample reason to want Pearl dead. The autopsy revealed that Pearl had been given a large amount of cocaine, which Jackson admitted purchasing. The African American driver whom Jackson had hired to drive them to Kentucky identified both Jackson and Walling. The driver, George H. Jackson, said at the trial that Jackson, who rode up front, was carrying a pistol. Pearl seemed drugged, and had cried and moaned the entire trip, but when the surrey stopped, she became even more agitated and Jackson, the driver, was frightened. When the men told him to stop the surrey and went off with the drugged girl, he whipped up the horse and raced back to Cincinnati. It was unclear why Jackson and Walling hired a driver who turned out to be a key witness to the crime. After all, they could have driven a hired carriage themselves. Detective John T. Norris suggested that they rented the carriage in a place they were not known; hired a stranger to drive it, and had planned to kill the driver, make it look like suicide, and plant evidence to implicate him in Pearl's murder.

It is painful to imagine the poor girl's feelings as she was "taken for a ride." Where did Jackson tell her they were going? To be married in Kentucky? Why was she screaming and crying in pain in the back of the surrey? Why did she not try to escape before they dragged her up the hill or ask the cabman for help? Some answers were forthcoming from Pearl Bryan's spirit at a February séance.

SENSATIONAL
IS THE LATEST REPORT ABOUT PEARL BRYAN'S MISSING HEAD

Anderson, Ind., February 21. The Daily Bulletin tonight publishes a most sensational report that Pearl Bryan's head was taken through this city last night by a Greencastle man, who went to Cincinnati for the head and came home this roundabout way carrying it in a hat box.

A very sensational séance was held last night in the private séance rooms at the residence of Sanford Bronnenberg, one of the best-known farmers in this county. Several Spiritualists gathered at Bronnenberg's, as they often did. After several spirits had materialized as they ordinarily do, it was noticed that a headless form had materialized over in the corner of the room. It was a horrible sight and intimidated those present. It was at last asked who it was and where the head should be. A woman's voice answered that it was Pearl Bryan. The spirit went on to tell of the murder, saying that Jackson was responsible for her death and had cut off her head.

The girl had taken some wine in which she thought were chemicals arranged by Walling. She became stupefied and they put her in a buggy. She remembers little else. She was held by Walling in a secluded spot, and while yet alive Jackson cut her throat and she saw the rest in spirit form. She saw her life blood trickling down and saw them take the head away. But where it is now she does not know. The form then dematerialized in the center of the room.

Cincinnati [OH] Enquirer 22 February 1896: p. 8

Another, rather less productive séance was held in Cincinnati.

A SÉANCE
IN WHICH THE SPIRITS TALK OF POOR
PEARL BRYAN

A weird scene was enacted at the house of a Spiritualistic medium last night, at which strong men trembled and women wept and went into hysterics. It was a special séance given by Mrs. Mary Garrett, the founder of the People's Religious Spiritualist Society, at her residence on Richmond Street. At 8 o'clock some 20 people had gathered in the parlor, and the Pearl Bryan murder was the sole topic of conversation.

Mrs. Garrrett herself was present, and joined in the discussion, expressing her fervent wish that through her the spirits might furnish a clew to the greatest murder mystery of the age. A few minutes after everybody adjourned to the séance room, where a music box furnished the entertainment before the spirit manifestations.

"No sooner were the lights put out than the trumpet, which before that had been peacefully resting in the middle of the room, beat a fearful tattoo. The last strains of "Nearer My God to Thee" floated on the air, when a childish treble was heard in the stillness, announcing itself as "Dollie," the control of the medium. Without further preamble the voice declared that the search for the murdered girl's head was all in vain.

"It's in the grate."

"Where?" somebody in the circle had the temerity to ask.

"On Fifth Street."

"Where on Fifth Street?" the inquisitive inquirer asked.

"I can't locate it at present."

"Can you give us the details of the crime?" someone asked.

"She was drugged in a woman's room. A surrey was hired and so was George Jackson, the colored man to drive them."

"How was the murder committed?" another one in the circle inquired.

"They used a razor first and a hatchet afterward."

This blood-curdling announcement threw several of the women present into hysterics, and the séance was declared ended.
Cincinnati [OH] Enquirer 21 February 1896: p. 8 HAMILTON COUNTY

NOTE: There were suggestions that Jackson had either taken the head to the Ohio Medical College furnace and burned it or put it down a sewer. In choosing the word "grate," the medium has covered both possibilities. Everything else mentioned had already been in the papers.

The imprisoned Jackson thought it was all ludicrous.

WITH A SMILE
SCOTT JACKSON ASKS A REPORTER A MOST GREWSOME QUESTION

Scott Jackson was sitting in his cell last night talking to an *Enquirer* reporter, when he was informed that the Spiritualists had been talking to Pearl Bryan's spirit.

"How did the spirit appear?" asked Jackson.

"Without a head," was the reply.

"Without a head? Why, that's the funniest thing I ever heard. How could a headless spirit talk?" said Jackson with a smile.
Cincinnati [OH] Enquirer 25 February 1896: p. 8 HAMILTON COUNTY

Yet by the time of the August Indiana Spiritualists' Camp Meeting, Pearl had fallen silent.

MRS MENDENHALL OF MUNCIE

Was next called upon, and the powers were evoked, but to no successful end. Neither Holmes nor the Greencastle girl would manifest themselves....

Mrs. Mendenhall, the materializing medium, stated that it would probably be years before Pearl would materialize owing to the sudden

and frightful manner in which she had departed from this life. She intimated that the relatives of the dead girl had come to her several times at
Muncie, and had sat for materialization, with no success. She says that
she has been continually trying to get the dead girl to come to her, but
she has not as yet had any success. She has sent the spirits in quest of her,
but she refuses to even try yet to make herself known to her friends. She
will, in time, however, Mrs. Mendenhall says, come to her friends and
explain the mystery. She says that the spirits of Pearl that mediums over
the country have caused to materialize are nothing more than fakes of
the lowest order. She says that Pearl Bryan has not reached that position
in the spirit world yet where it would be possible for her to materialize.
Cincinnati [OH] Enquirer 10 August 1896: p. 10

NOTE: "Holmes" is "Dr. Henry Howard Holmes," the alias of serial killer
Herman Webster Mudgett of Chicago's "Murder Castle." He had confessed
to murdering 27 victims, but police believed there could have been as many
as 200. He was executed May 8, 1896; Spiritualists had been trying to
contact him ever since to get him to reveal the identities of his victims.

As with any sort of horrific murder in the public eye, rumors and whis-
pers flew. An attorney named Clay claimed that Pearl Bryan was alive and
living within 40 miles of the city and that another woman had worn her
clothes "as a blind." A woman told the police chief that she had overheard
three negroes hired by Jackson and Walling planning to kill Pearl Bryan.
There was a plot to lynch the prisoners; someone smuggled a saw and other
tools to Walling so the men could break out of the Newport jail, but they
were afraid of being lynched if they left the prison.

On New Year's Eve 1896, Jackson claimed to the other prisoners that
five years previously at a New Year's bazaar the gypsy fortuneteller had predicted that unless he changed his ways, and associates, he and another man
would die a horrible death within five years. *Cincinnati [OH] Enquirer* 1
January 1897: p. 12.

It was also reported that Jackson and Walling attended church on the
Sunday after the murder, hearing a sermon from the Rev. Dwight L. Moody,
the evangelist, whose text was taken from Galatians: "Be not deceived; God
is not mocked; for whatsoever a man soweth, that shall he reap," with the
additional text "Your sin will find you out." *Cincinnati [OH] Enquirer* 25
Dec 1899: p. 5

Early in Walling's imprisonment, someone sent him a mystery package.

A DOLL'S HEAD
SENT THROUGH THE POST OFFICE TO
ALONZO WALLING

A package was received at the post office last night addressed to Alonzo Walling, which accidentally burst open, and incidentally caused several of the clerks to quake with fear.

The packaged contained the head of a doll, almost life size, and bore a crop of short auburn hair, not unlike that of the unfortunate victim of the awful tragedy.

For a few minutes there was some hesitancy among the clerks as to who would pick the package up, so life-like did it appear. The doll's head was finally placed in its receptacle and the cords fastened more firmly about it. To-day it will be delivered to Jailer Lew Kushman, in whose care it is consigned for Walling. There is nothing about the package to indicate who the sender was, although it was mailed in this city.
Cincinnati [OH] Enquirer 25 February 1896: p. 8 HAMILTON COUNTY

A little later, someone recalled that Alonzo Walling had visited Hamilton, Ohio on February 5th and it was suggested that he had deposited Pearl's head in a local graveyard in a bizarre sort of reverse body-snatching.

NOT FOUND
PEARL BRYAN'S HEAD NOT BURIED IN HUBER'S
COFFIN AT HAMILTON

Hamilton, Ohio. April 17. The remains of Albert Huber, who was buried in Greenwood Cemetery on February 5 last, the day that Alonzo Walling came up to Hamilton to visit his brother, was unearthed at 7:30 o'clock this evening.

Undertaker Charles Gath, William and Charles Huber, brothers of deceased, took it upon themselves to dig up the body of their brother, Albert Huber, in search of Pearl Bryan's head. They prevailed upon Superintendent Goshorn to allow them the privilege without the necessary formalities, and he reluctantly granted it.

The search was made without the consent or knowledge of Mayor Bosch, who is highly indignant. Superintendent Goshorn with two grave diggers set to work and soon unearthed the fast-decaying body of young Huber.

When the coffin was raised to the sod Undertaker Gath assisted in opening the dismal coffin, and midst the dull flare from flickering lanterns the corpse was drawn from its casket and a thorough search was made for the head. It resulted in a grewsome failure and one of the mysteries of Pearl Bryan's head was exploded.

Mayor Bosch had detailed four officers to patrol the cemetery, but Undertaker Gath and his assistant had got their work in before the officers could stop them. They met them at the gate of the cemetery and Undertaker Gath told Officer Cruzen what he had done and that the head had not been found.

Cincinnati [OH] Enquirer 18 April 1896: p. 4 BUTLER COUNTY

There was something about the horrible particulars, printed in every edition of the papers, which unhinged the mentally unstable. Thomas Hawkins, a Kentucky farmer, hung himself February 20th after he "became affected by reading of the Pearl Bryan murder." *Morning Herald* [Lexington, KY] 22 February 1896: p. 2

John Kottmeyer, a coal merchant, "closely followed the details of poor Pearl Bryan's murder...this is the cause of his derangement of mind." He also told how Jackson had cut the head up into small pieces. *Cincinnati [OH] Enquirer* 12 February 1896: p. 8.

Madness struck a Mrs. Reiser of Hamilton who was a "close student" of the mystery, "Charles Opmeyer, a well-known grocery clerk of Norwood," who became a "raving maniac," and Mrs. Maggie Jones of Clermont County who "was seized with a sudden fit of insanity... through reading the fate of Pearl Bryan as portrayed in a cheap novel." *Cincinnati [OH] Enquirer* 26 May 1896: p. 8

Pearl's missing head obsessed many a madman or woman.

A MANIAC
WHO THINKS HE IS DESTINED TO FIND PEARL BRYAN'S HEAD

Lexington, Ky. June 17. Malcolm Smith, aged 27, was incarcerated to-day and will be tried to-morrow for lunacy. Smith imagines that he is a mind-reader and chief of all the detectives in the world. To the *Enquirer* correspondent he said: "The Lord has given me this great power that enables me to know what everybody in the world is thinking of. I have been appointed by the Lord to find the head of Pearl Bryan. I know where it is now. Pearl's spirit told me it was in the Ohio River under the Brooklyn Bridge. When I dive for it and take it to Jackson and Walling they will kneel down and beg for mercy. I have the power also to rob banks without being arrested.

Cincinnati [OH] Enquirer 18 June 1896: p. 16

HEADLESS BODIES STALK ABOUT HER
PECULIAR DELUSION OF A WOMAN REVEALED
IN COURT

A strange woman clad in peculiar garb created no little excitement in the Probate Court yesterday. She called to see the Judge, but in his absence told a queer story to Chief Deputy James. She said she had stopped last night on West Seventh Street, where she had been horrified to see a young girl, whom she claimed to know, taken from the house and laid in the street with her head and arms cut off.

She declared that she could not walk the street without seeing headless bodies everywhere. Her condition is supposed to be due to reading the Pearl Bryan murder sensation. It was remarked that she would certainly land in Lunacy Court ere long. Her queer actions attracted quite a crowd.

Cincinnati [OH] Enquirer 1 August 1896: p. 16

It was reported in the papers that Scott Jackson was interested in Spiritualism. Some of his biggest jailhouse fans were Spiritualists and, significantly, the Spiritualists spoke out against capital punishment.

WHAT THE SPIRITS SAY

Anderson, Ind., March 15. At a séance at the Spiritualist Temple in this city, held last night by Medium Mrs. Eva Pfunter, of Cincinnati, the materialized spirits said that it would be wrong to hang Scott Jackson. They did not say whether he was guilty or not, but said that his spirit was a revengeful one, and would return to earth and prompt people to murder and to crime. The spirits said that they would have him at the Spiritual Temple in this city next Sunday, if he was executed on the 20th.

Cincinnati [OH] Enquirer 16 March 1897: p. 12

Jackson and Walling were jailed at Covington, Kentucky with another notorious murderer and the three prisoners made an uncanny pact.

LAUGHLIN
WILL COME BACK TO EARTH
IN SPIRIT FORM AND MANIFEST HIMSELF TO
JACKSON AND WALLING
A WEIRD COMPACT

A singular compact, and one that will be watched by Spiritualists especially with intense interest, has been made between Scott Jackson, Alonzo Walling and Robert Laughlin, the three men in the Covington Jail. Laughlin is doomed to die on the gallows on Saturday next, and the other two have every chance of meeting a similar fate at no distant day.

These three men, virtually standing each with one foot upon the threshold of eternity, have resolved to put to a close and crucial test the question that has baffled scientists and scholars—whether or not there is a life beyond the grave.

These three men, bound, as it were, in the shackles of fate, will shortly solve the greatest problem ever put before mankind. They have determined if feasible to pull apart the veil that separates future from past, and prove to the world surviving them that there is another life.

Jackson, among his friends, has many who are Spiritualists, and they have been exceptionally kind and good to him. Their hopes of a higher and brighter life beyond the tomb have made a deep and perceptible impression upon the mind of the condemned prisoner and on this subject more than anything else he has been induced to talk with his fellow prisoners.

Robert Laughlin, who is to be hanged next Saturday at Brooksville, Ky., was approached upon the subject, and readily consented to aid in the plan suggested by Jackson—that, if possible, he return in spirit form and make his presence known to his two companions, who will join him so shortly in the other world. Laughlin, if returning is possible, will materialize at a given hour to Jackson and at a specified time to Walling.

If materialization is not possible he is to give certain raps and signals that cannot be misunderstood.

Cincinnati [OH] Enquirer 3 January 1897: p. 4

NOTE: Laughlin was an Augusta, Kentucky man convicted of decapitating his invalid wife and 12-year-old niece, after he had assaulted the girl in front of his wife. He burned the house down to cover the crime and claimed that "masked men" had done the deed.

CONSUMMATION
OF A WEIRD COMPACT
CLAIMED BY COVINGTON SPIRITUALISTS
IT IS ALLEGED THAT LAUGHLIN HAS RETURNED
TO JACKSON AND WALLING IN SPIRIT FORM

According to rumors circulating about the jail in Covington, Scott Jackson and Alonzo Walling have experienced the fulfilment of a weird promise made by Robert H. Laughlin, who was confined with them in jail, and who was executed at Brooksville a week ago yesterday.

These three men, with the knowledge that their days on earth were numbered, made a compact that if the belief that spirits can return after death be true, Laughlin, who was first to step into the great beyond, was to return in spiritual form.

A WEIRD STORY

The following story is told by a prominent Spiritualist of Covington:

One night last week, at a well-attended séance in Covington, the form of a body materialized, but no one in the circle could recognize it, a fact that caused apparent regret to the materialized form who was unable at that time to express himself in language audible to these within the circle.

The form vanished momentarily, only to again assume a materialized shape, and by concentrated efforts of those present in extending sympathetic power the spirit at last made known the fact that it was that of Robert H. Laughlin, and he felt that one lady in the audience should now be able to at least bid him welcome.

The medium, under control, followed the phantom-like form to the lady indicated and told her that Laughlin wanted to convey his untiring love to "the boys," meaning Walling and Jackson, and to notify them that he had frequently visited them and was able to make rappings, but had not as yet developed sufficient strength to appear in full form.

To those in the circle explanations were unnecessary. They could fully understand the ill-adapted conditions surrounding the jail and how difficult it was to perfect a recognizable materialization under those existing conditions. After again giving expression to sincere thanks for assistance given by sympathetic believers. Laughlin's form vanished, with the promise to return again.

KNOWS JACKSON AND WALLING

The lady who had been expected to recognize Laughlin had performed for him many little acts of kindness through her friendship for Jackson and Walling, but had never seen Laughlin. She hears from both men regularly. This woman says that Jackson and Walling claim to have heard Laughlin spirit rapping. Frequently while playing cards the tinkle of a tin would be heard, as though someone was gently tapping on the tin cups, first in Jackson's and next in Walling's cell. As conditioned by the compact made by the man before Laughlin's departure, the two men have tried to maintain an air of secrecy through fear that the constant rapping and tapping would excite the fears and superstitious theories of the other prisoners, many of them such disbelievers in the faith that they would give unnecessary trouble to Jailer Wieghaus.

Jailer Wieghaus has been informed of the supernatural noises, but tries to make light of the suspected causes, as he knows that if the ignorant moonshiners in his charge once entertain the idea that spirits are frequenting the jail, there would be a panic among the prisoners.
Cincinnati [OH] Enquirer 17 January 1897: p. 8

Jackson and Walling received separate trials. Jackson's jury took less than two hours to find him guilty; the Walling jury deliberated only briefly before voting unanimously for his guilt.

On March 20, 1897, Jackson and Walling were hung on a single, white-washed gallows. They stood together on a double trap and the lever was arranged so that with one pull, both of the condemned men dropped together. Neither man's neck broke with the drop: they both strangled to death. Black flags announcing the execution were run up over Newport, Covington, and Cincinnati, the waiting crowds "expressing their satisfaction over the result."

The body of Scott Jackson was cremated. His mother was opposed to cremation, but as the directors of Forest Hill Cemetery had made it clear that they would not allow Jackson to be buried in the same ground as his victim, and Mrs. Jackson did not wish to suffer the mortification of their public refusal, she decided to bring her son's ashes to her home. This is the same woman who spoke out a few days before her son's death, bitter about the "persecution" he'd been subjected to and blackening the victim's name.

"It has been made to appear that the unfortunate girl who was the victim in this tragedy was the pure and innocent object of the villainy of one as black as Satan. I have seen her on the streets of Greencastle, and I did not wish my son to associate with her."
Cincinnati [OH] Enquirer 8 March 1897: p. 8

Pearl's body had been secretly returned to Greencastle and put into a holding vault at Forest Hill Cemetery. The young woman herself had at last been laid to rest on March 27, 1896. The *Cincinnati Enquirer* account of the funeral was quite brief, only mentioning the names of participants and the "snow white casket" borne from the vault by six of her high school classmates. It was said that people began to put Lincoln's head pennies on her stone, which has now been almost chipped out of existence by souvenir hunters, so that she would arise with a head on Resurrection Day.

Pearl's father, Alexander, died in 1901. Her mother, Susan, lingered until 1913. Seven of her twelve children died before her.

The Spiritualists had been faithful visitors to Jackson and Walling in the jail, bringing little treats and cheer, behaving just like modern-day serial killer groupies. After his execution, Jackson repaid their kindness by appearing at some of their séances.

SPIRIT OF SCOTT JACKSON TALKS TO THE SPIRITUALISTS AT THE INDIANA CAMP SAYS HE NEEDS SYMPATHY

It is claimed that the spirit of Scott Jackson manifested itself in a séance room at the Indiana Spiritualists' camp, east of this city, last night. He talked through a trumpet, but promised to materialize before the meetings were over. He stated he was groping in darkness, but was getting to the light. He said the feeling against him on earth kept him back, and he made a request that those present ask others to sympathize with him. He had nothing to say about the great murder mystery. Last year Pearl Bryan is alleged to have materialized in one of Mrs. Mendenhall's séances at the camp grounds, and given a complete story of the crime in which she said that Scott and Walling did not kill her. She has not been heard at the camp this year.
Cincinnati [OH] Enquirer 2 August 1897: 1.

For a long time the case of poor, pitiful Pearl was known only to true crime fans or local historians. The case languished in obscurity until 1993 when a book called *Hell's Gate: Terror at Bobby Mackey's Music World* was published. I was appalled when I read its lurid description of innocent Pearl Bryan being sacrificed by Satanists at the former slaughterhouse. Pearl after swine?

The nightclub's owner claimed that the building housed a "well of blood," (i.e. slaughterhouse drain) that Pearl's head had been thrown down the well, that the "Satanist" murderers cursed the spot and vowed to haunt everyone who had led them to the gallows. The building was full of demonic presences, was a Portal to Hell, etc. Troy Taylor's 2001 book *No Rest for the Wicked* invented and embellished further. With the advent of TV ghost hunting shows, the stories grew more lurid by the year. The wild tales are endlessly repeated on internet sites and even in recently published books by authors who should know better.

Let us be clear: the murderers of Pearl Bryan were not Satanists. There is not the slightest hint of such a thing in the contemporary news accounts. Jackson was called a demon, but that was a journalist's word for anyone who was unusually violent or had committed an especially vile crime. Forensic evidence at the murder scene showed that Pearl had tried to run, but had been brought down, fighting for her life as her head was hacked off. A demon's act, yes, but a demon with an angel's face, violet-blue eyes, and a silky blond mustache.

And what of the ghost of Pearl Bryan? She could not rest in her snow white casket at Greencastle, but returned to make an unforgettable appearance at a Cincinnati séance.

SPIRITS
OF JACKSON, WALLING, AND PEARL BRYAN
APPEAR AT A SEANCE

According to the prediction of the famous Sybil and trumpet medium, Mrs. Garrett, of 307 West Fourteenth Street, published in *The Enquirer* about one year ago, Jackson and Walling died together.

Last night, at the residence of this eminent spiritualist and medium, a special séance was conducted. From a sick bed where she has been suffering great anguish for weeks, Mrs. Garrett arose and presided at a circle, which was productive of most weird and remarkable results, in which the principals of the terrible tragedy just concluded by the ebon hands of death were largely concerned.

Three trumpets were brought in. One was about four feet long, one about two and one half feet, and the other about one and one half feet in length. The burning coal was removed from the grate in Mrs. Garrett's sick chamber. The transoms were then shaded and the lights extinguished after the trumpets had first been taken out and chilled in cooler atmosphere. The little circle was then formed with Mrs. Garrett near the grate, muffled in blankets, pillows and shawls, too ill to stand upon her feet alone.

THERE WAS SILENCE

For about one minute the people in the circle sat motionless staring at the inky darkness. Under the circumstances the effect of this was to produce an evil sensation on one in that silent circle at least. Then there appeared a flickering phosphorescent light in the center of the group, near the floor. At times it was dull and vaporish, but occasionally deepened in the intensity of its brilliance until it closely resembled the glow sometimes seen in the eye of a jaguar when crouched in shadows.

This jaguar's eye, if it may be so called, vacillated between the floor and the ceiling, a distance of perhaps 15 feet. Then it vanished altogether.

A piping voice next sounded inside the circle and was at once recognized. It said: "Please pray."

The request was granted and the Lord's Prayer was said in chorus. At its conclusion a voice, which was also recognized, said something of a personal nature to a lady in the circle and made its exit.

The atmosphere of the room seemed to then be slowly peopled with spirits who arrived upon the wings of each weird, ghastly minute that passed, and from their ethereal carriages were handed down with sibilant rustle of ghostly satins, and hastily prepared themselves for the reception that awaited them. These fleeting guests were heralded by Mrs. Garrett's control, who is none other than the spirit of her late husband. Mr. Garrett seemed to divine the eagerness of the circle to learn of the arrival of the spirits of Jackson and Walling on the misty shores he had but quitted for a few moments, and spoke in the full, rich tones of a strong man about 50 years of age.

COULD NOT TALK

"They are here," he said, beginning with the all-consuming subject, "but it will be some days before they can talk. Jackson and Walling are now seated together over there, and are still suffering the terrible tortures that were inflicted upon them. The first person to meet and greet them both was Pearl, who met them, and forgave them." At this the spirit of Mr. Garrett retired.

No sooner had the last one gone than did another appear. It was poor Pearl Bryan, and was recognized by many present, as her spirit has visited Mrs. Garrett's circle often. There was a piteous wail that seemed to grow to a volume of pathetic sounds and then die away almost to a whisper.

"Poor child," "Alas, dear, poor creature," and such other exclamations greeted the sound, which died away, and then came the request: "Kindly sing."

This, it was explained, was asked by the spirit that it might strengthen itself for some particular effort.

"Shall We Gather at the River," was sung by the members of the circle, soft and low, and at once another phosphorescent glow near the carpet in the center of the ring appeared.

"She is going to materialize," exclaimed one lady.

"Poor child, let us pray that she may do so," said another, and it was then apparent that the phosphorescent glow was widening and lengthening. Slowly it took shape and form, until, horrible to relate, what nearly resembled the decapitated trunk of a woman materialized. Only the glimmer of a thin white light could be seen, but its contour described the headless figure of a woman, dressed in flowing white, and an ague fell upon the little circle that played a gibbering tattoo with their dentistry.

THE LAST SCENE.

Another unearthly wail supplemented those seconds of horror, which lengthened out into an eternity whose ghastly mileposts gleamed like grave stones. The vision passed, and the wail that accompanied it ceased. Nerves that had been keyed up by the fingers of awe at last relaxed, but the sounds of hard breathing around the circle rasped and jarred the inky silence, until a baby voice, sweet as the carol of a bird and liquid clear, blew through those marvelous instruments—those trumpets—words that ran into charming sentences, like strings of flaring marigolds. It was a welcome relief, and the dainty spirit slew with childish prattle all the terror of the minute before. Strange as it may seem, a spirit, claiming to be that of Stephen A. Douglas, voiced an eloquent benediction that only a master mind could have worded, and the experience of that dark hour was concluded. When the light was brought the figure of the wonderful woman was found sitting bolt upright, with eyes wide open, staring straight into what may be nothing and what may be eternity. Her form was rigid and all signs of animation suspended. Her icy lips were bathed with spirits, and when the Enquirer reporter left, the ladies present were working with all their might to bring her back to consciousness.

Cincinnati [OH] Enquirer 22 March 1897: p. 8 HAMILTON COUNTY

Epilogue: The Silent Woman

She is the silent woman, like a British pub sign showing a decapitated female carrying a round of drinks. She does not speak, but wails piteously; raps on the tables of Spiritualists; is identified only by her shoes.

We put words into her missing mouth; project emotions into her missing brain. She is a blank slate for all our fears of innocence lost, of fallen women and bad men, of spirits that rise, headless, keening of our guilt.

Was she the innocent who "loved not wisely, but too well?"

Did she have any misgivings when she boarded the train for Cincinnati? Or was she unsuspecting, as a ballad suggested: "Poor Pearl! Poor girl, she thought she was going right. She had no dream of murder on that dark stormy night."

She fought for her life on that dark, stormy night. Did she truly meet and forgive her killers on the Other Side?

We do not know. Dead women tell no tales.

There is no one left to speak for poor, pitiful Pearl, only the words of a ballad:

> Deep, deep in a lonely valley
> Where the violets fade and bloom
> There sleeps my own Pearl Bryan
> So silent in the tomb.

Appendix

Spook Squibs

Chips from the Headstone of News

Whenever I take up a newspaper, I seem to see Ghosts gliding between the lines.
– Henrik Ibsen –

For the historical ghost hunter in a hurry, I present these short squibs, the antique equivalent of the "Fright Bite" chapters in *Haunted Ohio III, IV,* and *V.*

THINK IT IS A SPOOK

Martin's Ferry, March 10. This town is just now stirred to its innermost circles by what is supposed to be a real spook. For a week people of the most reliable veracity have been telling of seeing a figure clad in white and uttering the most unearthly noises in the neighborhood of Jefferson and Second Streets. Several efforts have been made by people to get a good look at the apparition, but it has invariably vanished into thin air upon the approach of mortal man. Its cries have been plainly heard, however, by many. Several people have banded together to catch the ghost or find who is playing the trick.
Plain Dealer [Cleveland, OH] 11 March 1894: p. 2 BELMONT COUNTY

Newark has a ghost. A speechless woman in black haunts a picnic grove near the town. When pursued she evaporates.
Plain Dealer [Cleveland, OH] 27 July 1881: p. 1 LICKING COUNTY

OBERLIN HAS A GHOST
THE SPOOK IS MUSCULAR AND A CROWD HAS BEEN ORGANIZED TO WAYLAY IT

Oberlin, O., Aug. 20. People living in the northern part of this place are greatly excited over a haunted house. In the house lives Marsh Kelley, his wife and brother-in-law. Reports have been out for some time, but last night the climax was reached.

About 1 o'clock this morning the inmates were awakened by sounds in the house and Kelley and his brother-in-law, A. Easterwood who sleep upstairs came down to investigate. On reaching the lower floor every door in the house was found to be open, and on entering the sitting room a huge ghost which they claim was over six feet tall, and robed in white grabbed them.

Kelley succeeded in getting out of the house immediately and awakened the neighbors, while Easterwood was so badly scared he fainted. A thorough investigation was made but no further developments were secured. A crowd has been secured, who will stay in the house tonight and try and catch the ghost.

Plain Dealer [Cleveland, OH] 21 August 1904: p. 7 LORAIN COUNTY

THE GHOST OF COLONEL CRAWFORD

Upper Sandusky, O., July 27. People here are telling weird stories about an apparition seen at night near here. It is said that the ghostly form of a man with a bloody head is seen moving around on a circle of fire. This is the spot where Colonel Crawford was tortured by the Indians nearly a hundred years ago and people say it is his ghost.

Plain Dealer [Cleveland, OH] 28 July 1888: p. 5 WYANDOT COUNTY

NOTE: Col. William Crawford was captured and tortured in retaliation for the massacre of the Moravian Indians at Gnadenhutten. (See *Haunted Ohio V: 200 Years of Ghosts*, "The Saddest Place in Ohio.")

Circleville has a ghost. It rises nightly in the graveyard on Mound Street and proceeds to the graveyard on North High Street—so it is said.

Cincinnati [OH] Daily Gazette 24 November 24 1877: p. 3 PICKAWAY COUNTY

In the southern part of Athens County, Ohio, an extensive elevation, denominated "Dead Man's Hill," is haunted by a phantom horseman. The clattering of equine hoofs may be heard nightly and the wail of an unfortunate being in agony is sometimes described to be heartrending. This apparition with a dead rider on its back sometimes dashes furiously toward travelers, through whom it passes like a misty cloud, leaving them clammy and almost dead with chill and terror. The noise of the approaching phantom steed is said to resemble the rushing sound produced by an eagle in its most rapid flight.

Philadelphia [PA] Inquirer 14 October 1889: p. 3 ATHENS COUNTY

SEES GHOST ENACT MURDER
OHIO MAN OVERCOME BY HORRIBLE NOCTURNAL
OUTDOOR VISION

Columbus, Ohio, Aug. 20. Absolutely sick with fright, with distended eyes, almost beyond the power of articulation, and clutching the air as though for support, Badger Curry staggered into the midst of a party of men at the corner of Rose Avenue and Oak Street shortly before midnight.

The men, alarmed at his appearance, made as though to move away, when he managed to say, "Don't go away or I'll go crazy," and after he had somewhat recovered himself he related the experiences that had so frightened him.

"I was passing through Franklin Park a little while ago, and just as I came out on the east side of the park, in an open place, I saw a woman struggling with a man, who appeared to be trying to carry her away. I rushed toward them to help the woman, when she threw her head back, and a saw a great gash across her throat from which blood was spurting, and just as I was about to yell for help both of them vanished in a second. Then it seemed to me as though someone passed a hand across my face, and I became terror stricken and ran."

Questioned about the conditions, Curry said: "I could see perfectly plain, as there was plenty of light and there was no place where anyone could have hidden."

Olympia [WA] Record 20 August 1904: p. 5 FRANKLIN COUNTY

A RESTLESS GHOST

Toledo, O., May 12. A ghost story from Paulding County has reached this city. The inhabitants of Arthur are said to be very much frightened and agitated over the report of a ghost which walks every night around Beaver Dam. The ghost was first seen by Frank Wells and several prominent citizens testify to the fact that whenever it is approached it walks across the mill pond. A citizens' committee will watch the ghost and measures have been taken to drag the pond, citizens generally believing that a murder has been committed and the body thrown into the pond.

Plain Dealer [Cleveland, OH] 13 May 1887: p. 5 PAULDING COUNTY

Howard Harroff, a murderer in prison at Youngstown, Ohio, believes that the ghost of his victim walks through the grated door into his cell every night. The conscience-stricken wretch screams out with terror, and implores the jailors not to leave him alone.

Macon [GA] Telegraph 11 August 1880: p. 2 MAHONING COUNTY

NOTE: Howard shot Marshall John Cone of Canfield.

Piqua, Ohio, reports a gigantic ghost that nocturnally wanders around with a dagger and clad only in huge rubber boots.

Albany [NY] Evening Journal 25 May 1871: p. 2 MIAMI COUNTY

HAUNTED TRACKS
A GHOST DRIVING RAILROAD EMPLOYEES OUT OF
THE COUNTRY

Youngstown, Ohio. October 13. Railroad men employed between Hazelton and Struthers claim that the track is haunted by a muscular ghost that has terrorized them and a number have resigned and sought employment elsewhere. An employee named Van Horn was attacked by the ghostly apparition and beaten until large welts were raised on his body, and when he reached Struthers fell exhausted. Several persons have been killed near the lonely place by trains and it is probable some practical jokers are working the ghost business, but they have been unable to catch him or bring him down with revolvers.

Cincinnati [OH] Enquirer 14 October 1891: p. 9 MAHONING COUNTY

A gigantic spirit horseman is terrorizing the town of Wapakoneta, O., following night travelers, cracking windows in houses seemingly without cause, frightening horses and cattle and making strange noises at night. So alarmed did the inhabitants become that they employed two detectives to watch for the spook. That night while both were asleep on a haystack it caught on fire, seemingly without cause, and both were cremated. Armed squads of men are now patrolling the country.

Omaha [NE] World Herald 23 January 1894: p. 1 AUGLAIZE COUNTY

NOTE: Detectives cremated by an incendiary poltergeist! That *would* be news. Except that the reality is less exciting. Here is the genuine story:

NOT TROUBLED WITH INSOMNIA
DETECTIVES FALL ASLEEP WHILE WORKING ON
A CASE
AND ARE NEARLY CREMATED.

Wapakoneta, Jan. 19. For several weeks past an alleged spook has been playing havoc with the wits of the family of John Reisenzehn of Freyburg. He has been struck while in the yard at night with small missiles. His daughter was struck with a stone and knocked down and lay unconscious for some time. The windows in the house have all been broken and the vandalism had become something unbearable. Last night two Wapakoneta detectives went out to lie in wait for the fellow doing the mischief. They hid in a straw stack and fell asleep. While asleep, the spook came upon them and set fire to the stack and came near cremating the detectives.

Plain Dealer [Cleveland, OH] 20 January 1894: p. 3 AUGLAIZE COUNTY

And the sequel:

GHOSTS IN COURT.
THE OLD MAN AND HIS SON AS PROPERTY DEPRECIATORS

Wapakoneta, Ohio, January 29. Two ghosts were in Squire Roger's Court this afternoon and were treated in a very earthly way. They were bound over to the next term of court in the sum of $500, and will then be expected to show a good reason for attempting the malicious destruction of property belonging to John Reisenzahn, of Freyburg. For some time the old and well-worn trick of "mysterious" stone throwing by unseen hands has been perpetrated on Mr. Reisenzahn's house until it bore resemblance to a besieged fort.

Saturday night two "detectives" concealed themselves in a haystack near the house to watch for spooks. They fell asleep, and during their slumbers the spirits set the haystack on fire to resent the interference of mortals with their pleasure. The detectives were rescued more dead than alive, being burned from head to foot.

Antone Reinike, Sr., and Antone Reinike, Jr., were found on the place and were arrested and identified as the "spooks." Their scheme was to lessen the value of the property, which they desired to purchase.

Cincinnati [OH] Enquirer 30 January 1894: p. 1 AUGLAIZE COUNTY

SAW NIECE'S GHOST, SHE SAID.
MRS. CLAUER FOUND DEAD SOON AFTER MAKING THIS ANNOUNCEMENT.

Springfield, Ohio, March 23. Mrs. Daniel Clauer, 40 years old, was found dead at her home here to-day. She was apparently in good health yesterday, but last night became frightened, and startled her relatives by declaring that she saw the ghost of her dead niece, Maria Grasla, who died a week ago. Mrs. Clauer's husband, who was an engineer at the State Odd Fellows Home, died suddenly two weeks ago.

The New York Times 24 March 1907 CLARK COUNTY

A TRUE GHOST STORY

I was a boy at the age of seven years at home with my father and mother. We were living in Cincinnati at the time. We were living in one room and there was a long porch in the front part. I saw the ghost with my own eyes. It was a big tall woman all dressed in white. She had a candle in her hand and [was] standing in front of the window. She looked so beautiful I thought she was an angel. She stood there about five or ten minutes. My father got up to see who she was but she disappeared just as soon as he opened the door.

My little sister was in the cradle at the time the ghost came to the window at 12 o'clock. She died the next day so I believe in a ghost. E.S.

Dayton [OH] Daily News 19 January 1914 HAMILTON COUNTY

NOTE: This was part of the 1914 ghost story contest sponsored by the *Dayton Daily News.*

A ghost at Shadesville goes around kicking citizens' chimneys down.

Plain Dealer [Cleveland, OH] 1 February 1881: p. 1 FRANKLIN COUNTY

MINER SCARED TO DEATH

Zanesville, O., Dec 25. Howard Mills, a miner living near Coaldale, was scared to death about midnight by some boys who rigged up a "ghost" which, with the aid of some thin paddles with hooks to swing through the air, was able to emit unearthly groans and shrieks. Mills was confronted with the machine while returning home late at night, and was so overwhelmed with the terrific noise and the suddenness of the apparition that he dropped dead in his tracks. He was a stalwart man, 47 years of age, and the father of six children.

The Ohio Democrat [Logan, OH] 2 January 1902: p. 1 MUSKINGUM COUNTY

New Philadelphia has a haunted well. A ghost clad all in white rises out of it every night at midnight.

Plain Dealer [Cleveland, OH] 28 February 1883: p. 4 TUSCARAWAS COUNTY

HAS NO HEAD
A REAL GHOST CAVORTING ABOUT THE COLUMBUS CITY PARK

Columbus, Ohio, December 4. A ghost is said to be haunting the City Park, and great excitement prevails on the South Side. Among a large number of persons who claim to have seen the supernatural being are William Bell and a young man named Sedlinger. They say that when returning home from a party last Friday night they took a short cut through the City Park. Just south of the Schiller monument they saw the figure of a man walking with outstretched hands slowly to and fro in the driveway in front of the monument. The glare of an electric light a few hundred feet distant enabled them to see the figure distinctly, and suddenly Sedlinger grasped Bell by the arm and said: "See, he ain' got any head."

While the badly frightened young men were consulting, the figure continued to walk to and fro, its arms extended as if imploring aid. The figure was draped from the shoulders to the knees in a grayish cloak or robe, which added to its ghostly appearance. They looked closely, but not a sign of a head could be seen. They decided it was a ghost, and a headless one at that, and they lost no time in getting off the grounds. They said nothing about their adventure next day for fear of being laughed at, but Sunday they happened to meet some friends who reside near the park, some of whom were telling about having seen the identical ghost they had seen and under much the same circumstances. Albert Dittlebach, a Socialist, and a stranger in the city, committed suicide by shooting himself in the mouth just at the spot where the ghost is said to have been seen. It is the theory of the superstitious South Side people that the ghost is Dittlebach's spirit returned.

Cincinnati [OH] Enquirer 5 December 1894: p. 4 FRANKLIN COUNTY

This sounded like something seen by men who had overindulged at a party, but here is the suicide's story:

SUICIDED IN A PARK

Columbus, O., Nov. 14. A. Dittelbach, 54, a German and a wine agent for Brandt & Company, Toledo, committed suicide in the City Park by shooting himself in the mouth late yesterday afternoon. He was despondent, though for what reason is not known, and had threatened several times in the past week to take his own life. Dittlebach has been in this city for several weeks, and it was thought has been reasonably successful in business. His acquaintances in Columbus believe he left no family.

Repository [Canton, OH] 14 November 1894: p. 4

A charming apparition in the shape of a headless, armless and footless ghost has made its appearance near Pleasant Point, Van Wert County. Must be a "pleasant point" indeed for nervous people.

Plain Dealer [Cleveland, OH] 19 April 1880: p. 1 VAN WERT COUNTY

Isador Wiseler, of Springfield, Ohio, called on Mrs. Cobb, a medium. A cross-eyed spirit asked him to remove his coat. He complied. She laid the coat on her arm, touched one of the sleeves with her finger tips and pulled from it thirty yards or so of the finest black lace. The sleeve showed no sign of disturbance. Then she applied one end of the lace to the coatsleeve, when it disappeared entirely within the cloth. The cross-eyed spirit asked him to touch the lace. He did so, and it gradually melted away until nothing remained. The spirit, he said, vanished then, mysteriously fading out of sight by degrees. It wore a gauze-like costume.

Philadelphia [Pa] Inquirer 24 June 1889: p. 3 CLARK COUNTY

The ghost of a young woman floats ahead of the Pittsburg & Lake Erie train as it traverses a marsh where a Mrs. Stewart was found murdered near Youngstown, O. The crews have become nervous wrecks, and declare that either the ghost or themselves must hand in a resignation.
Cincinnati [OH] Post 6 October 1888: p. 4 MAHONING COUNTY

Mt. Vernon has a ghost that flies in the air and blows a horn.
Plain Dealer [Cleveland, OH] 21 May 1887: p. 4 KNOX COUNTY

POLICEMAN PLAYS GHOST
HAUNTS OLD CANALBOAT TO HAVE FUN
WITH REPORTERS

Akron, O., Jan. 19.—Patrolman John Holland of the Barberton police force admitted that he was the "ghost" in the old canalboat near the Pennsylvania station, Barberton, which has been exploited in local newspapers and attracted thousands of people to the scene.

Holland hid in the cabin of the boat, wrapped in sheets, and was discovered by a crowd of school boys.

When questioned Holland said he posed as a "ghost" to have some fun with the reporters.
Plain Dealer [Cleveland, OH] 20 January 1914: p. 14 SUMMIT COUNTY

Canal Dover has a ghost that jumps off a bridge into the canal every night at midnight.
Plain Dealer [Cleveland, OH] 14 January 1885: p. 1 TUSCARAWAS COUNTY

A ghost haunts a church in Canal Fulton and plays the organ, but it is not the ghost of Johnny Morgan.
Plain Dealer [Cleveland, OH] 17 September 1881: p. 4 STARK COUNTY

NOTE: Johnny Morgan was a character in a popular song of the 1880s. The chorus began: Johnny Morgan played the organ, the father beat the drum; The sister played the tambourine, the brother went pom pom…

A few nights ago Henry Waters, a youth, whose home is near Youngstown, Ohio, was aroused from his sleep by something in the room. He sat bolt upright in bed. The moon shone through a window, and as young Waters looked towards the light he saw a tall figure in ghostly attire slowly approaching. He spoke, but the ghost made no reply. Then he grasped his revolver, and thus armed and thus emboldened said: "If you are a man I kill you; if you are ghost this won't hurt you." He pulled the trigger and report came, but as with quick motion the ghost lifted an arm Waters heard the bullet rebound against the headboard of the bed. This sent a cold chill through the youth, but he discharged his revolver again and again, and then, wild with fear, hurled it at the intruder. At that moment the ghost threw off his disguise, several other parties to the joke came laughing in and lights were struck. The merry-makers had drawn the bullets from the pistol, leaving enough powder to make a report, and at each discharge the play-ghost had thrown a bullet against the headboard. All this the practical jokers expected Waters to enjoy, as he was a jovial fellow, but they found him first dazed, then incoherent, then raving, and now, as his parents fear—a maniac.

New Hampshire Patriot and State Gazette [Concord, NH] 16 March 16 1882: p. 2
MAHONING COUNTY

SKY SCRAPER HOODOOED

Columbus, Ohio. Jan. 20. Declaring the Columbus Savings and Trust Company's skyscraper now in course of erection to be "hoodooed" all the workmen on the structure quite today. There have been 21 accidents since the building was started and the climax came when a bricklayer fell nine stories to his death.

Grand Forks [ND] Herald 21 January 1905: p. 2 FRANKLIN COUNTY

NOTE: The bricklayer was Alfred F. Smith, who fell to his death on 20 January.

A howling ghost troubles the citizens of Newcomerstown.
Plain Dealer [Cleveland, OH] 13 September 1882: p. 1 TUSCARAWAS COUNTY

A GHOST WITH A GRIEVANCE
THE FAMILY IT HAUNTS HAS APPEALED TO
THE SQUIRE
AGAINST ITS RACKET.

Zanesville, May 18. The family of Joseph Purcell, who lives on North Third Street, this city, are greatly excited over strange noises, which they say are made by the spirit of Clyde Shires. The spirit has been at it now for four weeks, and the family desire to sleep. They have appealed to a Justice of the Peace to stop the racket, but that official has declined to issue a summons, on the grounds that none of his officers were sufficiently acquainted with Shires' spirit to make the service.

The spirit rappings, as interpreted by the Purcell family, inform them that Shires, who was convicted of an assault upon a young lady in a family where he was adopted, is not guilty of the offense, and that he intends to haunt those who prosecuted the case. Thus far his haunting has been solely on the premises of the Purcells, who had nothing to do with the case. Shires died shortly after his conviction.

Pittsburg [PA] Dispatch 19 May 1892: p. 9 MUSKINGUM COUNTY

The colored citizens of Maysville are annoyed by a real ghost. This troublesome visitor is supposed to be the spirit of Harry Boyd, a well-to-do hack driver, who died very suddenly.

Portsmouth [OH] Times 22 January 1881: p. 2 SCIOTO COUNTY

WROUGHT UP OVER STRANGE MANIFESTATIONS IN A FARMHOUSE

Cleveland, O., Sept.4 The village of Chagrin Falls is wrought up over the strange manifestations in the farmhouse of Henry Bancroft. Mr. Bancroft is 75 years old, and a well-respected resident of the village. Beginning with Wednesday morning articles in his home began to catch fire, apparently from nothing, and to burn violently.

Napkins, socks, aprons, towels and the like suddenly flare up and are consumed. This happens only in the day time. Mrs. Bancroft's dress caught fire while on her. Opinion is divided between the supernatural and the belief that some evil-minded person is making use of a chemical compound to annoy the Bancrofts.

Marietta [OH] Daily Leader 6 September 1897: p. 1 CUYAHOGA COUNTY

REAL SPOOK
HOVERS AROUND CABIN WHERE BEATTY
KILLED HIMSELF
SAY THE FARMERS

Hamilton, Ohio February 17. The village of Somerville is shaking in its boots over the nightly appearance of a ghost, vouched for by Farmers Dan Thomas and his neighbor Andy Neanover, both of whom have made affidavit before Mayor Ben Bake, of Somerville, to actually seeing the estray from spiritland. Thomas and Neanover last night lay for the ghost, whose haunts are in an abandoned log cabin, where 35 years ago Dan Beatty hanged himself. The ghost appeared, and, both men swear, ran after them waving its bony and flesh-beshredded arms. They ran to the Thomas home and his ghostship vanished in a pale blue flame.

Cincinnati [OH] Enquirer 10 February 1910: p. 3 BUTLER COUNTY

Cambridge has a mysterious woman in white.

Steubenville [OH] Herald Star November 11, 1909: p. 2 GUERNSEY COUNTY

Bibliography

The Anomalist http://www.anomalist.com

Anonymous, *The Mysterious Murder of Pearl Bryan or The Headless Horror: a full account of the mysterious murder known as the Fort Thomas tragedy, from beginning to end : full particulars of all detective and police investigations : dialogues of the interviews between Mayor Caldwell, Chief Deitsch and the prisoners*, Barclay & Co., [1896]

Arment, Chad, *Boss Snakes: Stories and Sightings of Giant Snakes in North America*, Coachwhip Publications, 2008

———*Varmints: Mystery Carnivores of North America*, Coachwhip Publications, 2010

Dr Beachcombing's Bizarre History Blog http://www.strangehistory.net/

Bondeson, Jan, *A Cabinet of Medical Curiosities*, W.W. Norton, 1999

Brandon, Jim, *Weird America: A Guide to Places of Mystery in the United States*, E.P. Dutton, 1978

Citro, Joseph A. *Green Mountain Ghosts, Ghouls & Unsolved Mysteries*, Mariner Books, 2012

———Joe Citro's *Weird Vermont*, Bat Books, 2012

———*Passing Strange: True Tales of New England Hauntings and Horrors*, Mariner Books, 2001

———*Vermont's Haunts: Tall Tales & True from the Green Mountains*, Bat Books, 2011

Clark, Jerome, *Unnatural Phenomena: A Guide to the Bizarre Wonders of North America*, ABC-CLIO, 2005

Cohen, Anne B., *Poor Pearl, Poor Girl! The Murdered-Girl Stereotype in Ballad and Newspaper*, The University of Texas Press, 1973

Coleman, Loren, *Mysterious America*, Pocket Books, 2007

Finucane, Ronald C., *Appearances of the Dead: A Cultural History of Ghosts*, Prometheus, 1984

Fort, Charles, Jim Steinmeyer, intro., *The Book of the Damned: The Collected Works of Charles Fort. Four Complete Volumes: The Book of the Damned, New Lands, Lo!, and Wild Talents*, Tacher, 2008

Fortean Times http://www.forteantimes.com/

Lesy, Michael, *Wisconsin Death Trip*, University of New Mexico Press, 2000

Okonowicz, Ed, *Possessed Possessions: Haunted Antiques, Furniture, and Collectibles*, Myst & Lace, 1996

———*Possessed Possessions 2: More Haunted Antiques, Furniture, and Collectibles*, Myst & Lace, 1998

Slade, Paul, http://www.planetslade.com/pearl-bryan.html

Woodyard, Chris, *The Face in the Window: Haunting Ohio Tales*, Kestrel Publications, 2013

———*The Headless Horror: Strange and Ghostly Ohio Tales*, Kestrel Publications, 2013

———*The Ghost Wore Black: Ghastly Tales from the Past*, Kestrel Publications, 2013

General Index

Index by County